Does It Take a Village?
Community Effects on
Children, Adolescents, and Families

Does It Take a Village?
Community Effects on
Children, Adolescents, and Families

Edited by

Alan Booth
Ann C. Crouter
The Pennsylvania State University

LEA LAWRENCE ERLBAUM ASSOCIATES, PUBLISHERS
2001 Mahwah, New Jersey   London

Lawrence Erlbaum Associates, Inc., Publishers
10 Industrial Avenue
Mahwah, NJ 07430

Cover design by Kathryn Houghtaling Lacey

Library of Congress Cataloging-in-Publication Data

Does it take a village? : community effects on children, adolescents,
    and families / [edited by] Alan Booth, Ann C. Crouter.
        p.   cm.
    Includes bibliographical references (p.) and index.
    ISBN 0-8058-3242-4 (c: alk. paper) --ISBN 0-8058-3243-2 (p: alk. paper)
            1. City children—United States. 2. Urban Youth—United States.
            3. Environment and children—United States. 4. Child rearing—United States.
            5. Child development—United States. 6. Adolescent psychology—United States.
            7. Neighborhood—United States. 8. Community-based child welfare—United States.
            9. Community-based family services—United States. I. Booth, Alan, 1935-- .
            II. Crouter, Ann C.

        HT206.D64   1999
        362.7'0973   dc21   99-38654

The final camera copy for this work was prepared by the author, and therefore the
publisher takes no responsibility for consistency or correctness of typographical style.
However, this arrangement helps to make publication of this kind of scholarship possible.

Printed in the United States of America

10 9 8 7 6 5 4 3 2 1

Contents

Preface

"It takes a village to raise a child" is a saying seemingly imbued with wisdom that cuts across time and place. Indeed, studies from a variety of disciplines have found evidence that community and neighborhood factors play a role in people's decisions to marry and have children (in or out of marriage), family stability, childrearing strategies, and children's psychosocial functioning and educational achievement. As studies have become more sophisticated, however, there has been increasing debate about community and neighborhood effects; indeed, some studies have found little evidence that they make an independent contribution, net of residents' own personal characteristics. Given this ambiguity in findings, and the important policy and program ramifications of this area of research, the time is right to bring together a talented, interdisciplinary group of researchers and program experts to consider what is known about how communities and neighborhoods make their mark on families, children, and adolescents.

This book focuses on the mechanisms that link community characteristics to the functioning of the families and individuals within them (e.g., community norms, economic opportunities, reference groups for assessing relative deprivation, and social support networks). Contributors underscore those features of communities that represent risk factors for children, adolescents, and their families, as well as those characteristics that underlie resilience and thus undergird individual and family functioning. Several authors with applied expertise review the state of the art in terms of policies and programs designed to strengthen communities and neighborhoods as settings for children, youth, and families. On the basis of the research evidence to date, some innovative community- and neighborhood-based programs and policies have been implemented to address problems that appear to have their roots in community organization. Although some programs have achieved results, others have not. The reasons for these mixed results are not clear and deserve attention.

As a society, the U.S. has heavy investments both in research and in programs based on the idea that communities affect families and children, yet important questions have arisen about the validity of the link between communities, children, and families. Because the topic is so prominent in public discussion of family and child problems and because the research evidence is so diverse, this volume is an appropriate vehicle to advance knowledge about these matters. In so doing, we hope to be able to answer the question of whether—and how—it takes a village to raise a child and what can be done to help communities achieve this essential task more effectively. The chapters in this book address these issues; they are based on the presentations and discussion from a national symposium on community effects on children, adolescents, and families held at The Pennsylvania State University, November 5-6, 1998, as the sixth in a series of annual symposia focused on family issues.

Acknowledgments

There are many to thank for assistance with the symposium. We are indebted to the National Institute of Child Health and Human Development, The Pennsylvania State University Population Research Institute, College of Liberal Arts, College of Health and Human Development, College of Agricultural Sciences, Prevention Research Center, Department of Anthropology, Department of Economics, Department of Education Policy Studies, Department of Human Development and Family Studies, Department of Psychology, Department of Sociology, Crime, Law and Justice Program, and Women's Studies Program for funding the symposium. We appreciate the advice and encouragement of members of the Population Research Institute throughout the process of planning and conducting the symposium. The contributions of Erin Lesser, Diane Mattern, Kris McNeel, Sherry Yocum, and Kim Zimmerman in assisting with the administration of the symposium were invaluable. Special thanks to professors Clancy Blair, Connie Flanagan, Daniel Lichter, and Wayne Osgood for their excellent work in presiding over the four sessions and for their contributions to the flow of ideas during the sessions.

—Alan Booth
—Ann C. Crouter

List of Contributors

Frank Avenilla
The Pennsylvania State University

Dale A. Blyth
University of Minnesota

John O. G. Billy
*Battelle Centers for Public Health
Research and Evaluation*

Linda M. Burton
The Pennsylvania State University

James P. Connell
*Institute for Research and Reform
in Education*

Greg J. Duncan
Northwestern University

Mark Greenberg
The Pennsylvania State University

Jill E. Korbin
Case Western Reserve University

Anne C. Kubisch
*Roundtable on Comprehensive
Community Initiatives for Children
and Families, The Aspen Institute*

Barrett A. Lee
The Pennsylvania State University

Douglas Massey
University of Pennsylvania

Stephen W. Raudenbush
University of Michigan

Robert J. Sampson
University of Chicago

Susan Singley
The Pennsylvania State University

Stephen Small
University of Wisconsin–Madison

Scott J. South
*State University of New York
at Albany*

Margaret Beale Spencer
University of Pennsylvania

Mercer L. Sullivan
Rutgers University

Andrew Supple
University of Wisconsin–Madison

Ralph B. Taylor
*Temple University and National
Consortium on Violence Research*

I

How do Communities Undergird or Undermine Human Development? What are the Relevant Contexts and What Mechanisms are at Work?

1

How do Communities Undergird
or Undermine Human Development?
Relevant Contexts and Social Mechanisms

Robert J. Sampson
University of Chicago

A long-standing tradition of ecological research has documented the negative conditions for children associated with concentrated urban poverty and related dimensions of structural disadvantage such as racial segregation. The range of child and adolescent outcomes correlated with multiple forms of concentrated disadvantage includes infant mortality, low birthweight, teenage childbearing, dropping out of high school, child maltreatment, and adolescent delinquency (for a recent overview and set of empirical studies, see Brooks-Gunn, Duncan, & Aber, 1997). Much less understood, however, are the reasons for these correlations. As Jencks and Mayer (1990) and Sampson, Morenoff, and Earls (1999) argued, if "neighborhood effects" on child and adolescent outcomes exist, presumably they are constituted from social processes that involve collective aspects of community life. What are the collective processes that make for a healthy neighborhood environment for children and adolescents? How are neighborhood mechanisms measured? What are their structural sources of variation? Are neighborhood mechanisms embedded in citywide processes that transcend local boundaries? In short, and in the words of the National Family Symposium, "Does it take a village?"

In this chapter, I attempt to answer these questions by focusing attention on the neighborhood processes themselves. Drawing in large part from an ongoing research program in Chicago, I present a general theoretical approach to community social organization that specifies what neighborhoods supply for children and adolescents. I discuss the ways in which structural characteristics (e.g., economic segregation, residential instability) and spatial externalities promote or inhibit mechanisms of neighborhood social organization. I illustrate my argument with analyses that combine independent sources of data on crime, child health, and ecological structural differentiation with a survey of more than 8,500 residents of 343 neighborhoods in Chicago. Because of time constraints, I distill basic findings and present a map that, although simple, paints the big picture.[1]

Although briefly, I address also some of the challenges facing current research, including thorny conceptual and methodological issues like selection or

---

[1] Detailed results are available on request. The work described in this chapter stems from a collaborative project with Earls, Morenoff, and Raudenbush.

endogeneity bias, the mis-specification of enduring neighborhood effects, simultaneity, measurement mismatches, and the explanation of events versus individual differences. Linking methodological issues (especially measurement strategy) with theory is, I believe, necessary for the advancement of knowledge. However, I leave it to Duncan to tackle the lion's share of methodological issues, and I leave it to Connell to inform us about policy interventions. I plan to stick mainly with neighborhood-level theory, its implications for research design, and illustrative findings.

ECOLOGICAL DIFFERENTIATION AND COMMUNITY STRATIFICATION

I begin by summarizing the large body of research looking at ecological differentiation in U.S. cities by socioeconomic and demographic factors. Research traditions rooted in *social area analysis* and *factorial ecology* (for a review see Sampson & Morenoff, 1997) have established a number of structural characteristics that vary systematically between neighborhoods along dimensions of socioeconomic stratification (e.g., poverty, wealth, occupational attainment), family and life-cycle status (e.g., female-headed households, child density), residential stability (e.g., home ownership and tenure), racial composition, and urbanization (density). Considerable attention in recent years has been devoted to the concentration of multiple forms of social and economic disadvantage in urban neighborhoods.

Probably the best known explanation for this phenomenon is Wilson's (1987) theory of *concentration effects*. Wilson argued that the social transformation of inner-city areas in the United States from the 1970s to the 1990s resulted in an increased concentration of the most disadvantaged segments of the urban Black population—especially poor, female-headed families with children. At the national level in 1990, fully 25% of poor Blacks lived in concentrated poverty neighborhoods compared to only 3% of poor Whites (see Jargowsky, 1997). The concentration of poverty and joblessness (Wilson, 1996) has been fueled by macrostructural changes related to the deindustrialization of central cities where low-income minorities are disproportionately located. These changes include a shift from goods-producing to service-producing industries, the increasing polarization of the labor market into low-wage and high-wage sectors, and relocation of manufacturing out of the inner city. The related out-migration of middle- and upper-income Black families from the inner city has also, according to Wilson (1987), removed an important social buffer that could potentially deflect the full impact of prolonged joblessness and industrial transformation. Wilson (1996) argued that the social milieu of increasing stratification among Blacks differs from the income-mixing characteristic of inner-city neighborhoods in previous decades. The consequences of these differential ecological distributions are potentially profound because they mean that relationships between race and child outcomes are systematically confounded with differences in community contexts.

Focusing instead on racial segregation, Massey and Denton (1993) described how increasing economic dislocation interacts with the spatial concentration of a minority group to create a set of structural circumstances that reinforce the effects of social and economic deprivation. They showed that, in a segregated environment, exogenous economic shocks that cause a downward shift in the distribution of minority income not only bring about an increase in the poverty rate for the group as a whole, but also cause an increase in the geographic concentration of poverty. This geographic intensification of poverty occurs because the additional poverty created by macroeconomic conditions is spread unevenly over the metropolitan area. The greater the segregation, "the smaller the number of neighborhoods absorbing the shock, and the more severe the resulting concentration of poverty" (Massey, 1990, p. 337). At the other end of the income distribution, Massey (1996) noted the growing geographic concentration of (predominantly White) affluence, suggesting a society increasingly bifurcated by wealth. Although for different reasons, then, both Wilson and Massey conceptualized race-linked social change as a structural characteristic reflected in local environments.

Consequences for Children and Adolescents

Indicators of socioeconomic (dis)advantage and racial isolation are not only concentrated ecologically; they tend to be clustered with a set of troublesome behaviors that likewise seem to be increasing in concentration. In a case study of Cleveland, for example, Chow and Coulton (1992) sought to determine whether there was a social transformation of urban neighborhoods in the 1980s. Rather than simply documenting the spread of negative social conditions and the growth of a so-called "underclass," they searched for evidence of structural change in the ecological distribution and interrelationship of adverse conditions such as violent crime, drug addiction, teenage pregnancy, and welfare dependency. Comparing ecological structures for a wide range of social indicators in two time periods, 1980 and 1989, they showed that the earlier period was characterized by an evenly distributed three-factor structure defined by unruliness (e.g., weakened social control of adolescents), family disruption (e.g., family composition and maternal and child health), and dangerousness (crime and drug arrests). By 1989, however, these social conditions became more interrelated, and one factor, which they called *impoverishment*, emerged as the dominant construct. More generally, ecological research in numerous cities has shown that social problems such as crime, public disorder, school dropout, and child maltreatment are significantly clustered and correlated with concentrated poverty, family instability, and residential turnover (see also Coulton, Korbin, Su, & Chow, 1995; Sampson, 1992).

The neighborhood concentration of child-linked social problems actually has a long history. Discovered by Shaw and McKay (1942/1969) in the 1920s, the same Chicago neighborhoods characterized by poverty, residential instability, and high rates of crime and delinquency were also plagued by high rates of infant mortality, low birthweight, tuberculosis, physical abuse, and other factors detrimental to child development. Shaw and McKay (1942/1969) thus argued that delinquency "is not an isolated phenomenon" (p. 106) and went on to document the close association of delinquency rates with a host of social problems that directly influence children.

This general empirical finding continues to the present day, as illustrated by recently compiled data on seemingly disparate outcomes (Morenoff, 1999). Table 1.1 reflects the ecological "comorbidity" of rates of homicide, infant mortality, low birthweight, accidental injury, and suicide for Chicago census tracts. In this table, *high-high* specifically refers to a tract being above the mean on both the outcome variable and its spatial lag (defined further later). *Low-low* refers to tracts below the mean on both. Taken for the period 1995-1996, the data show very high levels of spatial clustering for all outcomes except suicide. For example, of tracts with high homicide rates that are spatially contiguous to other tracts high in homicide, fully 94% are in the high-high cluster for low birthweight, 80% are high-high for infant mortality, and more than half are high-high in accidental injuries. Other combinations across homicide, low birthweight, infant mortality, and injury show similar spatial clustering. Not surprisingly, suicide is somewhat distinct, although even here the spatial clustering is not trivial.

I claim, then, that empirical research on ecological differentiation has established a reasonably consistent set of "neighborhood facts" relevant to children and adolescence.

1.   There is considerable race-linked social inequality between neighborhoods and local communities, evidenced by the clustering of indicators of socioeconomic status (SES) (both advantage and disadvantage) with racial isolation. Even in areas of race-ethnic homogeneity, however, economic segregation is common (Jargowsky, 1996, 1997).
2.   Myriad social problems tend to come bundled together at the neighborhood level, including but not limited to crime, adolescent delinquency, social and physical disorder, low birthweight, infant mortality, school dropout, and child maltreatment.
3.   Third, these two sets of clusters are themselves related — neighborhood predictors common to many child-adolescent "outcomes" include concentrated poverty, racial isolation, family disruption, and residential instability (Sampson, 1992).
4.   Empirical results have not varied much with the operational unit of analysis. The ecological stratification of local communities in U.S. society by factors such as social class, race, family status, and crime is a robust phenomenon that emerges at multiple levels of geography, whether local community areas, census tracts, or other neighborhood units.
5.   The ecological concentration of poverty, racial isolation, and social disadvantage appears to have increased significantly during the 1980s and 1990s, as has the concentration of affluence at the upper end (Jargowsky, 1996, 1997; Massey, 1996).

Table 1.1

Cross Classification of Chicago Neighborhoods by Spatial Clustering of "Co-Morbidity" Outcomes: 1995-1996

	Homicide		Low Birthweight		Infant Mortality		Accidental Injuries		Suicides	
	High–High	Low–Low	High–High	Low–Low	High–High	Low–Low	High–High	Low–Low	High–High	Low–Low
Homicide[1]										
High–High			93.6%		78.9%		55.0%		18.3%	
Low–Low				84.7%		66.3%		73.2%		28.9%
Low Birthweight[2]										
High–High	83.6%				78.7%		55.7%		17.2%	
Low–Low		94.2%				72.5%		74.9%		27.5%
Infant Mortality[3]										
High–High	78.9%		88.1%				54.1%		15.6%	
Low–Low		92.0%		90.5%				73.0%		29.2%
Accidental Injuries[1]										
High–High	81.1%		91.9%		79.7%				17.6%	
Low–Low		88.5%		81.5%		63.7%				28.7%
Suicides[1]										
High–High	26.7%		28.0%		22.7%		17.3%			
Low–Low		50.5%		43.1%		36.7%		41.3%		

Notes:
[1] Age- and sex-adjusted death rate per 10,000 persons
[2] Rate per 100 live births
[3] Rate per 1,000 live births

Despite globalization, urbanization, and modernity, neighborhoods and residential differentiation thus remain persistent in U.S. society. As any real estate agent or homeowner (especially those with children) will attest, location does seem to matter. The next logical question is that of why a neighborhood matters. Taken together, the five facts on neighborhood differentiation yield a potentially important clue in thinking about this question. If numerous and seemingly disparate child outcomes are linked together empirically across neighborhoods and are predicted by similar structural characteristics, there may be a common underlying cause or mediating mechanism. Hence, rather than seeking specific or unique theories for each and every different outcome, another strategy is to develop a more general theory. The next section articulates such a theoretical approach by going beyond economic and demographic factors to probe the associated *social mechanisms* relevant to child and adolescent development.

FACILITATING MECHANISMS AND UNDERMINING RISKS

At a general level, I conceptualize community social organization as the ability of a community structure to realize the common values of its residents and maintain effective social controls (Kornhauser, 1978; Sampson & Groves, 1989). *Social control* should not be equated with repression or forced conformity. Rather, social control refers to the capacity of a social unit to regulate itself according to desired principles—to realize collective, as opposed to forced, goals (Janowitz, 1975; Sampson, 1999). This conception is similar to Tilly's (1973) definition of *collective action*, namely, the application of a community's pooled resources to common ends. One of the most central of such common goals or ends is the desire of community residents to live in orderly environments free of predatory crime. Extant research also points to a substantial consensus among Americans of all stripes on the virtues of neighborhoods characterized by economic sufficiency, efficacious schools, adequate housing, and especially a healthy and safe environment for children (Kornhauser, 1978).

It is important to note that a focus on the capacity of communities to achieve common goals does not require cultural or sociodemographic homogeneity. Ethnically diverse populations can and do agree on goals such as safety for children. Social conflicts can and do rend communities along the lines of economic resources, race, political empowerment, and the role of criminal justice agents in defining and controlling social deviance (e.g., drug use, gangs, panhandling). It is around the distribution of resources and power that conflict usually emerges, not the content of core values (Kornhauser, 1978). The goal of community is thus the reconciliation of partial with general perspectives on the common good (Selznick, 1992).

I also define communities ecologically in terms of neighborhoods and local community areas, rather than elevating solidarity to the major criterion for definition. Like Tilly (1973), that is, I "choose to make territoriality define communities and to leave the extent of solidarity problematic" (p. 212). When formulated in this way, dimensions of local social organization and control are analytically separable not only from structural sources of variation (e.g., racial segregation, concentrated poverty, instability), but also from child outcomes that may result.

Social Capital and Collective Efficacy

My theoretical focus on social control is theoretically compatible with more recent formulations in the social science literature of what has been termed *social capital*. Coleman (1990) defined social capital as a resource embodied in the relations among persons and positions that facilitates action (see also Coleman, 1988). Bourdieu (1986) wrote of the "actual or potential resources which are linked to possession of a durable network of more or less institutionalized relationships of mutual acquaintance and recognition" (p. 249). Putnam (1993) defined social capital in a broader fashion as "features of social organization, such as networks, norms, trust, that facilitate coordination and cooperation for benefit" (p. 36). It follows that communities high in social capital are better able to realize common values and maintain social controls.

Unfortunately, the concept of social capital has come to mean so many things in recent empirical inquiry that it has lost much of its meaning. Coleman's formulation has been either used too expansively or, more frequently, recast into individual-level terms (Sampson et al., 1999). Yet Coleman's (1990) narrative descriptions, such as his comparison of social capital available to mothers in Detroit and Jerusalem, referred to the extraindividual properties of social-organizational structures embedded in local communities. This is important, for social capital tied to local community context is analytically distinct from (and may be no less consequential than) the more proximate family processes and structures observed inside the home (Sampson et al., 1999). Indeed, recent efforts seem to have bypassed the essential theoretical claim of Coleman (1990): Social capital is lodged not in individuals but in the structure of social organization (p. 302).

Consider the social-organizational context of childrearing that extends beyond families "under the roof." Neighborhoods characterized by an extensive set of obligations, expectations, and interlocking social networks connecting adults facilitate the informal social control and support of children (Furstenberg & Hughes, 1997). For example, when parents know the parents of their children's friends, they have the potential to observe the child's actions in different circumstances, talk to each other about the child, compare notes, and establish norms (Coleman, 1988). Such intergenerational closure of local networks provides the child with social capital of a collective nature. One can extend this model to closure and norm establishment among networks involving parents and teachers, religious and recreational leaders, businesses that serve youth, and perhaps even agents of criminal justice (Sampson, 1992).

Neighborhoods are differentially characterized not only by network-related structures such as intergenerational closure, but also by cultural expectations for the informal social control and mutual support of children. The expectation that neighborhood residents can and will intervene on the behalf of children depends on conditions of mutual trust and shared values among neighbors. As Putnam (1993) put it, "Trust lubricates cooperation" (p. 171). Private ties notwithstanding, then, it is the linkage of mutual trust and the shared willingness to intervene for the common good that defines the neighborhood context of what Sampson, Raudenbush, and Earls (1997) termed *collective efficacy*. This term is meant to signify an emphasis on shared beliefs in a neighborhood's conjoint capability for action to achieve an intended effect, and hence an active sense of engagement on the part of residents. As Bandura (1997) argued, the meaning of efficacy is captured in expectations about the exercise of control, elevating the "agentic" aspect of social life over a perspective centered on the accumulation of "stocks" of social resources. This conception of collective efficacy is consistent with the redefinition of social capital by Portes and Sensenbrenner (1993) in terms of "expectations for action within a collectivity" (p. 1323).

Institutions and Public Control

The present focus on informal social control and collective efficacy should not be read as ignoring institutions or the wider political environment in which local communities are embedded. The institutional component of social control theory is the resource stock of neighborhood organizations and their linkages with other organizations, both within and outside the community. Neighborhood organizations reflect the structural embodiment of community cohesion, and thus the instability and isolation of local institutions are key factors underlying the structural dimension of social organization. Kornhauser (1978) argued that when the horizontal links among institutions within a community are weak, the capacity to defend local interests is weakened. Moreover, institutional strength is not necessarily isomorphic with strong personal ties in a neighborhood. Many communities exhibit intense private ties (e.g., among friends, kin) yet still lack the institutional capacity to achieve social control.

Vertical integration is potentially even more important. Bursik and Grasmick (1993) highlighted the importance of *public* control, defined as the capacity of local community organizations to obtain extralocal resources (e.g., police, fire services; block grants) that help sustain neighborhood social stability and local controls. More generally, Hunter (1985) argued that parochial social control— within-community social order based on interpersonal networks and the interlocking of local institutions—"leaves unresolved the problems of public order in a civil society" (p. 216). The problem is that public order is provided mainly by institutions of the state, and we have seen a secular decline in public (citizenship) obligations in society accompanied by an increase in civil (individual) rights. This imbalance of collective obligations and individual rights undermines social control. According to Hunter (1985), local communities must therefore work together with the forces of public control to achieve social order, principally through interdependence among private (family), parochial (neighborhood), and public (state) institutions such as the police and schools.

Routine Activities

A concern with ecology suggests another often overlooked mechanism in discussions of neighborhood effects: how land use patterns and the ecological distributions of daily routine activities bear on children's well being. The location of schools, the mix of residential with commercial land use (e.g., strip malls, bars), public transportation nodes, and large flows of nighttime visitors, for example, are relevant to organizing how and when children come into contact with other peers, adults, and nonresident activity. The *routine activities* perspective in criminology (Cohen & Felson, 1979) provides the important insight that predatory crime requires the intersection in time and space of motivated offenders, suitable targets, and the absence of capable guardians. Rooted in social control theory, the routine activity approach assumes a steady supply of motivated offenders, and focuses instead on how targets of opportunity and sanction mechanisms combine to explain criminal events. This strategy has appeal in thinking about a range of child and adolescent behaviors, such as drinking, early sexual behavior, smoking, and "hanging out," that reflect natural desires yet can yield negative outcomes both personally and for others (e.g., teen childbearing, low birthweight, low achievement, poor health). For example, not only do mixed-use neighborhoods offer greater opportunities for expropriative crime, they offer increased opportunity for children to congregate outside the home in places conducive to peer-group influence (Stark, 1987). Seemingly prosaic, an intriguing finding from criminology is that the incidence of delinquency is predictable from proximity to a McDonald's restaurant (Brantingham & Brantingham, 1984). Big Macs are not the problem, of course; the unsupervised activity space and peer contagion is.

    In short, because illegal and "deviant" activities feed on the spatial and temporal structure of routine legal activities (e.g., transportation, work, entertainment, and shopping), the differential land use of neighborhoods is a key to comprehending the ecological distribution of situations and opportunities conducive to a wide range of potentially troublesome adolescent behaviors. In particular, the ecological placements of bars, liquor stores, strip-mall shopping outlets, subway stops, and unsupervised play spaces play a direct role in the distribution of high-risk situations for children. The ecology of routine activities is not usually thought of in the "neighborhood effects" literature, much less as a mechanism. I suggest, however, that it holds considerable promise as an explanatory mechanism, especially in combination with the sociodemographic and collective action features just discussed. Indeed, decisions to locate high-risk businesses (concerning children's development) are often targeted to lower income communities known to lack the organizational capacity to resist.   Thus, one arena where collective efficacy is likely to matter greatly is in the differential ability of neighborhoods to organize against local threats such as disorderly bars, licensing of new liquor stores, and the mixing of strip malls with residential and school land use.

STRUCTURAL DIFFERENTIATION AND SPATIAL EXTERNALITY

Summarizing and simplifying, this review suggests that local neighborhoods vary considerably in three classes of mechanisms relevant to children, adolescents, and families: rules (shared action-expectations and social controls for guiding children's behavior), resources (e.g., social capital and institutional), and routines (prevalence and mix of different kinds of behavioral settings). These "three R's" (Wikström, 1998) are interwoven with the larger social ecology of neighborhoods. In this section, I sketch how both local and extralocal sources of structural differentiation noted earlier are linked to the rules, resources, and routines of neighborhood-level social organization. I then turn to a description of research in Chicago that addresses selected ingredients of this general theoretical argument.

Coleman's (1988, 1990) theory in particular and systemic ecological theory in general (Kasarda & Janowitz, 1974) hypothesized that the continuity of community structure helps explain the emergence of resources such as social capital and control. Sampson et al. (1999) defined stability not as lack of change, but rather the social reproduction of neighborhood residential structure, typically when population gains offset losses and home values appreciate. Although often overlooked in the urban poverty debate, a high rate of residential turnover, especially excessive population loss, fosters institutional disruption and makes it that much harder for residents to sustain interpersonal ties. Residential instability not only stymies the formation of new social networks, but in severing existing social ties, it also initiates a disruptive process that ripples outward and hence bears on the entire system of social networks (Coleman, 1990; Sampson et al., 1999). Financial investment also provides homeowners with a shared interest in supporting the commonweal of neighborhood life. Residential tenure and home ownership are thus hypothesized to promote collective efforts to maintain neighborhood exchange values and social control (see also Logan & Molotch, 1987).

Another major component of ecological differentiation stems from unequal resource distribution and racial segregation. As already noted, economic stratification by race and place fuels the neighborhood concentration of cumulative forms of disadvantage (Massey & Denton, 1993; Wilson, 1996), intensifying the social isolation of lower income, minority, and single-parent residents from key resources supporting collective social control. Sampson et al. (1997) argued that the alienation and dependency wrought by resource deprivation and racial exclusion act as a centrifugal force that stymies collective efficacy. Even if personal ties are strong in areas of concentrated disadvantage, they may be weakly tethered to expectations for collective action. The concentration of single-parent households also makes it harder to maintain the supervision of adolescents, thus facilitating a peer-controlled system (Sampson, 1987). Overall, then, the capacity to achieve collective social control and establish social capital for children is likely to be attenuated in neighborhoods with multiple forms of disadvantage.

Not only has poverty become more concentrated in recent years, so too has the ecological sorting of residents by resources such as education, occupation, and income (Brooks-Gunn, Duncan, Kato, & Sealand, 1993; Massey, 1996; Sampson et al., 1999). Recent scholarship has thus argued for the importance of separating the upper tail of the SES distribution from the bottom tail of so much research. Brooks-Gunn et al. (1993), for example, found that it was the positive influence of concentrated SES, rather than the presence of low-income neighbors, that enhanced adolescent outcomes. Yet the tendency of research on child development has been to focus quickly and narrowly on poverty, neglecting the growing phenomenon of concentrated wealth. Following Sampson et al. (1999), I correct for this tendency by explicitly considering the role of concentrated affluence in generating aspects of social capital and collective efficacy for children.

There are other structural characteristics that bear on the ability of local communities to effectively engage in collective childrearing and social control. The density of adults relative to children is one structural indicator of the child-centered nature of neighborhood life. Another factor is the sheer density of the population relative to land space. Quite apart from the latent capacity for action inherent in any community, dense levels of population concentration and the accompanying anonymity form a structural limit to what can be achieved through relational ties.

Metropolitan and Spatial Inequality

To fully understand neighborhood-level mechanisms and the ecology of routine activities, we must also take into account extralocal forms of metropolitan inequality. Research on the political economy of U.S. cities has shown that structural differentiation is shaped, both directly and indirectly, by the decisions of public officials and businesses. For example, the decline and destabilization of many central city neighborhoods has been facilitated not only by individual preferences, as manifested in voluntary migration patterns, but by government decisions on public housing that concentrate the poor, incentives for suburban sprawl in the form of tax breaks for developers and private mortgage assistance, highway construction, economic disinvestment in central cities, and haphazard zoning on land use (Logan & Molotch, 1987).

The embeddedness of neighborhoods within the larger system of citywide spatial dynamics is equally relevant. Recent research on population change shows that population abandonment is driven as much by spatial diffusion processes (e.g., changes in proximity to violent crime) as by the internal characteristics of neighborhoods (Morenoff & Sampson, 1997). In particular, housing decisions are often made by assessing the quality of neighborhoods relative to what is happening in surrounding areas. Parents with young children appear quite sensitive to the relative location of neighborhoods and schools in addition to their internal characteristics.

Sampson et al. (1999) thus argued that the benefits for children that might accrue from neighborhood collective efficacy and community social organization are conditioned by the characteristics of spatially proximate neighborhoods, which in turn are themselves linked to adjoining neighborhoods. In this sense, a major source of variation in social support for children stems from spatially linked inequalities that characterize the wider metropolitan system. Moreover, because the resources of social capital and the active processes generated by collective efficacy are nonexclusive, their benefits may spill over to influence neighboring communities. In other words, like a good school or a desirable park, the collective practices of child supervision and neighborly exchange may accrue not just to residents of that neighborhood but to those in surrounding areas, thus producing *spatial externalities* (Sampson et al., 1999). Black neighborhoods are situated in more disadvantaged larger environments than are similarly endowed White neighborhoods, suggesting that spatial externalities to collective efficacy and social capital may be one of the ecological mechanisms that help explain the sharp differences in children's outcomes by the racial composition of neighborhoods (Sampson et al., 1999).

TESTING NEIGHBORHOOD-LEVEL THEORY

There are a daunting number of complex challenges to assessing the neighborhood-level framework just articulated. Indeed, methodological issues such as differential selection of individuals into communities (compositional or endogeneity effects), the importance of indirect neighborhood effects, measurement error and shared method variance, spatial dependence, and simultaneity bias represent serious challenges to drawing definitive conclusions on the role of neighborhood context (Cook, Shagle, & Degirmencioglu, 1997; Duncan & Raudenbush, 1998; Tienda, 1991). Neighborhoods are also much more heterogeneous internally and thus less "monolithic" than commonly believed (Furstenberg, Cook, Eccles, Elder, & Samoroff, 1999).[2] Duncan has done a beautiful job laying out these challenges, and, better yet, possible solutions. Although a full discussion is beyond the scope of this chapter, the following methodological issues are important enough to merit brief comment.

---

[2] The same might be said of individuals, although it rarely is. There is much more intra-individual variability (heterogeneity) in all sorts of human phenomena (from committing crime to depression) than our theories seem to allow. The assumption of stability is deep-rooted in the social sciences (Kagan, 1980) despite considerable evidence suggesting a more complex pattern.

Selection Effects

That there is differential selection of neighborhoods by individuals (parents, not children) is no doubt true, but so also is the reverse. That is, neighborhoods can in a sense be said to "choose" or allocate individuals. As Bickford and Massey (1991) argued, public housing has in large part represented a federally funded, physically permanent institution for the isolation of low-income Black families and must therefore be considered an important structural constraint on ecological area of residence. Even among those with the financial wherewithal, however, neighborhoods act on and often reject the individual choices of newcomers. As Sugrue's (1996) poignant research on postwar Detroit revealed, neighborhood associations were the vehicles exploited by Whites to forcibly keep Blacks from moving into White working-class areas (e.g., by means of arson, threats, violence). When access *is* allowed, rejection of individuals' "selection" decisions can take on other means. What is the phenomenon of "White flight" if not a choice by Whites to reject Black newcomers through exit rather than voice? Moreover, in this case, the neighborhood of choice by the inmovers is significantly altered by the choice of outmovers, and, sociologically, is thus no longer the same neighborhood. Whether through active segregation in housing allocation, threats of violence, or exit, the unfortunate historical reality suggests that neighborhood composition is not easily reduced to individual selection. More generally, when sorting and allocation represent ecological processes embodied in public policy and historical patterns of racial subjugation, concerns about individual differences (or selection) take on a new light.

Endogeneity Bias

Implied by the selection argument is *endogeneity bias*, or the notion that if individuals' choices of context are freely made, the collective properties of context are an outcome rather than cause. I agree with Duncan and Raudenbush (1998) on the importance of this problem, although I also think that the endogeneity argument blurs the relational insight of sociology—social life is both interdependent and emergent. I refer to the dynamic interplay of how actors make interdependent choices, the environmental consequences of which are often beyond our control and exert unpredictable (exogenous) influences. Put differently, even if choices are made, which they are, contexts themselves exert emergent effects that are not easily predictable from the characteristics of the individuals entering those contexts. As an analogy, consider dyadic relationships in marriage. Although what people bring to a marriage relationship matters, the qualities of the *relationship itself* are not easily predictable from those individual differences (see Johnson & Booth, 1998). Part of the reason, of course, is that individuals do not easily control the social interactional features of life. Further thought suggests even more complexity at the neighborhood level where the number of social interactional and situational possibilities increases. It is also worth noting that neighborhood-effects research typically examines aggregated individual characteristics, to the neglect of factors like income inequality, variance in cultural expectations, and social network cohesion—none of which has an individual analog.

Overcontrol and Indirect Effects

Most research on neighborhood effects seems to me to be inconsistent with the logical expectations set forth by a major stream of neighborhood theory—enduring (developmental) effects. Most neighborhood research estimates a *direct effect* model whereby a host of individual, familial, peer, and school variables are entered as controls along with current neighborhood characteristics (of residence). However, this strategy confounds the potential importance of long-term community influences on the development of personal traits and dispositions, learning patterns from peers, family socialization, school climate, and so on. Indeed, static models that try to estimate the direct effect of neighborhood on a status (e.g., delinquent or nondelinquent, level of academic achievement) may be partitioning out relevant variance in a host of mediating and developmentally appropriate variables. If there is a developmentally mediated history, then null direct effects of current neighborhood context is just what we should expect. The problem is that indirect or mediated effects are likely to be complex and in large part extrafamilial. I thus agree with Duncan and Raudenbush (1998) on the need for more multilevel, developmental research.

Event-based Models

Another disconnect between theory and design is again tied to the common practice in neighborhood-effects research of looking solely at the characteristics of the individual's current residential environment. Not only may past environments matter in developmental (enduring) accounts—situational theorists point to context-specific effects. However, correlating characteristics of the neighborhood of one's current residence with individual outcomes implicitly assumes context-*invariant* effects, because in many (most?) cases, the behaviors that comprise the outcomes (e.g., stealing, smoking, drinking, cutting class) unfold in different neighborhood contexts (e.g., schools, parks, center-city areas). Consider the nature of routine activity patterns in modern U.S. cities, where residents traverse the boundaries of multiple neighborhoods during the course of a day (Felson, 1987). Adolescents occupy many different environmental contexts outside of home, especially in the company of peers. Even children experience more familial and residential environments than we might expect (Burton, Price-Spratten, & Spencer, 1997). This is a problematic scenario for neighborhood research seeking to explain contextual effects on individual differences in some behavioral status. In fact, it is logically possible for there to be no variation across neighborhoods in the prevalence of some behavior (such as crime), yet the manifestations of the behavior (crime events) could be highly concentrated in a few neighborhoods (e.g., because of low social control). This sort of situational neighborhood effect *on events* (typical of drug markets, for example, where buyers come from afar) is completely confounded in current practice. It thus pays to take seriously contextual theories, most notably routine activity theory, that focus more on behaviors and events than on individuals—that is, how neighborhoods fare as units of control, guardianship, and socialization over their own public spaces. Here the unit of analysis becomes the neighborhood and the phenomenon of interest rates of child behavior within its purview. From a sociological view, I think that we should not be so concerned with whether it was "Sally" or "Joe" who committed the act, but with the distribution of acts. Individuals are replaceable.

Intraclass Correlations

I think Duncan and Raudenbush (1998) had it exactly right in calling for caution in interpreting low intraclass correlation coefficients (ICCs) for neighborhoods. Large neighborhood differences (and intervention effects) are not incompatible with low ICCs. I would only add that if my critiques have any merit, then the informative status of ICCs and sibling correlations is ambiguous. Note as well that the low *explained variance* critique of ICCs rings rather hollow when one considers state-of-the-art results for individual prediction. Indeed, it seems ironic that the best individual models (without a lagged dependent variable on the right hand side of the equation) typically explain about the same amount of variance in dependent variables (roughly 10%) as ICCs. More generally, recent expectations for neighborhood effects are too high and have been fostered, I believe, by advocates and activists, not researchers. Duncan and Raudenbush's (1998) sober analysis was thus a timely tonic.

Toward a Science of Ecometrics

As interest in the social sciences turns increasingly to the integration of individual, family, and neighborhood processes, another methodological problem arises — potential mismatch in the quality of measures. Standing behind individual measurements are decades of psychometric research, producing measures that often have excellent statistical properties. In contrast, much less is known about measures of ecological settings. Neighborhood-level research in particular is dominated by the study of poverty and other demographic characteristics drawn from census data or other government statistics that do not provide information on the collective properties of administrative units. Equally important, the methodology needed to evaluate neighborhood measures is in its infancy. Raudenbush and I thus proposed moving toward a science of ecological assessment by developing systematic procedures for directly measuring neighborhood mechanisms, and by integrating and adapting tools from psychometrics to improve the quality of neighborhood-level measures. The details of this methodology and strategy, which we labeled *ecometrics*, are described elsewhere (Raudenbush & Sampson, 1999a, 1999b; Sampson et al., 1997). Overall, we integrated a latent-variable approach with hierarchical linear models (HLM), linked to a strategy to account for selection bias. The models adjust for measurement error in predictors and outcomes, differential social composition, and nonindependence of observations within neighborhoods. In Raudenbush and Sampson (1999a), we also developed a model of statistical inference for estimating indirect (mediating) effects in multilevel latent variable models.

In the following data analytic section, I build on this approach by combining survey methods, census data, and administrative records on health and crime to get at some of the theoretical mechanisms discussed earlier. Drawing in particular on original survey data collected across a large number of ecologically defined units, I briefly highlight the association of structural antecedents and spatial proximity with dimensions of collective efficacy for children and two independently measured outcomes: homicide and low birthweight.

DATA AND METHOD

The data stem from a study explicitly designed to examine neighborhood mechanisms in structural context—the Project on Human Development in Chicago Neighborhoods (PHDCN). The extensive social class, racial, and ethnic diversity of the population was a major reason Chicago was selected for the study. To operationalize ecological neighborhoods, Chicago's 865 census tracts were combined to create 343 neighborhood clusters (NCs). The main consideration in forming NCs was that they should be ecologically meaningful units composed of geographically contiguous and socially similar census tracts. NCs are smaller than Chicago's 77 community areas (average size: 40,000) but large enough to approximate local neighborhoods; they average around 8,000 people. Major geographic boundaries (e.g., railroad tracks, parks, freeways), knowledge of Chicago's local neighborhoods, and cluster analyses of census data were used to guide the construction of relatively homogeneous NCs with respect to distributions of racial-ethnic mix, SES, housing density, and family structure.

The Community Survey (CS) of the PHDCN was conducted in 1995, when 8,782 Chicago residents representing all 343 NCs were personally interviewed in their homes.[3] The basic design for the CS had three stages: at Stage 1, city blocks were sampled within each NC; at Stage 2, dwelling units were sampled within blocks; and at Stage 3, one adult resident (18 or older) was sampled within each selected dwelling unit. Abt Associates carried out the screening and data collection in cooperation with PHDCN, achieving a response rate of 75%.

Explaining Violence

Sampson et al. (1997) developed a two-part scale of collective efficacy to examine rates of violence. One component of the construct was shared expectations about *informal social control*, represented by a five-item, Likert-type scale. Residents were asked about the likelihood ("Would you say it is very likely, likely, neither likely nor unlikely, unlikely, or very unlikely?") that their neighbors could be counted on to take action if (a) children were skipping school and hanging out on a street corner, (b) children were spray-painting graffiti on a local building, (c) children were showing disrespect to an adult, (d) a fight broke out in front of their house, and (e) the fire station closest to home was threatened with budget cuts. The second component was *social cohesion*, measured by asking respondents how strongly they agreed (on a 5-point scale) that "People around here are willing to help their neighbors"; "This is a close-knit neighborhood"; "People in this neighborhood can be trusted"; and (reverse coded) "People in this neighborhood generally don't get along with each other"; and "People in this neighborhood do not share the same values." Social cohesion and informal social control were closely associated across neighborhoods ($r = .80$, $p < .001$), suggesting that the two measures were tapping aspects of the same latent construct. Because we also expected theoretically that shared intentions to intervene on behalf of the neighborhood would be enhanced under conditions of social cohesion and trust, we combined the two scales into a summary measure of *collective efficacy*. The aggregate-level or *ecometric* reliability was very good (.85).[4]

---

[3] By *neighborhood*, the survey protocol stated: "we mean the area around where you live and around your house. It *may* include places you shop, religious or public institutions, or a local business district. It is the general area around your house where you might perform routine tasks, such as shopping, going to the park, or visiting with neighbors." The survey also asked each respondent to name and map their ego-defined neighborhood using ecological referents. More than 70% of respondents reported that their neighborhood had a name, and the mean number of blocks reported in the neighborhood was approximately 25. There is thus some evidence that respondents report the size of their neighborhood to match up fairly well with the size of the constructed NCs (which contain about 2.5 census tracts, on average). Nonetheless, it should be emphasized that the NC sampling frame and the merger of census data required the use of administratively defined boundaries. The use of administrative units as local communities in sociological research is not ideal, but it is virtually a necessity when the interest is macrolevel variations across a large number of areas. Our use of spatial models in later analyses addresses the issue of artificial boundaries by capturing the citywide influence of all other neighborhoods weighted by geographical distance. Moreover, following Lee and Campbell (1997), we introduced controls for differing perceptions of neighborhood boundaries and names. These controls did not influence the results.

[4] Distinct from individual-level reliability (e.g., Cronbach's alpha), neighborhood reliability is defined as: S $[t_{00}/(t_{00} + s^2/nj)] / J$, which measures the precision of our estimate, averaged across the set of J (343) neighborhoods, as a function of the sample size (n) in each of the j neighborhoods and the proportion of the total variance that is between groups (t_{00}) relative to the amount that is within groups (s^2). A magnitude of greater than .80 suggests that we are able to reliably tap parameter variance in collective efficacy at the neighborhood level.

Using this measure, Sampson et al. (1997) found that collective efficacy had a strong negative relationship with violence, controlling for concentrated disadvantage, residential stability, and immigrant concentration.[5] Our analytic procedure also adjusted for a core set of 11 individual-level characteristics (e.g., age, sex, SES, race-ethnicity, home ownership) and measurement error. The results showed that whether measured by official homicide events or violent victimization as reported by residents, neighborhoods high in collective efficacy had significantly lower rates of violence. This finding held up even when controlling for prior levels of neighborhood violence that may have depressed later collective efficacy (e.g., because of fear). In this model, a two standard-deviation elevation in collective efficacy was associated with a 26% reduction in the expected homicide rate (Sampson et al., 1997, p. 922). Concentrated disadvantage and residential stability were also strongly related to collective efficacy in theoretically expected directions (t ratios = -10.74 and 5.61, respectively). Moreover, the association of disadvantage and stability with rates of violence was significantly reduced when collective efficacy was controlled. Thus a reasonable inference is that structural characteristics influence violence in part through the social mechanism of neighborhood collective efficacy.

Replication and Extension

For the National Family Symposium, I replicated the basic analysis by implementing three major changes. First, I considered additional neighborhood-level structural variables of theoretical interest as discussed earlier. *Concentrated affluence* taps the upper end of the SES distribution and is defined by percent of families with income more than $75,000, percent with a college education, and percent of the civilian labor force employed in professional or managerial occupations. To account for demographic imbalances across neighborhoods in age structure, I controlled for *youth concentration* as defined by the ratio of adults (18+) to children under 18. *Population density* was also considered, defined as persons per square kilometer.

Second, in collaboration with Morenoff and building on the recent work of Buka, Rich-Edwards, Raudenbush, and Earls (1998), I examined a conceptually distinct outcome that is independent of survey, census, *and* crime records — the percentage of low birthweight babies born to mothers residing in the neighborhood. Not only is this outcome measured separately (from vital statistics) thus eliminating shared method variance, it addresses rather well the simultaneity prob-

---

[5] Based on census data for 1990, *concentrated disadvantage* was a principal-components scale representing economic disadvantage in racially segregated urban neighborhoods. It was defined by percent below the poverty line, percent receiving public assistance, percent unemployed, percent female-headed families with children, and percent Black. The second scale captured areas of *concentrated immigration*. The variables that defined this dimension are percent Latino (some 70% of Latinos are Mexican American in Chicago) and percent foreign born. Consistent with a long line of urban research, the third scale was neighborhood *residential stability*, as defined by percent of residents 5 years and older residing in the same house as 5 years earlier and percent owner-occupied homes.

lem identified by Duncan and Raudenbush (1995). It is implausible to argue that low birthweight babies cause a reduction in informal social control and cohesion. It is probably the case that residents are largely unaware of the state of aggregate birth outcomes in the neighborhood, and even if they were, it is not the sort of fear-inspiring phenomenon hypothesized to undermine social order (cf. Skogan, 1990). By contrast, there is a strong theoretical literature that specifies collective aspects of social cohesion and local ties as a protective factor in health outcomes among women (see Morenoff, 1998).

Third and perhaps most important, I examined the notion of a spatial external-ity which, once accrued in a given neighborhood, benefits or puts at risk not only residents of that area but also others who live nearby (Sampson et al., 1999). Meth-odologically, this led to a model of *spatial dependence* whereby neighborhood ob-servations are interdependent and characterized by a functional relationship be-tween what happens at one point in space and what happens elsewhere. Spatial dependence may also arise as a result of the inexact correspondence between the neighborhood boundaries imposed by census geography and the ecological proper-ties that constrain social interaction. Following Sampson et al. (1999), I modeled spatial interdependence by introducing a *spatial lag*, Wy, as a key explanatory vari-able. For a given observation i, a spatially lagged variable, Wy_i, is the weighted average of values in neighboring locations, $S_j w_{ij} y_j$. In the present case, the weights matrix is expressed as first-order contiguity, which defines neighbors as those NCs that share a common border or corner.[6] Addressing the spatial theory introduced before, I defined $y = rWy + Xb + e$, where y is a N by 1 vector of observations on the dependent variable, Wy is a N by 1 vector of spatial lags for the dependent variable, r is the spatial autoregressive coefficient, X is a N by K matrix of observations on our (exogenous) explanatory variables with an associated K by 1 vector of regres-sion coefficients b, and e is a N by 1 vector of normally distributed random error terms, with means 0 and constant (homoskedastic) variances.[7]

Table 1.2 displays the maximum likelihood (ML) spatial regression results for rates of homicide (age and sex adjusted) and low birthweight in 1995-1996, controlling for prior levels of each outcome (1989-1990). Because of the strong temporal stability in homicide and low birthweight, the time-lag specification pre-sents a conservative test and helps to control for omitted variable bias. The results show at least three interesting and parallel results. Note first the strong spatial

---

[6] Although this specification of the weights matrix limits the calculation of Wy to contiguous first-order neighbors, the model incorporates the spatial dynamics of the entire city through what is called a spatial multiplier. That is, spatial dependence is modeled as a ripple effect, through which a change in X at location I affects not only the value of y at location I but also at all other locations (Sampson et al., 1999).

[7] Spatial dependence may also be treated as a "nuisance," in the form of a *spatial error* model (Anselin, 1988). The decision of which modeling approach is more appropriate rests largely on theoretical considerations, but it can also be tested with a variety of diagnostic statistics. The spatial lag models are more consistent with a theoretical ap-proach that considers spatial dependence as a substantive phenomenon rather than as a nuisance. Moreover, overall the lag models outperformed the corresponding spatial error models in diagnostic tests (for details see Sampson et al., 1999). The maximum-likelihood (ML) estimation of the spatial lag model is based on the assumption of normal error terms.

Table 1.2
Maximum Likelihood Estimates for the Spatial Lag Regression of Logged Rates of Homicide and Low Birthweight on Neighborhood Structural Predictors and Collective Efficacy:
Vital Statistics (1995-1996), PHDCN Survey (1995), and Census Data (1990)

	Logged age- & sex-adjusted rates of homicide per 10,000 persons (1995-1996)			Logged rates of low birthweight per 100 live births (1995-1996)		
	Coeff.	SE	z-value	Coeff.	SE	z-value
Intercept	0.72	0.13	5.36 **	1.21	0.15	8.28 **
Concentrated Disadvantage	0.12	0.08	1.42	0.13	0.04	3.04 **
Concentrated Affluence	-0.09	0.06	-1.49	-0.07	0.03	-2.16 *
Immigrant Concentration	-0.25	0.06	-4.10 **	-0.15	0.03	-4.51 **
Residential Stability	0.04	0.05	0.91	0.01	0.03	0.21
Adults per Child[1]	-0.39	0.34	-1.17	-0.18	0.19	-0.98
Population Density[2]	0.41	0.92	0.45	0.62	0.50	1.24
Collective Efficacy	-0.09	0.03	-3.41 **	-0.03	0.01	-2.21 *
Logged Prior Level (1989-90)	0.20	0.06	3.39 **	0.15	0.05	3.08 **
Spatial Proximity	0.31	0.06	5.60 **	0.26	0.06	4.70 **
Pseudo R^2	0.64			0.68		
Log-Likelihood	-262.95			-56.74		
Likelihood ratio test for lag	31.04 **			20.08 **		
Diagnostic tests (p values)						
Spatial error dependence	0.04 *			0.70		
Heteroskedasticity	0.00 **			0.01 **		

** $p < 0.01$
* $p < 0.05$

[1] Coefficients and Standard Errors have been multiplied by 100
[2] Coefficients and Standard Errors have been multiplied by 100,000

effect after controlling for the internal characteristics of neighborhoods. Substantively, the results suggest that spatial proximity to neighborhood "hot spots" of criminal violence increases a NC's level of homicide (z-ratio = 5.60) regardless of social structural characteristics like concentrated poverty, affluence, and residential stability. There is a spatial profile to rates of low birthweight as well—being located in "hot spots" of health risk seems to have a diffusion effect. This spatial component may arise from lack of institutional resources and easy access to health care. It might also capture a network-based transmission of health information, where pregnant women are influenced to act in certain ways based on what people around them are doing, or what people close to them advise them to do (Morenoff, 1999). Whatever the specific mechanism, spatial proximity matters whether we are predicting variations in violence or low birthweight unaccounted for by previous levels of risk.

The second parallel finding is that collective efficacy exhibits a consistent negative association with rates of both homicide and low birthweight (z-ratios = -3.41 and –2.21, respectively), controlling for spatial dependence and structural factors. The association of residential stability with these outcomes is also significantly reduced once collective efficacy is controlled (reduced form not shown). Interestingly, however, once spatial proximity, collective efficacy, and structural characteristics are controlled, immigrant concentration continues to have a significant negative (protective?) effect on both homicide and low birthweight. In addition, the direct effects of concentrated disadvantage and affluence remain for low birthweight. The mediating role of collective efficacy is thus smaller for low birthweight than for homicide.

Third, note the stability in outcomes over time. Prior homicide exhibits a large positive association with the 1995-1996 homicide rate, and prior rates of low birthweight predict later rates of low birthweight. If prior homicide and low birthweight serve to pick up multiple elements of stress and exposure to violence not captured by the socioeconomic variables, then the spatial proximity and collective efficacy results take on added significance.

What are the Sources of Collective Efficacy?

Having looked at two outcomes, I now turn to a description of analyses that attempt to unpack the sources and spatial context of collective efficacy. Table 1.3 shows that ecological segregation at both ends of the socioeconomic distribution is important for understanding variations in collective efficacy. Neighborhoods characterized by the concentration of affluence exhibit significantly higher levels of collective efficacy (z-ratio = 4.53), controlling for poverty, stability, and other structural features.[8] At the other end of the socioeconomic distribution, cohesion and shared expectations for social control are much lower in neighborhoods of disadvantage (z-ratio = -5.66). Apparently, there is something about the concentration of multiple forms of disadvantage that depresses shared expectations for efficacious action. The data also suggest that we not overlook density and stability. In particular, regardless of concentrated poverty and affluence, race-ethnic composition, and age composition, stable neighborhoods exhibit significantly higher levels of collective efficacy than do unstable neighborhoods. Although

---

[8] As expected, concentrated disadvantage and affluence are inversely related, but not so much as to present severe multicollinearity problems. The magnitude (-.56) is in fact relatively modest. No correlation among predictors is greater than .7.

Table 1.3
Maximum Likelihood Estimates for the Spatial Lag Regression of
Collective Efficacy on Neighborhood Structural Predictors:
PHDCN Survey (1995) and Census Data (1990)

	Coeff.	SE	z-value
Intercept	0.735	0.154	4.78
Concentrated Disadvantage	-0.809	0.143	-5.66
Concentrated Affluence	0.544	0.120	4.53
Immigrant Concentration	-0.158	0.125	-1.26
Residential Stability	0.439	0.104	4.20
Adults per Child	-0.011	0.007	-1.62
Population Density[1]	-0.087	0.019	-4.65
Spatial Proximity	0.224	0.058	3.85

Pseudo R^2	0.66
Log-Likelihood	-517.00
Likelihood ratio test for lag	14.27 **
Diagnostic tests (p values)	
Spatial error dependence	8.86 **
Heteroskedasticity	7.90

** $p < 0.01$
* $p < 0.05$

[1] Coefficients and Standard Errors have been multiplied by 1,000

concentrated poverty seems to be the privileged construct in mainstream urban research, these results call for a renewed look at residential stability and the perquisites of concentrated affluence (Sampson et al., 1999).

Perhaps most important, the results show how forms of metropolitan spatial inequality translate into inequalities across areas in collective efficacy for children. Above and beyond the internal characteristics of residential environments —including both wealth and poverty—the potential benefits for children of collective efficacy are linked to a neighborhood's ecological position in the larger city. For example, collective efficacy in surrounding neighborhoods (themselves conditioned by structural conditions in surrounding neighborhoods) exhibits a direct positive relationship (z-value = 3.85) with a neighborhood's internal pattern of collective efficacy after taking into account demographic composition and the set of ecological controls.

To better appreciate the core substantive findings in visual form, Sampson et al. (1999) developed a fourfold typology of spatial association: *high-high*, for NCs where large (i.e., positive) values of y_i are surrounded by large values Wy_i; *low-low*, for small (i.e., negative) y_i surrounded by small Wy_i; *high-low*, for large y_i surrounded by small Wy_i; and *low-high*, for small y_i surrounded by large Wy_i. The first two categories are types of positive spatial association, whereas the latter two categories are examples of negative spatial association.

Figure 1.1 adapts this typology for the scale of collective efficacy. One notes the clustering of low-low values on the near northwest side of the city and in large sections of the south side, areas that coincide with the concentration of poverty within Chicago's inner city. The cases that hold considerable theoretical interest are those that display "off-diagonal" patterns of negative or positive spatial association. For example, in Fig. 1.1, NCs with a dotted pattern exhibit a high degree of collective efficacy, but they are located in proximity to other NCs with far less shared willingness to intervene in support of local social control. One can see that many of these high-low areas are isolated ecological pockets surrounded by neighborhoods with much lower collective efficacy. The predicament faced by these types of neighborhoods, similar to what Pattillo (1998) described in a middle-class African American neighborhood, often entails an intense collective effort by residents just to maintain a reasonable level of social control.

The opposite type of negative spatial association is found in NCs shaded by a hatched gray pattern (see Fig. 1.1). These NCs have a low level of collective efficacy but adjoin a cluster of neighborhoods where collective efficacy is higher. This type of neighborhood, despite lacking the crucial element of *internal* collective efficacy, nonetheless is likely to derive considerable benefits from the spillover of collective efficacy in surrounding areas. Note that the low-high areas are located mostly in the far northwest and southwest portions of the city—predominantly White neighborhoods that pick up advantages simply by their location. Note also that there are significantly fewer neighborhoods in the low-high than high-low cell.

In essence, the patterns observed in Fig. 1.1 reflect the main story behind the multivariate models in Tables 1.2 and 1.3. Some neighborhoods—especially White ones—gain advantages simply by their proximity to other neighborhoods with high levels of collective efficacy. Such spatial externalities have been largely overlooked in prior research, suggesting that collective efficacy is relational in character at a higher level of analysis than the individual and even local neighborhood. These results likewise suggest that the concept of advantage (or disadvantage) be expanded beyond the often simplistic notion of rates of neighborhood poverty (for further analyses and theoretical discussion, see Sampson et al., 1999).

Figure 1.1
Spatial Association of Collective Efficacy (CE)
Across Chicago Neighborhoods: PHDCN Survey, 1995

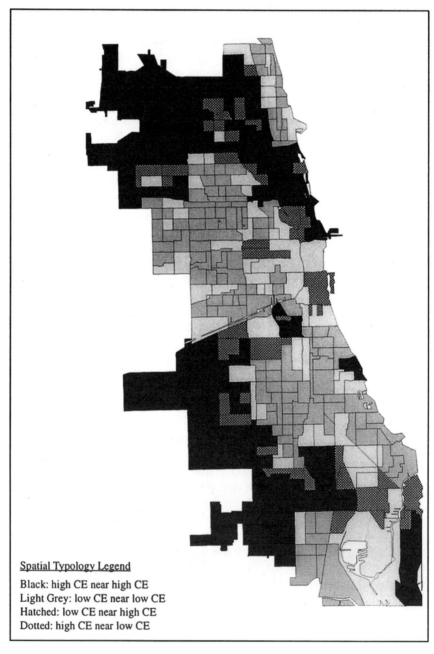

Spatial Typology Legend

Black: high CE near high CE
Light Grey: low CE near low CE
Hatched: low CE near high CE
Dotted: high CE near low CE

SUMMARY AND CONCLUSION

There is little doubt that numerous problems hinder the estimation of "neighborhood effects" in research on children, families, and adolescence. Many of these complex challenges have been discussed in this chapter. Still, I would like to conclude on a positive note by arguing that we know quite a bit; I further defend this knowledge as rigorous. As reviewed in this chapter, the evidence is solid on the spatial differentiation of U.S. cities along socioeconomic and racial lines, which in turn corresponds to spatial differentiation of neighborhoods by multiple child and adolescent outcomes. These conditions are interrelated and appear to vary in systematic ways with hypothesized social mechanisms such as collective efficacy with respect to informal social control. Extralocal neighborhood mechanisms also appear with considerable strength, suggesting that spatial externalities operate above and beyond internal neighborhood dynamics of race, class, and family status. Although individual differences obviously play a part, for these patterns to arise solely because of individual selection or endogeneity bias seems implausible. Paraphrasing one of my favorites, something ecological is happening here, even if we don't know fully what it is.

Furthermore, I think the National Family Symposium demonstrated that methodological advances are rapidly improving our prospects for better understanding both individual and neighborhood processes simultaneously. Duncan's paper with Raudenbush (1998) made this clear. Consider just the "Moving to Opportunity" experiment alone—these results are exciting and suggest a new generation of innovative methodological approaches to estimating unbiased neighborhood effects. It is my hope that some headway has also been made in the present chapter as well. At the least, I think a take-away message is that neighborhood-level variations in social mechanisms *can* be measured reliably with a survey (see also Raudenbush & Sampson, 1999b). Although there is considerable within-neighborhood variation in reports of neighborhood context, the measures considered were nonetheless reliable at the neighborhood level. Even after adjusting for confounding individual level factors, the dimensions of collective efficacy for children varied systematically with structural and spatial contexts as expected theoretically.

Based on these encouraging results, new research projects are underway to further probe neighborhood mechanisms. Morenoff (1999) is attempting to unpack in more depth the sources and consequences of ecological comorbidity in multiple health-related outcomes. A cross-national comparative project is also exploring the generalizability of neighborhood-level mechanisms to the European context. Sampson and Wikström (1998) replicated a subset of the collective efficacy items in a survey of more than 200 Stockholm neighborhoods in 1996. Preliminary analyses suggest that although the levels of concentrated disadvantage and collective efficacy differ dramatically by city, the general pattern of relationships looks similar. For example, concentrated poverty is negatively related, and residential stability is positively related, to collective efficacy in a very similar fashion across neighborhoods in both Chicago and Stockholm. Collective efficacy in turn predicts lower crime rates in both cities in almost exactly the same way.

There is, finally, the prospect that neighborhood-level theory has advanced in tandem with methodology, providing better specification of the conditions under which neighborhoods matter in modern society. Here, too, I hope to have made a contribution, sharpening our understanding of how to respond to the substantive question posed at the outset by this volume: Does it take a village to raise children? To me the question is the wrong one, for all human behavior is situated in context. The better question is: How do variations in neighborhood structures and social mechanisms influence the contexts and thus manifestations of child development? Although the current fascination with neighborhood effects has set up unrealistic expectations, my answer is that the three neighborhoods R's (rules, resources, and routines) do matter—especially when we reorient our vision to bring events, developmentally mediated history, context-specific situations, and spatial externalities into sight.

ACKNOWLEDGMENTS

This chapter draws in part from *Beyond Social Capital: Structural Sources and Spatial Embeddedness of Collective Efficacy for Children* (Sampson, Morenoff, & Earls, 1999), with grateful acknowledgment to the American Sociological Association. I thank Jeffrey Morenoff for his role in the analysis, especially in providing Fig. 1.1 and the comorbidity health data.

REFERENCES

Anselin, L. (1988). *Spatial econometrics: Methods and models.* Dordrecht: Kluwer Academic.

Bandura, A. (1997). *Self efficacy: The exercise of control.* New York: Freeman.

Bickford, A., & Massey, D. (1991). Segregation in the second ghetto: Racial and ethnic segregation in American public housing, 1977. *Social Forces, 69,* 1011–1036.

Bourdieu, P. (1986). The forms of capital. In J. Richardson (Ed.), *Handbook of theory and research for the sociology of education* (pp. 241–258). New York: Greenwood Press.

Brantingham, P. L., & Brantingham, P. J. (1984). Mobility, notoriety and crime: What can be done to reduce crime and fear? *Journal of Environmental Systems, 11,* 89–99.

Brooks-Gunn, J., Duncan, G., & Aber, L. (Eds.). (1997). *Neighborhood poverty: Policy implications in studying neighborhoods.* New York: Russell Sage Foundation.

Brooks-Gunn, J., Duncan, G., Kato, P., & Sealand, N. (1993). Do neighborhoods influence child and adolescent behavior? *American Journal of Sociology, 99,* 353–395.

Buka, S., Rich-Edwards, J., Raudenbush, S., & Earls, T. (1998). *Neighborhood support and birthweight of urban infants.* Unpublished manuscript. Cambridge, MA: Harvard University School of Public Health.

Bursik, R. J., & Grasmick, H. (1993). *Neighborhoods and crime: The dimensions of effective community control.* New York: Lexington.

Burton, L., Price-Spratlen, T., & Spencer, M. (1997). On ways of thinking about measuring neighborhoods: Implications for studying context and developmental outcomes for children. In J. Brooks-Gunn, G. Duncan, & L. Aber (Eds.), *Neighborhood poverty: Policy implications in studying neighborhoods* (pp. 132–144). New York: Russell Sage Foundation.

Chow, J., & Coulton, C. (1992). *Was there a social transformation of urban neighborhoods in the 1980s?* Cleveland, OH: Case Western Reserve University.

Cohen, L., & Felson, M. (1979). Social change and crime rate trends: A routine activity approach. *American Sociological Review, 44*, 588–608.

Coleman, J. S. (1988). Social capital in the creation of human capital. *American Journal of Sociology, 94*, S95–S120.

Coleman, J. S. (1990). *Foundations of social theory.* Cambridge, MA: Harvard University Press

Cook, T., Shagle, S., & Degirmencioglu, S. (1997). Capturing social process for testing mediational models of neighborhood effects. In J. Brooks-Gunn, G. J. Duncan, & L. Aber (Eds.), *Neighborhood poverty: Policy implications in studying neighborhoods* (pp. 94–119). New York: Russell Sage Foundation.

Coulton, C., Korbin, J., Su, M., & Chow, J. (1995). Community level factors and child maltreatment rates. *Child Development, 66*, 1262–1276.

Duncan, G., & Raudenbush, S. (1998, November). *Neighborhoods and adolescent development: How can we assess the links?* Paper presented at the National Family Symposium, "Does it take a village? Community effects on children, adolescents, and families," Pennsylvania State University.

Felson, M. (1987). Routine activities and crime prevention in the developing metropolis. *Criminology, 25*, 911–931.

Furstenberg, F., Cook, T., Eccles, J., Elder, G. H. Jr., & Samenoff, A. (1999). *Managing to make it: Urban families and adolescent success.* Chicago: University of Chicago Press.

Furstenberg, F. & Hughes, M. E. (1997). The influence of neighborhoods on children's development: A theoretical perspective and research agenda. In J. Brooks-Gunn, G.J. Duncan, & L. Aber (Eds.), *Neighborhood poverty: Policy implications in studying neighborhoods* (pp. 23–47). New York: Russell Sage Foundation.

Hunter, A. (1985). Private, parochial and public social orders: The problem of crime and incivility in urban communities. In G. Suttles & M. Zald (Eds.), *The challenge of social control* (pp. 230–242). Norwood, NJ: Ablex.

Janowitz, M. (1975). Sociological theory and social control. *American Journal of Sociology, 81*, 82–108.

Jargowsky, P. (1996). Take the money and run: Economic segregation in U.S. metropolitan areas. *American Sociological Review, 61*, 984–998.

Jargowsky, P. (1997). *Poverty and place.* New York: Russell Sage Foundation.

Jencks, C., & Mayer, S. (1990). The social consequences of growing up in a poor neighborhood. In L. Lynn & M. McGeary (Eds.), *Inner city poverty in the United States* (pp. 111–186). Washington, DC: National Academy Press.

Johnson, D. R., & Booth, A. (1998). Marital quality: A product of the dyadic environment or individual actors? *Social Forces, 76*, 83–904.

Kagan, J. (1980). Perspectives on continuity. In O. Brim & J. Kagan (Eds.), *Constancy and change in human development* (pp. 26-74). Cambridge, MA: Harvard University Press.

Kasarda, J., & Janowitz, M. (1974). Community attachment in mass society. *American Sociological Review, 39*, 328–339.

Kornhauser, R. (1978). *Social sources of delinquency.* Chicago: University of Chicago Press.

Lee, B., & Campbell, K. (1997). Common ground? Urban neighborhoods as survey respondents see them. *Social Science Quarterly, 78*, 922–936.

Logan, J., & Molotch, H. (1987). *Urban fortunes: The political economy of place.* Berkeley: University of California Press.

Massey, D. S. (1990). American apartheid: Segregation and the making of the underclass. *American Journal of Sociology, 96*, 338–339.

Massey, D. S. (1996). The age of extremes: Concentrated affluence and poverty in the twenty-first century. *Demography, 33*, 395–412.

Massey, D. S., & Denton, N. (1993). *American apartheid: Segregation and the making of the underclass.* Cambridge, MA: Harvard University Press.

Morenoff, J. (1999). *Unraveling paradoxes in public health: Race and ethnic group differences in pregnancy outcomes and the neighborhood context of health.* Doctoral dissertation, Department of Sociology, University of Chicago.

Morenoff, J., & Sampson, R. J. (1997). Violent crime and the spatial dynamics of neighborhood transition: Chicago, 1970–1990. *Social Forces, 76*, 31–64.

Pattillo, M. E. (1998). Sweet mothers and gangbangers: Managing crime in a black middle-class neighborhood. *Social Forces, 76*, 747–774.

Portes, A., & Sensenbrenner, J. (1993). Embeddedness and immigration: Notes on the social determinants of economic action. *American Journal of Sociology, 98*, 1320–1350.

Putnam, R. (1993, Spring). The prosperous community: Social capital and community life. *The American Prospect*, 35–42.

Raudenbush, S., & Sampson, R. J. (1999a). Assessing direct and indirect effects in multilevel designs with latent variables. *Sociological Methods and Research* (in press).

Raudenbush, S., & Sampson, R. J. (1999b). 'Ecometrics': Toward a science of assessing ecological settings, with application to the systematic social observation of neighborhoods. *Sociological Methodology* (in press).

Sampson, R. J. (1987). Urban black violence: The effect of male joblessness and family disruption. *American Journal of Sociology, 93*, 348–382.

Sampson, R. J. (1992). Family management and child development: Insights from social disorganization theory. In J. McCord (Ed.), *Advances in criminological theory* (Vol. 3, pp. 63–93). New Brunswick: Transaction Books.

Sampson, R. J. (1999). What 'community' supplies. In R. Ferguson & W. T. Dickens (Eds.), *Urban problems and community development* (pp. 241–292). Washington, DC: Brookings Institution Press.

Sampson, R. J., & Groves, W. B. (1989). Community structure and crime: Testing social-disorganization theory. *American Journal of Sociology, 94*, 774–802.

Sampson, R. J., & Morenoff, J. (1997). Ecological perspectives on the neighborhood context of urban poverty: Past and present. In J. Brooks-Gunn, G. Duncan, & L. Aber (Eds.), *Neighborhood poverty: Policy implications in studying neighborhoods* (pp. 1–22). New York: Russell Sage Foundation.

Sampson, R. J., Morenoff, J., & Earls, F. (1999). *Beyond social capital: Structural sources and spatial embeddedness of collective efficacy for children. American Sociological Review* (October, in press).

Sampson, R. J., Raudenbush, S., & Earls, F. (1997). Neighborhoods and violent crime: A multilevel study of collective efficacy. *Science, 277*, 918–924.

Sampson, R. J., & Wikström, P-O. (1998). *Crime and community in comparative perspective: Chicago and Stockholm.* Paper presented at the annual meeting of the American Society of Criminology, San Diego, CA.

Selznick, P. (1992). *The moral commonwealth: Social theory and the promise of community.* Berkeley: University of California Press.

Shaw, C., & McKay, H. (1969). *Juvenile delinquency and urban areas.* Chicago: University of Chicago Press. (Original work published 1942.)

Skogan, W. (1990). *Disorder and decline: Crime and the spiral of decay in American neighborhoods.* Berkeley: University of California Press.

Stark, R. (1987). Deviant places: A theory of the ecology of crime. *Criminology, 25*, 893–910.

Sugrue, T. (1996). *The origins of the urban crisis: Race and inequality in post-war Detroit.* Princeton, NJ: Princeton University Press.

Tienda, M. (1991). Poor people and poor places: Deciphering neighborhood effects on poverty outcomes. In J. Huber (Ed.), *Macro–micro linkages in sociology* (pp. 244–262). Newbury Park, CA: Sage.

Tilly, C. (1973). Do communities act? *Sociological Inquiry, 43*, 209–240.

Wikström, P-O. (1998). Communities and crime. In M. Tonry (Ed.), *Handbook of crime and punishment* (pp. 241–273). New York: Oxford University Press.

Wilson, W. J. (1987). *The truly disadvantaged: The inner city, the underclass, and public policy.* Chicago: University of Chicago Press.

Wilson, W. J. (1996). *When work disappears: The world of the new urban poor.* New York: Knopf.

2

Taking Neighborhoods Seriously

Barrett A. Lee
The Pennsylvania State University

Robert Sampson's chapter and the others to follow in this volume demonstrate the considerable progress made in assessing the effects of community context. A decade ago, one of our symposium participants, John Billy, and his colleagues at Battelle began an extensive literature review with the depressing observation that "contextual analysis is widely regarded as a quagmire of social science research and an area devoid of significant findings" (Billy et al., 1989, p. 6). Although difficulties certainly remain, it should be clear that this area of inquiry has come a long way. Gone, for the most part, are the days when dummy variables were used to capture the "total influence" of spatial units, or when one or two place characteristics were thrown into an individual-level model as an afterthought. The best research now applies multilevel statistical techniques to data obtained via several different methods and for a large number of contexts (Brooks-Gunn, Duncan, & Aber, 1997). With respect to outcomes for children and families, we are in a much better position to determine not only if it takes a village but which aspects of village life matter most.

The villages of principal interest at century's end are located in large cities. Chicago's neighborhoods, the cases for Sampson's study, qualify as the archetype, thanks to the efforts of the scholars affiliated with the Chicago School and their intellectual descendants. Ironically, the group of specialists whose lineage can be traced most directly to the Chicago School—urban sociologists—have not been major contributors to the latest round of work on community effects. As a card-carrying member of that group, I confess to being a bit embarrassed by this. Perhaps we are too wedded to aggregate units, or perhaps the problems involved are so thorny as to require the sort of multidisciplinary approach that has emerged. Whatever the reason, the primary professional identities of investigators at the forefront of community context research typically fall outside urban sociology and the other urban specialties.

Sampson represents a partial exception to this rule. Though a criminologist by training, he draws heavily on—and helps sharpen—concepts and ideas that have a long tradition in urban sociology. The basic model underlying his chapter is simple yet compelling. He proposes that if neighborhood structural features influence infant health, delinquency, academic achievement, and other outcomes, they should do so indirectly, through mechanisms of local social organization.

The outcomes should also be shaped by the position that a neighborhood occupies in the larger urban setting, specifically by its proximity to areas of advantage or disadvantage elsewhere in the city. In contrast to more individual- or family-oriented perspectives on human development, Sampson's model stresses community-level processes. As he puts the matter, "Something ecological is happening here, even if we don't know fully what it is" (chap. 1, this volume, p. 35).

Most urban sociologists, myself included, are very comfortable with the main elements of the model. The devil, as always, is in the details: how these elements are framed, operation-alized, and tested. Sampson's chapter constitutes a thought-provoking primer on the complexities involved in conducting neighborhood research. My task is to highlight some of the lessons to be learned from his work. Simply stated, what do we need to know about neighborhoods in order to take them seriously?

DOES ONE SIZE FIT ALL?

An initial lesson has to do with the slipperiness of the neighborhood concept. For practical reasons, many investigators rely on the census tract as the best available approximation of a neighborhood, implicitly assuming that one size fits all. To his credit, Sampson adopts a more enlightened strategy. His neighborhood clusters (groups of tracts) have been formed on the basis of multiple criteria, including demographic similarity, physical barriers and landmarks, and local knowledge of Chicago neighborhoods. Respondents' definitions have also been measured, using survey questions about their neighborhood's name, size, and boundaries. Sampson finds a reasonable congruence between the investigator-imposed clusters and the subjectively defined units with respect to size; respondents identify areas averaging about 25 blocks.

What best reveals the character of the neighborhood concept, however, is the dispersion that undoubtedly exists around that 25-block mean. A colleague and I collected similar data in 1988 from a sample of Nashville, Tennessee residents (Lee & Campbell, 1997). Although the neighborhoods defined in our survey average roughly the same size (19.1 blocks) as their Chicago counterparts, the range extends from 1 block to more than 900. Table 2.1 documents the large standard deviations in neighborhood definitions present within adult sex, race, and age categories. In parallel fashion, the 12.6-block mean obtained for a separate sample of 100 Nashville teenagers (not shown) is dwarfed by its 29.5-block standard deviation. This pattern of variation holds even among Nashvillians who share the same neighborhood, leading us to conclude that they must "see it through very different eyes" (Lee & Campbell, 1997, p. 931).

Table 2.1
Definition of Neighborhood Size by Sex, Race, and Age

| | Neighborhood Size (in Blocks) | | |
	Mean	SD	N of Respondents[a]
Sex			
Male	24.2	85.1	265
Female	15.6	60.5	333
Race			
White	19.4	70.0	464
Black	19.4	80.9	134
Age			
18-29	13.9	36.7	104
30-39	11.9	18.5	158
40-49	34.7	130.1	113
50-59	28.7	102.3	88
60 +	14.0	26.4	131
Total	19.1	71.7	612

Note. [a]Based on all adults who participated in the interview stage of a 1988 Nashville, TN survey and who have complete (non-missing) data on the variable(s) of interest. See Lee and Campbell (1997) for additional details.

Substantial intraindividual variation seems likely as well. One's spatial sense of neighborhood could depend on the behavioral domain in question (e.g., neighboring vs. local facility use), and it may expand and contract over the life course as one's action space and local investments change. Such variation reminds us that the neighborhood units of greatest salience to residents are socially constructed rather than formally demarcated (Rapoport, 1977). While we cannot fix the elastic nature of the concept, we should at least take it into account. Sampson has done this in a separate analysis, controlling for perceived neighborhood size.

STRUCTURE AND ORGANIZATION

The significance of the subjective realm carries over to neighborhood structure, the components of which include an area's racial mix, level of poverty or affluence, residential stability, and the like. Because different people view the same setting differently, they may be more or less aware of—and affected by—its features. The duality of context was recognized by Logan and Collver (1983), who asserted that "[r]esidents perceptions of what their community and other communities are like are as important to urban theory as the information on objective characteristics on which most urban research is based" (p. 432). The implication here is that the impact of structure may be misestimated if we neglect how it is subjectively processed and interpreted. To give but one illustration, the collective perception of local income inequality could have a bigger impact on trust among neighbors and their willingness to intervene than does its objective counterpart. Perceptions of this type serve as conduits for the indirect effects of structure.

Sampson's chapter raises the related question of which neighborhood structural dimensions deserve attention. The conventional approach is to stick to aggregated demographic data from the census. For certain purposes, though, this compositional treatment of structure can prove inadequate. To better understand crime, information on patterns of neighborhood land use and routine activities might be helpful, as Sampson acknowledges (also see Greenberg & Rohe, 1984). Similarly, aspects of the built environment—the presence of porches or stoops, cul-de-sac streets, and so forth—could affect the frequency of social interaction among residents (Athanasiou & Yoshioka, 1973; Caplow & Forman, 1955). Enlarging the notion of what structure means has practical consequences: investigators must be prepared to pay the price for using several methods of data collection. Sampson does not incorporate nondemographic dimensions of structure in the present chapter, but I gather that he will be able to do so in the future. I hope we hear more about the Chicago study's employment of observational techniques, one of which entailed videotaping neighborhood physical characteristics from a van during an exhaustive drive through each site.

Local social organization lies at the heart of Sampson's model and provides the means through which structural attributes are thought to operate. There is much to commend collective efficacy, intergenerational closure, and the other organizational mechanisms identified by Sampson: they are on target theoretically, they have been measured independently of neighborhood structure and outcomes, and they mediate (although not fully) the influence of the former on the latter. My reservation about these mechanisms has to do with the potentially one-sided picture of social organization that they offer. The analysis considers the extent to which positive organizational properties are present in a particular spatial context. Does their absence take us to the negative end of the scale or simply to the midpoint? One can imagine that outright hostility or conflict among neighbors might be worse from a developmental perspective than is a low level of efficacy. Alternatively, conflict and efficacy may coexist as separate dimensions.

The likelihood of such a scenario increases when we broaden social organization to include local institutions. Neighborhood associations, churches, and schools are generally portrayed in a positive light, as part of an area's resource stock. However, they can also be neutral or, in some cases, divisive. Churches often serve congregations from outside the neighborhood and may give little back in exchange for the parking problems they create. Schools draw the wrath of neighbors because of their weak academic programs and "open campus" policies. Neighborhood associations tend to have small, unrepresentative memberships that favor owners over renters. Against this backdrop, Sampson's statement that local institutions "reflect the structural embodiment of community cohesion" (p. 13) strikes me as an empirical question rather than fact. At a minimum, we need to do more than count these institutions or assert their significance. Our objective should be to discern the degree to which they engage residents, and in what ways (Furstenburg & Hughes, 1997, pp. 40-41). Likewise, we should not assume that informal aspects of local organization are an unqualified good. Dense networks among neighbors, for example, may allow rumor and misinformation to circulate rapidly, inflating one or two burglaries into a crime wave and elevating fear.

A PATCHWORK PATTERN

I like the careful manner in which Sampson distinguishes between neighborhood and local social organization. The temptation, frequently succumbed to in the urban literature, is to make some threshold level of organization a neighborhood prerequisite, claiming that a sufficient degree of collective efficacy (or some other property) must be present for a "true neighborhood" to exist. Instead, Sampson examines variation in collective efficacy across spatially defined settings. An intriguing complication is that there can also be variation within such settings. Those who regard the neighborhood as a "community of limited liability" argue that people become active in local life to the extent that their interests are affected (Hunter & Suttles, 1972; Janowitz, 1967). As a result, homeowners and families with young children may be more involved than renters or the childless because of their greater stake in the quality of the residential environment. This suggests that collective efficacy and other manifestations of local organization are spread in patchwork fashion over social groups and physical spaces in the typical neighborhood.

The patchwork pattern is particularly evident in the Nashville study I mentioned earlier. Campbell and I oversampled racially mixed neighborhoods to see if spatial proximity between Blacks and Whites translates into meaningful forms of social integration. Our research indicates that, despite circumstances favorable to integration, relationships with neighbors remain distinct for the two groups (Lee & Campbell, 1998). Employing concepts and measures from network analysis to examine local social organization, we find that African Americans' neighbor networks are narrow but deep; although ties are maintained to few neighbors, these ties are considered close or intimate in nature, they have been in place for a long time, and they are used often. Whites' networks, by comparison, are broad, shallow, and rarely activated. Most striking, however, is the lack of overlap between these networks. Even when living side by side in the same setting, over 80% of Blacks' ties and over 95% of Whites' ties are to same-race neighbors. Mixed areas thus appear to contain multiple social worlds rather than a single fabric into which all residents are woven.

The larger lesson here is to be critical of the assumption that neighborhoods constitute internally homogeneous entities. Neither aspects of social organization nor structural features (housing tenure, race, poverty, etc.) are evenly distributed in most areas. Casual observation supports such a conclusion, as does a body of evidence on the heterogeneity present in a growing number of neighborhoods (Allen & Turner, 1995; Cook, Shagle, & Degirmencioglu, 1997; Denton & Massey, 1991). In operational terms, then, means and percentages should be supplemented with measures of dispersion, diversity, and dissimilarity. Failure to take this extra step threatens the accuracy of comparisons between settings. For example, equally high mean scores on collective efficacy in two neighborhoods could be produced by very different distributions of survey responses, which in turn could have different consequences for the outcomes of interest. To bring the matter closer to home, would you prefer to live in an area where efficacy is uniformly average, or in one where the average level results from extremely high and low pockets? I know how I would answer this question.

CAUSAL ISSUES

When considering neighborhood heterogeneity, it is important to remember the temporal dimension as well as the spatial and social. Neighborhood structure and local organization are not constant; they change over time in complex, intertwined ways. Once again, the limited liability model helps us see the connection. It proposes that organization ebbs and flows, prompted in many instances by events that threaten residents' investments and well-being. Neighbors may mobilize politically to oppose the encroachment of commercial activity or they may "join hands with the badge" in response to a rise in crime.

Such efforts, when successful, probably enhance the sense of collective efficacy, convincing residents that their neighborhood can control its own destiny. When they fail—especially when they fail repeatedly—both objective conditions and perceived quality of life are likely to suffer. The reputation of the area declines, reducing demand among homeseekers. Incumbents are more inclined to move out or to let their property deteriorate. Demographic composition shifts. What these hypothetical possibilities indicate is that neighborhood structure not only shapes social organization but can be altered by it. In a similar manner, outcomes such as crime can have feedback effects on organization and structure, modifying a community's capacity for control (Morenoff & Sampson, 1997; Taylor, 1995). The causal terrain, in short, turns out to be more rugged than that

Table 2.2
Location of Helpers in Black and White Support Networks[a]

Type of Support/ Location of Helpers	Black Sample	White Sample	N of Respondents
Finding a ride[b]			
% Inside neighborhood	28.5	33.6	663
% Outside neighborhood	71.5	66.4	663
Finding a job[b]			
% Inside neighborhood	20.9	9.9	496
% Outside neighborhood	79.1	90.1	496
Loaning money[b]			
% Inside neighborhood	13.6	7.3	590
% Outside neighborhood	86.4	92.7	590
Caring for family during illness[b]			
% Inside neighborhood	18.6	11.4	614
% Outside neighborhood	81.4	88.6	614
Making an important decision[b]			
% Inside neighborhood	22.8	11.0	615
% Outside neighborhood	77.2	89.0	615
All types of support[c]			
% Inside neighborhood	24.3	19.2	671
% Outside neighborhood	75.7	80.8	671

b. See note a of Table 2.1 for a description of the data source. The sample is 24-25% Black in each panel of this table.
c. Limited to respondents who named one or more helpers providing the specific type of support identified in the panel.
d. Limited to respondents who named one or more helpers providing any of the types of supported identified in the first five panels.

implied by a cross-sectional analysis. Neighborhood ecology and social life evolve together. The arrows all point in one direction only when we force them to, by taking a "slice" out of a cyclical process.

The dynamic nature of neighborhoods raises another type of causal issue, about the role of exposure in producing outcomes (Tienda, 1991). In its present form, Sampson's model assumes that relatively current features of neighborhood structure and organization should be decisive. This assumption gains or loses credibility depending on what proportions of residents' lives are lived in that setting. Insofar as the neighborhood has changed, oldtimers will have been exposed to a range of conditions for differing durations. Newcomers bring experiences from other neighborhoods with them, experiences that may be reinforced or reversed by—or, most confusing of all, attributed to—the present place of residence. Readers will recognize such "imported" experiences as a variant of what has been termed the endogeneity or selection problem (Duncan, Connell, & Klebanov, 1997; also see Duncan, chap. 8, this volume). In this instance, however, previous neighborhood conditions rather than individual or family characteristics are implicated in the process through which households get sorted into particular locations.

Even among people who have lived in a neighborhood for the same length of time, the setting may differ in its centrality to them and hence in its likely impact. My own research documents a clear racial difference in the localization of support networks. Members of our Nashville sample were asked to whom they would turn for a ride, assistance in finding a job, a large loan, care of the family if the respondent were ill, and guidance in making an important decision. The average number of helpers identified is 5.4, with a range from 0 to 20. Table 2.2 reports what percentage of these helpers live inside and outside respondents' neighborhoods. For each kind of support except transportation, African Americans are more likely to contact neighbors than are Whites, who tend to look beyond the immediate residential area (Lee & Campbell, 1998).

A similar difference might be expected between single professionals whose careers take them far afield, stretching their social networks, and families whose children play and go to school in the neighborhood. Of course, exposure among child-rearing families can vary tremendously as well. Daycare arrangements, the strictness of parental supervision, and activities away from home may partially shield some children from the residential context, whereas others run free, subject to whatever the context has to offer. Presumably the intensity of exposure, not just the amount, differs between these two groups, particularly if peer contacts are greater for the latter.

CONTEXTS BIG AND SMALL

As Sampson points out, exposure has a broader ecological meaning than the one just described. Neighborhoods are exposed to each other on the basis of proximity, with organizational features of surrounding areas predicted to influence social control mechanisms in a given setting. Normally we would expect some sort of spillover or contagion, that is, a positive spatial association, and the proximity coefficients in Sampson's final regressions do take a positive sign. However, roughly one third of the neighborhood clusters exhibit organizational patterns that contrast with those in adjacent areas. It is fascinating to speculate about the processes responsible for this negative spatial association. Does disorder in one place encourage a strong response in another? Perhaps in-migrants to an area who have come from nearby "problem" neighborhoods engage in efficacy-enhancing behaviors that are intended to insure the success of their own fresh starts but that also diffuse throughout their new location, altering it for the better. Or perhaps some neighborhoods simply occupy well-insulated ecological niches and remain sheltered from outside influences.

The main insight, though, is quite the opposite: neighborhoods are not islands unto themselves. Rather, they are embedded in a higher level context that generates measurable outcomes within them. This context can take forms other than an assemblage of localities within the metropolis. Sometimes the metropolitan area as a whole, or the central city at its core, represents a relevant context. As an illustration, policies concerning general assistance payments and the delivery of social services are often set by local government and (in theory) apply to all neighborhoods throughout the municipality, although the benefits may actually trickle down in a spatially differentiated fashion. More concretely, Galster, Mincy, and Tobin (1997) showed that metropolitan-wide economic restructuring drives changes in neighborhood poverty rates and that Black neighborhoods are especially vulnerable to the impact of restructuring. Note that in both of these examples, the potential exists for significant variation across macro contexts (in welfare policy or economic conditions) as well as for the variable influence of such contexts on neighborhoods. To properly nest neighborhoods in these larger domains—and ultimately to separate the effects of the two—we need to move from single-city to multicity studies. Chicago is one big context among many.

In a volume such as this, I would be remiss in my duty if I failed to note that a key lower level context—the family—matters, too. The way the analysis is currently arranged obscures the importance of family variables relative to characteristics of larger contexts. It also has little to say about whether these variables mediate the influence of neighborhood properties or interact with them. Similar concerns apply to neighborhood- and school-based peer groups, both of which have the potential to affect childhood and adolescent outcomes directly or indirectly but are omitted from consideration.

In light of Sampson's previous forays into multilevel modeling (Sampson, 1991; Sampson, Raudenbush, & Earls, 1997) and the rich data that he has in hand, I suspect family and peer-group matters will be addressed soon enough. Even if they are not, I will continue to be impressed with the ability of his present line of work to energize and advance our thinking regarding how best to incorporate neighborhoods into the study of human development. He has already shed more light on the operation of neighborhood structure and social organization than have most card-carrying urban sociologists. For that we should all be grateful.

REFERENCES

Allen, J. P., & Turner, E. (1995). Ethnic differentiation by blocks within census tracts. *Urban Geography, 16*, 344–364.

Athanasiou, R., & Yoshioka, G. A. (1973). The spatial character of friendship formation. *Environment and Behavior, 5*, 43–66.

Billy, J. O. G., Grady, W. R., Hayward, M. D., Pullum, T. W., Brewster, K. L., Moore, D. E., Klepinger, D. H., & Rader, B. A. (1989). *Effects of contextual factors on fertility regulation and fertility* (Vol. 1). Seattle, WA: Battelle Human Affairs Research Centers.

Brooks-Gunn, J., Duncan, G. J., & Aber, J. L. (Eds.). (1997). *Neighborhood poverty* (Vols. 1 & 2). New York: Russell Sage Foundation.

Caplow, T., & Forman, R. (1955). Neighborhood nteraction in a homogeneous community. *American Sociological Review, 20*, 357–366.

Cook, T. D., Shagle, S. C., & Degirmencioglu, S. M. (1997). Capturing social process for testing mediational models of neighborhood effects. In J. Brooks-Gunn, G. J. Duncan, & J. L. Aber (Eds.), *Neighborhood poverty* (Vol. 2, pp. 94–119). New York: Russell Sage Foundation.

Denton, N. A., & Massey, D. S. (1991). Patterns of neighborhood transition in a multiethnic world: U.S. metropolitan areas, 1970–1980. *Demography, 28*, 41–63.

Duncan, G., Connell, J. P., & Klebanov, P. K. (1997). Conceptual and methodological issues in estimating causal effects of neighborhoods and family conditions on individual development. In J. Brooks-Gunn, G. J. Duncan, & J. L. Aber (Eds.), *Neighborhood poverty* (Vol. 1, pp. 219–250). New York: Russell Sage Foundation.

Furstenberg, F. F., & Hughes, M. E. (1997). The influence of neighborhoods on children's development: A theoretical perspective and a research agenda. In J. Brooks-Gunn, G. J. Duncan, & J. L. Aber (Eds.), *Neighborhood poverty* (Vol. 1, pp. 23–47). New York: Russell Sage Foundation.

Galster, G., Mincy, R., & Tobin, M. (1997). The disparate racial neighborhood impacts of metropolitan economic restructuring. *Urban Affairs Review, 32*, 797–824.

Greenberg, S. W., & Rohe, W. H. (1984). Neighborhood design and crime: A test of two perspectives. *Journal of the American Planning Association, 49*, 48–61.

Hunter, A. J., & Suttles, G. D. (1972). The expanding community of limited liability. In G. D. Suttles (Ed.), *The social construction of communities* (pp. 44–81). Chicago: University of Chicago Press.

Janowitz, M. (1967). *The community press in an urban setting* (2nd ed.). Chicago: University of Chicago Press.

Lee, B. A., & Campbell, K. E. (1997). Common ground? Urban neighborhoods as survey respondents see them. *Social Science Quarterly, 78*, 922–936.

Lee, B. A., & Campbell, K. E. (1998). Neighbor networks of Black and White Americans. In B. Wellman (Ed.), *Networks in the global village*. Boulder, CO: Westview.

Logan, J. R., & Collver, O. A. (1983). Residents' perceptions of suburban community differences. *American Sociological Review, 48*, 428–433.

Morenoff, J. D., & Sampson, R. J. (1997). Violent crime and the spatial dynamics of neighborhood transition: Chicago, 1970–1990. *Social Forces, 76*, 31–64.

Rapoport, A. (1977). *Human aspects of urban form*. Oxford, UK: Pergamon.

Sampson, R. J. (1991). Linking the micro- and macro-level dimensions of community social organization. *Social Forces, 70*, 43–64.

Sampson, R. J., Raudenbush, S. W., & Earls, F. (1997). Neighborhoods and violent crime: A multilevel study of collective efficacy. *Science, 277*, 918–924.

Taylor, R. B. (1995). The impact of crime on communities. *Annals of the American Academy of Political and Social Science, 539*, 28–45.

Tienda, M. (1991). Poor people and poor places: Deciphering neighborhood effects on poverty outcomes. In J. Huber (Ed.), *Macro-micro linkages in sociology* (pp. 244–262). Newbury Park, CA: Sage.

3
The Prodigal Paradigm Returns: Ecology Comes Back to Sociology

Douglas Massey
University of Pennsylvania

Sometime around 1967, U.S. sociology lost its way and spent the next two decades wandering the wilderness. From the founding of the discipline until the late 1960s, sociology had been fundamentally concerned with issues of space. Indeed, according to Park's widely cited dictum, social relations *were* spatial relations. In building theories and conducting empirical research, U.S. sociologists concerned themselves fundamentally with understanding how ecological factors shaped and constrained interpersonal behavior and social structure. No analysis of socioeconomic stratification or race relations was complete without describing ecological configurations of class, race, and socioeconomic resources, and outlining how their intersection influenced the life chances and social worlds experienced by individuals.

Ironically, it was one of the discipline's great sociologist-ecologists who played a pivotal role in facilitating ecology's ill-advised exit from mainstream sociology, although this was clearly not his intent. In an essay, Duncan (1959) pointed out the obvious fact that the structure of human societies stemmed from the interplay among population, social organization, environment, and technology. In subsequent years, this observation became reified as the POET framework, and under this conceptual banner, the center of ecological gravity spun outward toward the periphery. As succeeding generations of ecologists elaborated ever more refined models using variables grouped under these four rubrics, ecology drifted off on its own self-referential path, and key ecological insights gradually disappeared from sociological theorizing in core areas such as socioeconomic inequality and racial subordination.

A few years later, Duncan teamed up with Blau to publish *The American Occupational Structure* (1967), which set a new standard for research in social stratification. Ultimately institutionalized as the status attainment model, the methodologies developed by Blau and Duncan soon came to dominate the fields of race, ethnicity, and gender, as well as social stratification. During the 1970s and 1980s, sociologists at the University of Wisconsin and elsewhere estimated a plethora of path models to trace out the direct and indirect effects of family background on individual achievement and scrutinized a profusion of occupational mobility tables to study the transmission of status across time and the generations.

The concepts and methods of the status attainment model—and hence much of U.S. sociology—were profoundly aspatial and unecological. Processes of racial, ethnic, and socioeconomic stratification were conceptualized as occurring in a social realm that was strangely divorced from any specific location in space or time. As ecologists drifted off to estimate their self-referential models of spatial structure, mainstream sociologists simply bid them farewell and went on discussing stratification in a way that was devoid of concrete referents in the real world. As a result, U.S. sociology largely failed to notice the monumental shifts in the distributions of income, wealth, and residence that transformed U.S. society after 1970.

Sociology's romance with quantitative methods and individual-level data was partly an outgrowth of the computer revolution and partly a response to the imperial incursions of economics into domains hitherto reserved for sociology. Computerization enabled widespread access to detailed surveys, high-powered statistics, and complex methodologies, thus allowing sociologists to be as obscure, arcane, and seemingly hard-nosed as economists. Although the quantitative revolution may have enhanced the prestige, visibility, and scientific respectability of sociologists within the academy, its focus on individual-level data and processes came at the cost of understanding the importance of social context in human behavior. Ongoing debates about the causes and consequences of poverty, in particular, became fundamentally disengaged from the ecological context within which they occurred.

By the mid-1980s, status attainment research had largely ground to a halt, with investigators specifying ever smaller twists on ever more complicated path models to push around a fixed amount of variance in ever more trivial ways. At the same time, increasingly complicated log-linear analyses were yielding ever more modest insights into mobility processes. In general, the ratio of sociological insight to analytic complexity seemed to be reaching a point of diminishing returns. Few outside the discipline paid much attention to sociologists, and the high ground on issues such as race, poverty, and inequality was captured by conservative theorists who offered sweeping general paradigms to explain everything, usually in highly individualistic terms.

The event that changed U.S. sociology and reintroduced space forcefully back into mainstream of research was the publication, in 1987, of Wilson's book, *The Truly Disadvantaged*. He argued that whatever disadvantages individuals might experience by virtue of growing up and living in a poor family, they incurred *additional* penalties for growing up and living in a poor neighborhood. In other words, ecological context mattered in very fundamental ways that went well beyond individual characteristics or family circumstances. Wilson was the first U.S. sociologist to realize that the world had changed, and that poverty had become much more *geographically concentrated* since 1970. He coined the term *concentration effects* to describe the additional disadvantage—above and beyond individual and family problems—that poor people incurred by virtue of growing up and living in areas of concentrated poverty.

Suddenly space mattered a great deal to social scientists, and across disciplines there was a mad rush to specify, model, and estimate neighborhood effects on various socioeconomic outcomes related to poverty. Unfortunately, after two decades of being lost in the aspatial wilderness, sociologists had few data, methods, or studies capable of documenting contextual effects, a fact that Jencks and Mayer (1990) quickly discovered when they combed the research literature to discern the degree of support for Wilson's ideas.

In subsequent years, studies of neighborhood effects have proliferated, and although the quality of the data, methods, and results is variable, it seems clear, as Sampson said in chapter 1, that "something ecological is happening here, even if we don't know fully what it is." His presentation to the conference represents an attempt to specify an ecological model of how neighborhood contexts are caused and the consequences they have for people and families, focusing particularly on the mechanisms that mediate between neighborhood characteristics and individual- or family-level outcomes.

In an attempt to order the many hypotheses and ideas introduced by Sampson, I have taken the liberty of creating my own graphic rendition of his conceptual scheme, shown in Fig. 3.1. Basically, Sampson views local neighborhood conditions as arising from broad structural forces in society—shifts in the social and spatial distribution of income, race, and ethnicity, reinforced by the practices of public and private institutions. Together, these forces determine fundamental neighborhood conditions such as the concentration of affluence and poverty, the degree of racial-ethnic isolation, the mix of local land uses, residential stability, and population density. A particularly important concept is that of *spatial externalities*, which Sampson employs to account for the fact that neighborhoods do not exist in isolation; rather they are situated among other neighborhoods and influenced by their characteristics. Thus, the most important fact about a neighborhood may not be its own crime rate, but the crime rate in surrounding neighborhoods.

Much of the early research growing out of Wilson's book sought only to confirm and document the *existence* of contextual effects, focusing on estimates of effects along the path I have labeled "d" in the figure. What Sampson seeks to do is move the field beyond the mere documentation of effects to begin theorizing and testing just *how* those effects come about. To this end, he proposes specific social mechanisms associated with pathways "b," "c," and "d" in the model, and then uses data from a specially designed survey to estimate them. Neighborhood conditions are a dynamic reflection of individual choices, of course, and although Sampson does not specifically discuss or model pathway "e," I'm sure he would agree that individual and family behaviors feed back on neighborhood circumstances in nonrecursive fashion.

Although I concur with the general thrust of Sampson's argument and believe that his careful empirical research should serve as an exemplar to others in the field, I too have given the issue of neighborhood effects some thought and have

developed two theoretical ideas germane not only to Sampson's model and research, but to fundamental ways of thinking about and estimating neighborhood
effects. First, I think that sociologists spend way too much time thinking about,
studying, and documenting poverty and its concentration, and not nearly enough
time analyzing affluence and its geographic concentration (see Massey, 1996).
This asymmetry is misplaced because it gainsays the obvious interrelationship
between what happens to those at the top and the bottom of the socioeconomic
hierarchy, and because wealthy people living in areas of concentrated affluence
are disproportionately those making decisions that affect the life chances of poor
people living in areas of concentrated poverty.

Sampson and others realize this fact and recently began to include indicators
of concentrated affluence as well as poverty in their statistical models. Although
it constitutes a step in the right direction, I have never been very satisfied with this
approach. It seems to me that, conceptually, a high concentration of affluence and
a high concentration of poverty simply represent opposite ends of a common continuum, and that, empirically, their inclusion in the same model creates serious
multicolinearity problems in our statistical models. From my own work on neighborhood effects (see Massey & Shibuya, 1995), I know that the percentage of
persons classified as affluent and the percentage classified as poor are very strongly
and negatively correlated across neighborhoods.

I thus recommend that social scientists abandon trying to measure the *separate* effects of concentrated affluence and poverty, and try instead to measure a
neighborhood's position on an underlying *continuum* of concentrated affluence
and poverty. Specifically, I offer the following index of "concentration at the
extremes" to substitute for separate indices of concentrated poverty and
affluence:

$$ICE_i = \frac{A_i - P_i}{T_i} \tag{1}$$

where A_i equals the number of families or persons classified as affluent in neighborhood i, P_i is the number of families or persons classified as poor in neighborhood i, and T_i is the total population of neighborhood i. Within any neighborhood,
the index has a theoretical range of -1 through 0 to +1, where negative one indicates that all families or persons in the neighborhood are poor; positive one indicates they are all affluent; and zero indicates that the affluent and the poor are
exactly balanced. Dividing their difference, total population size expresses the
degree of imbalance relative to the total size of the neighborhood, recognizing that
is the *proportional* imbalance between affluence of poverty within a neighborhood that really matters. If the poor outnumber the affluent by three to one, but
95% of those in the community are middle class, then the social effects of the
imbalance are likely to be quite small.

Figure 3.1
Schematic Diagram of Sampson's Theory of Social Control

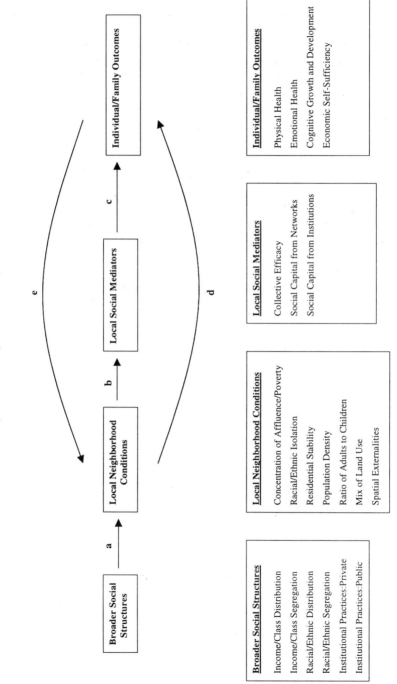

A second criticism that I have of research on neighborhood effects is the apparent disconnect between the theories about how neighborhoods influence individual outcomes and the way they are modeled statistically. To date, virtually all researchers (myself included) have measured neighborhood effects *additively,* in essence arguing that while it is disadvantageous to be from a poor family, and disadvantageous to live in a poor neighborhood, the total disadvantage is simply the sum of these separate effects, yielding a model of the form:

$$IO \quad = \quad f(IC, FC, NC) \quad\quad\quad (2)$$

where IO refers to some individual outcome, IC indicates a set of individual characteristics, FC is a vector of family characteristics, and NC stands for a relevant set of neighborhood variables.

As I read Wilson and other theorists of contextual effects, however, and as I think about neighborhood effects myself, I see their influence as much more *interactive.* Clearly it is disadvantageous to live in a poor family and disadvantageous to live in a poor neighborhood, but the total disadvantage of experiencing both at the same time is much greater than their simple sum. Framing the argument in terms of my earlier conceptualization of concentrated affluence or poverty as a continuum, I argue that living in a neighborhood of concentrated poverty accentuates and exacerbates whatever disadvantages come from living in a poor family, and that living in a neighborhood of concentrated affluence reinforces and strengthens the advantages of coming from an economically privileged family, yielding an interactive model of the following form:

$$IO \quad = \quad f(IC, FC, NC, IC*NC, FC*NC) \quad\quad (3)$$

Given the usual collinearity among individual, family, and neighborhood conditions, it may be easier to detect neighborhood effects interactively than additively. Obviously, however, one cannot just estimate all possible interactions between neighborhood conditions and individual or family characteristics. Rather, the choice of *which* interactions to pursue and how to specify them must be guided very carefully by theory. One general strategy for estimation might be to divide the sample into three groups: those living in areas of concentrated poverty (say, neighborhoods with ICE values below -.30), those living in areas of concentrated affluence (those with ICE values of +.30 and greater), and those living in areas that are homogenously middle class (ICE values between -.30 and +.30). One could then estimate the effect of schooling, for example, on the odds of employment separately for people living in affluent, poor, and middle class areas and compare the resulting regression coefficients. If the concentration of affluence or poverty indeed conditions the effect of education on employment, then we expect the size of the coefficient to increase as one moves from poor through middle class to affluent social settings.

None of these comments is meant as a criticism of Sampson's very fine chapter. On the contrary, his attempt to synthesize theory and undertake careful empirical analyses based on this synthesis is precisely the sort of work that needs to be done if we are to make any headway in measuring and understanding neighborhood effects. It also represents a welcome step in the broader intellectual movement to reinsert ecology into the mainstream of sociological thought on racial, ethnic, gender, and class stratification.

REFERENCES

Blau, P. M., & Duncan, O. D. (1967). *The American occupational structure*. New York: Free Press.

Duncan, O. D. (1959). Human ecology and population studies. In P. M. Hauser & O. D. Duncan (Eds.), *The study of population* (pp. 678–687). Chicago: University of Chicago Press.

Jencks, C., & Mayer S. E. (1990). The social consequences of growing up in a poor neighborhood. In L. E. Lynn, Jr., & M. G. H. McGeary (Eds.), *Inner city poverty in the United States* (pp. 111–186). Washington, DC: National Academy of Sciences.

Massey, D. S. (1996). The age of extremes: Concentrated affluence and poverty in the 21st century. *Demography, 33*, 395–412.

Massey, D. S., & Shibuya, K. (1995). Unravelling the tangle of pathology: The effect of spatially concentrated joblessness on the well-being of African Americans. *Social Science Research, 24*, 352–366.

Wilson, W. J. (1987). *The truly disadvantaged: The inner city, the underclass, and public policy*. Chicago: University of Chicago Press.

II

How do Neighborhoods Enhance or Interfere with Families' Abilities to Raise Children?

4

Resiliency and Fragility Factors Associated with the Contextual Experiences of Low Resource Urban African American Male Youth and Families

Margaret Beale Spencer
University of Pennsylvania

There has been a quite interesting and unvarying finding from our program of research in low resource communities that suggests a particular human capital investment strategy of minority families. The patterned finding for African American families stands in opposition to many social science presumptions concerning the group and its cultural values. In general, independent of economic resources and years of completed education, families are consistent in their valuing of competence and positive youth outcomes. Parents consistently report a desire to rear healthy children and report a definite valuing of schooling as the critical conduit for life course success (e.g., Spencer, 1983, 1990).

However, particularly for low income families more generally and minority group members and communities specifically, neighborhoods vary widely in their direct and indirect support of those values and patterns of human capital investment in its children. There is no context more significant than the neighborhood school, where themes of individual-context discontinuity are played out throughout the middle childhood and adolescent years. Similarly, there is no other group for whom the early and persistent theme of discontinuity bodes more poorly than for African American, urban, male teens. For that reason, this chapter focuses specifically on their neighborhood experiences.

Presented as a five-part synthesis statement, first, I present an alternative theoretical framework for interpreting youths' development in environments that do not always provide the best individual-context fit. Second, I use the framework to describe the special risks and challenges faced by African American male youth because it affords a culturally sensitive perspective for interpreting evoked reactions to chronic contextual risk. Third, the theoretical perspective is offered as a heuristic device for analyzing parental strategies as key socialization methods for buffering youths' stress experienced in both the neighborhood and school contexts. Parental supports are viewed as critical for supporting youths' subsequent fragility even in the presence of apparent resiliency.

Fourth, I use adolescent self-reports as descriptive indicators for illustrating the importance of other socialization contexts such as the peer group and the church;

parental reports of youth competencies suggest specific buffers and sources of positive identification. Empirical data are presented that suggest how experiences in the neighborhood context (e.g., autonomy pursuits) may reinforce particular reactive coping responses (e.g., hypermasculine coping strategies) that tend to interfere with achievement pursuits in a second critical context: the school. Additional empirical demonstrations are used to illustrate important parental strategies as perceived by youth (e.g., monitoring and simple "hassling" behaviors) for maximizing adolescent males' achievement behavior (i.e., grade point average) and school completion (i.e., high school attainment). Hypermasculinity is a featured factor in the several analyses presented. It is a reactive coping style frequently used by urban youth in high-risk communities, particularly by males. Although usually not acknowledged as such, this particular reactive strategy may be helpful to psychological survival in challenging neighborhoods, albeit in the short run. Because it is a form of *foreclosure*, in the long run, the response style has negative correlates with other contexts such as schools and peer groups.

Finally, coming full circle as the chapter's conclusion, the data are interpreted and integrated from the perspective of the theoretical framework initially introduced, and specific policy recommendations are advanced.

INTRODUCTION

As described by Bronfenbrenner (1975) quite early on, the roots of normative development and alienation continue to be attributed to many societal institutions; the family holds sway as a critical contributor given the rapidly changing family structure. The rate and myriad structural and economic changes set the stage for adolescent alienation. The general assumption has been that the economic stresses of single-parent families led to diminished interaction among parents and youth. Other "manifestations of progress" such as "fragmentation of the extended family, the separation of residential and business areas" and the "breakdown of neighborhoods..." also contribute to and further inhibit adolescents from building meaningful relationships with adults (Bronfenbrenner, 1975, p. 54). It is assumed that the decrement in adult contact and supervision eventually leads adolescents to depend on peers for socialization and support. Bronfenbrenner (1975) suggested that "attachment to age-mates appears to be influenced more by a lack of attention and concern at home than by any positive attraction of the peer group itself" (p. 55). He noted that the family is not the singular blame for the isolation of youths. In fact, the family might be thought of as merely a victim of the circumstances in which it finds itself. Bronfenbrenner acknowledged that the increasing demand for and dependency on daycare and schools as socializing agents for children may also be viewed as important contributors to the isolation of children in that each serves to physically insulate children from the rest of the community.

Made quite explicit by Bronfenbrenner, then, is the potential opposite and negative influences of the larger context on families' impact and support of its youth as parents attempt to carry out their adult developmental tasks (see Havighurst, 1953). Nowhere is this "interference" more evident than in families of color who encounter racially linked structural barriers that not only interfere with adulthood requirements of instrumentality in the care of its young, but compromise parents' own psychological resources. Structural racism in American society stems from systematic, institutionalized practices resulting in the subordination and devaluation of minority groups and the setting up of life course barriers for all of its members' life course experiences.

Structural Barriers as Life Course Challenges

The consequences of structural racism for minority youth are twofold. First, minority youth in America often live and mature in high-risk environments characterized by systemic, structural barriers to individual success. These obstacles include conditions within the family, neighborhood, and school contexts and interactions between these different contexts, along with the relationships between these settings and the larger social, economic, and political forces in U.S. society. Second, instances of resilience—success and competence displayed by vulnerable minority youth in spite of adverse living conditions—often go unrecognized, thus denying individuals a sense of success and accomplishment; accordingly, resiliency should still be associated with future psychological fragility that requires sustained support during subsequent developmental periods and the critical transitions between. To illustrate, a singular dose of early intervention against inequitable life course conditions administered during the preschool years alone—perhaps as Head Start programming—is inadequate. The inoculating impact is ineffective given the chronic and multidimensional expressions of structural racism as one moves forward across the life course.

Part of the cultural experience of visible and stigmatized minority group members is the challenge of coping across the life course with myriad expressions of structural racism. Accordingly, a lack of understanding of cultural context leads to a misinterpretation of minority youth behavior and development. Even when successes are acknowledged, the factors that lead to success and resilience in high-risk environments are not identified and considered. Identification of these factors, along with their implementation within intervention efforts, is crucial to promoting the resiliency of minority youth. Affording consistent supports along the developmental pathway limits the "wear and tear" associated with the combating of structural barriers experienced, and the consequent psychological fragility, even for resilient youth. Needed are conceptual models that consider the identification and enhancement of resiliency-promoting factors from a contextually and developmentally sensitive perspective.

The analysis of structural racism typically focused on societal-historical conditions leading to racial subordination. Theorists such as Wilson (1987, 1991) and Eggers and Massey (1992) examined the relationship between structural changes in the urban economy and poverty among inner-city African Americans. This knowledge is useful in understanding the context and stress engagement that many inner-city Black youth encounter. It is also useful in guiding macrolevel policy that may alleviate structural barriers to success. Moreover, these analyses also help to refute research with a more conservative political agenda, which blames the circumstances of minorities on public dependence (Murray, 1984) or cultural pathology (D'Souza, 1995). The sociological approach, however, does not examine the psychological processes involved in racism, namely, how minority youth *perceive* structural barriers and cope with them.

To complement the sociological delineation of structural racism, my approach for understanding resiliency also focuses on the appropriate psychological factors. The ways in which minority youth perceive their environments and cope with contextual stressors mediate the relationship between structural barriers and outcomes. These perceptual processes vary by developmental status. By understanding these processes, we can begin to design developmentally and culturally sensitive interventions for promoting competence and success in spite of structural barriers.

Of note is that an examination of structural racism poses somewhat of a paradox within the realm of developmental psychology. Whereas sociology focuses on the analysis of social structures and related processes, and anthropology has considered issues of cultural context, psychology has traditionally highlighted individual attitudes and behaviors. Psychological approaches to racism often focus on proximal manifestations such as prejudice (Bonilla-Silva, 1996; Wellman, 1993), but ignore the underlying structural and sociohistorical factors that create the foundation for psychological expressions (Bonilla-Silva, 1996). Moreover, research on prejudice tends to neglect more subtle, unconscious instances of racism, and it often focuses mainly on the attitudes of the prejudiced person rather than on the recipients of prejudice.

Challenges in the Conceptualization of Minority Youth Development

As described elsewhere, the literature for minority youth suffers from several flaws (Spencer, 1995, 1999; Swanson, Spencer, & Petersen, 1998). First, the literature tends to be non-developmental; too frequently youth are conceptualized as "short adults" as opposed to perspectives that consider simultaneously the contributions of unavoidable cognitive, psychosocial, and biological maturational processes (Spencer, 1990). Unlike this volume, social science efforts generally ignore the character of the context. Theoretical perspectives narrowly focus on problem outcomes and themes as opposed to coherent conceptual frameworks that afford an understanding of normative life course developmental processes and transitions; the oversight is particularly salient between the early years to middle childhood that serve as the history for adolescence and youthful transitions into young adult-hood. Culture is too infrequently integrated except for a statement of ethnicity and race; similarly, historical factors generally remain unaddressed (Spencer, 1985; Spencer & Markstrom-Adams, 1990). Consequently, I introduce an alternative theoretical framework that affords a more sensitive way of conceptualizing and demonstrating the linkages between context character (i.e., as representative sources of risk and stress), family-relevant mediating variables (i.e., as stress buffers), and youth outcomes (i.e., both coping strategies and coping products). The approach represents an identity-focused cultural ecological (ICE) perspective.

A PHENOMENOLOGICAL VARIANT OF ECOLOGICAL SYSTEMS THEORY

As a way of influencing an extremely important neighborhood setting—the school—teacher training programs and intervention and prevention efforts fre-quently fail to use developmentally appropriate and contextually sensitive theory to guide their efforts. The problem leaves educators inadequately prepared and emotionally unready to understand the fragile adolescent psyche of urban African American male youths who, in addition to combating structural barriers, also ex-perience the traditional normative adolescent stressors (see Spencer & Dornbusch, 1990). On the one hand, youths demonstrate a cognition-determined *hyperawareness of self* and, in addition, demonstrate a heightened awareness of and sensitivity to the perceptions and inferred evaluations of others. As a way of capturing human complexities across the life course, although particularly helpful during the stressful teen years, my alternative theoretical framework affords an ICE perspective.

As a helpful heuristic device, an ICE perspective expands the ecological sys-tems perspective of Bronfenbrenner by placing issues of context and character within a phenomenological frame. Although useful for all individuals as a life course model, it provides a welcome advantage in its sensitivity to cultural and context variations. The approach provides for a developmentally sensitive "fram-ing" of context-family-youth relationships because the social cognition-depen-dent character of phenomenological processing is contingent on the actual devel-opmental status of the individual. Thus, for a family living in a community with few apprenticeship (work) opportunities or recreational options, the absence of these resources means something entirely different if one is concerned with a pre-school or middle-childhood youngster versus an adolescent in the throes of pre-paring for early adulthood responsibilities while simultaneously exploring iden-tity possibilities. Accordingly, I emphasize the utility of an ICE perspective. It is supported by a theoretical framework that is governed by the individual's devel-opmental sensitive and context linked experiences. I refer to this undergirding framework as a *Phenomenological Variant of Ecological Systems Theory* or its acronym, PVEST (see Spencer, 1995, in press; Spencer, Dupree, & Hartmann, 1997; Swanson, Spencer, & Petersen, 1998) (see Fig. 4.1).

PVEST is an inclusive theoretical framework and synthesis. Although the term phenomenological is cumbersome and represents a long-standing philosophical history, as used by psychologists, it simply underscores and emphasizes the individual's unique perceptions of an experience that is frequently overlooked. Phenomenology refers to the suspending of one's perceptions that others think in a particular customary way and attempting, instead, to enter into the distinctive world from the outside. In sum, the term suggests the placing of oneself into the other's shoes or experiences (see Ellenberger, 1958). Given the heavy stigma under which youth struggle, the perspective provides an opportunity for integrating youths' meaning-making processes into our theorizing concerning their context-specific developmental experiences.

As a heuristic device, the framework serves as a mechanism for analyzing contributing effects of multileveled context characteristics as uniquely experienced by an individual. The framework provides a method for understanding the linkages among a variety of risks, stressors, coping responses, identity processes, and

Figure 4.1
A Phenomenological Variant of Ecological Systems Theory (PVEST)

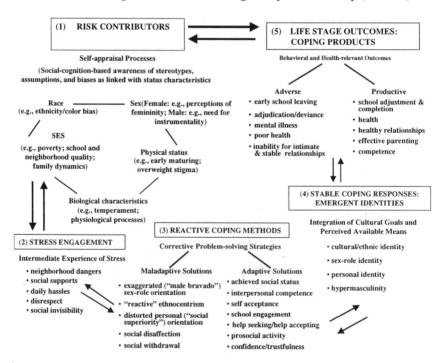

patterned outcomes. It is the nature of the outcomes, we feel, that may further exacerbate or diminish risks and associated stressors that require subsequent and specific coping responses that become linked to patterned identity formation processes. That is, as suggested by Fig. 4.2, coping outcomes at one stage may serve to exacerbate one's context-linked experiences at subsequent developmental periods.

PVEST represents an undergirding theoretical synthesis that guides our ICE perspective about adolescent-family relationships, specifically, and human developmental processes, more generally (see Spencer, 1995, 1999; Spencer, Dupree, & Hartmann, 1997; Swanson, Spencer, & Petersen, 1998). The undergirding theoretical synthesis itself is relatively new (Spencer, 1995; Spencer, Dupree, & Hartmann, 1997; Swanson, Spencer, & Petersen, 1998); however, my views concerning the salience of identity and its linkages to context quality are long-standing (see Spencer, 1982a, 1982b, 1983, 1985; Spencer, Kim, & Marshall, 1987; Spencer & Markstrom-Adams, 1990; Spencer & Dornbusch, 1990; Spencer, Swanson, & Cunningham, 1991). These inclusive themes do not represent the norm.

Figure 4.2
PVEST and an ICE Perspective Suggest the Exacerbating Influences (i.e., through the nested ecologies) of Coping Outcomes (either productive or adverse) for the Experiences of Risk and Stress and Associated Necessary Coping Processes (i.e., manifested as coping strageties and identity formation efforts)

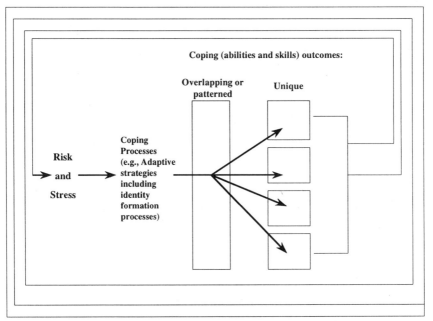

Analyses of Family Influences on Youth Development and Parent-Child Relationships.

As a developmentally fragile period of the life course, the teen years mimic sets of conflicting behaviors, often vacillating between immature, childlike behavior in certain contexts and mature, adult behavior in other settings. Parental characteristics, behaviors, and relationships provide important feedback and set expectations. Particularly, the expectations for progressive autonomy provide potential for parent-youth conflicts when behavior is inconsistent with parental expectations. While attempting to negotiate the desire for greater autonomy and experiencing an increase in parental conflict, studies have demonstrated the importance of the parent-child relationship in the structuring of positive relationships, a confident sense of identity, and successful separation and autonomous functioning (Steinberg, 1987, 1988). Most developmental theorists, including Steinberg, do not consider the experiences of minority youth. However, developmental themes such as independence and autonomy needs are also relevant for them; the context is simply different given generally unaddressed issues of structural racism.

Achieving independence from parents is a critical psychosocial task that adolescents must accomplish in becoming autonomous, self-sufficient, productive, and competent adults. Perceiving roles and boundaries as a challenge to autonomy is a characteristic adolescent response. However, the quality, type, and requirement for boundaries will vary depending on the characteristics of the context. To illustrate, specific expectations and requirements around issues such as maintaining a curfew or staying "on task" relative to academic performance must be negotiated. Negotiated outcomes must be successful relative to the parent-child relationship and also to the theme of concern (e.g., resiliency): academic performance and school completion achieved irrespective of the chronic presence of structural barriers. The responses of parents to neighborhood police presence, recreational space options, and work apprenticeship options may further vary in significant ways as a function of the child's gender. For example, parents of African American male youths perceive police presence in neighborhoods as a source of hassles for boys and as a potential neighborhood resource for girls (Spencer, Swanson, & Glymph, 1996). The findings noted also raise concerns about differential perceptions of neighborhood resources, and, potentially, how parental perceptions of a particular context affect differential male and female socialization practices and developmental outcomes.

Socialization efforts and challenges confronted by minority parents. When examined over time, parents are often viewed as providing different socialization experiences for males and females. Significant attention has been given to analyzing father-absence and female-headed households and subsequent identity processes. Often males are encouraged to be physical and allowed significant independence, whereas females are frequently assisted rather than encouraged toward independence and mastery. Although men tend to encourage more gender-associated activities in their young people, both parents tend to be generally attentive and controlling toward same-sex children. The latter finding indicates that males and females may present differential outcomes to father-absence versus mother-absence (Ruble, 1988). To illustrate, it has been suggested that boys who are reared in female-headed homes without a positive male figure often lack adequate identification with a male role model. Accordingly, these youngsters may overcompensate a sense of masculinity by demonstrating excessively aggressive, assertive, and often antisocial behavior patterns (see Cunningham, 1993, 1994; Ketterlinus & Lamb, 1994). This tendency may have disastrous implications for educational experiences that occur, most often, in female-predominate learning environments where women represent the source of directives for academic performance and behavioral expectations (see Spencer, 1999).

Harris, Gold, and Henderson's (1991) study examined the influence of father-absence on gender-role orientation and achievement for a sample of African American and White older female adolescents. Although prior findings indicate that fathers play an important role in forming more traditional traits in daughters, Harris et al. expected females without fathers to exhibit greater masculine-linked attributes and have higher achievement motives. Their findings indicated that for their African American girls, although not supported for the overall sample, data patterns indicated significantly higher achievement needs and higher masculinity and androgynous attributes. The extent to which this finding reflects a characteristic of female-headed (father-absence) outcomes or represents part of the cultural socialization experience associated with the multiple roles of African American females is a critical consideration. Ladner's (1972) research on sex role development suggested that positive characteristics of adulthood, including strength and independence, are less sex-role differentiated among poor African American adolescents than among their Anglo, middle class counterparts. Ladner suggested that multiple gender roles have been a reality for African American women for generations. Their identity has been defined in terms of additional roles other than mother and wife; this is in contrast to White, middle class U.S. women for whom dual roles are a more recent phenomenon. There may be important implications for competing male adolescent youths' masculinity needs.

As reported in Swanson and Spencer (1997), traditional masculinity as experienced in Western societies includes engaging in certain behaviors that are not socially sanctioned, but that nevertheless validate masculinity. Male adolescents may perceive themselves masculine and, in fact, believe that others will also perceive them in that way, if they engage in risk-taking behaviors that may include premarital sex, alcohol, and drugs, and participating in delinquent activities. For African American male youths who feel frequently challenged due to myriad expressions of structural racism, risk-taking behavioral patterns may be viewed as more salient for guaranteeing their view of self as a man. It is not surprising, then, that girls and boys perceive neighborhood police presence as having very different meanings and serving quite different potential sources of stress and self-definition.

Although often anecdotally reported, African American parents frequently describe the additional developmental task of having to instruct their young males in how to respond to police officers for insuring that behavior is not misconstrued as threatening or aggressive. This childrearing strategy reduces the probability that their Black sons become victim to police brutality at worst or simple harassment at best (see Cunningham, 1994). Thus, for minority parents, childrearing efforts require the provision of explicit explanations of minority status and its meaning and significance relative to race, gender, body type, physical size, and responses to authority. U.S. culture and the minority experience are themes explained by some parents to their sons. Such formally shared and stated explanations are not the norm (see Spencer, 1983, 1990), yet the dialectic and attendant stress remain even when not made explicit. In the context of such a culture, youth having similar experiences can exhibit either resiliency and school adjustment or problem behavior and academic disengagement. Thus, a phenomenological approach, one that emphasizes *how* the individual perceives or makes sense of an experience, is useful in identifying specific points in need of intervention or support for enhancing school adjustment.

As one intervention type, reports from mentoring programs (e.g., see Mincy, 1994) suggest that supportive and stable input from a mentor improves life chances. The ICE perspective provided by PVEST affords a dynamic interpretive framework for analyzing why traditional programs work better for some individuals than for others. Understanding why and how particular intervention strategies behave may aid the customization of supportive programming for diverse clients as each moves across the life course trajectory in search of an efficacious self. Too often, the complexity of these processes is not well understood for youth who daily struggle with difficult conditions, and they are stereotyped as lacking appropriate moral fabric given the patterning of stage-specific coping products and unchanged and unacknowledged difficult social conditions.

In his discussion of gender-role socialization, Steinberg (1999), citing Hill and Lynch (1983), stated "This idea called the Gender Intensification Hypothesis is that many of the sex differences observed between adolescent males and females are due not to biological differences but to an acceleration in the degree to which youngsters are socialized to act in stereotypically masculine and feminine ways" (p. 269). They suggested that with adolescence "girls become more self-conscious and experience more disruption in the self-image than boys." Of course, they did not rule out contributions of biology, but suggested that some areas of sex role socialization show *intensification*. For example, it may be more important to act in ways that are consistent with sex-role expectations and that meet with approval in *the peer group*" (Steinberg, 1999, p. 267). More often than not, particularly for minorities and low-resource youngsters, given the problem of stigmatization, racism, and socioeconomic inequities, youths often infer a lack of *respect* frequently accorded others as they pursue an orientation of *habitual right action*;

that is, consistently manifesting behavior narrowly equated with principled and moral values. As noted, these efforts frequently occur in hostile contexts or minimally supportive environments as they pursue greater independence and respond to autonomy needs.

The development of autonomy becomes a particularly critical developmental task during adolescence as youths find themselves moving into positions that demand responsible and independent behavior. One aspect of independence is *value autonomy*. As described by Steinberg, "Value independence is more than simply being able to resist pressures to go along with the demands of others; it means having a set of principles about what is right and what is wrong, about what is important and what is not" (Steinberg, 1999, p. 278). It involves changes in youths' views about moral, political, ideological, and religious issues. In addition, youths often believe that their academic efforts are not respected by the school system or by their peers. Thus, the exaggerated sex role orientation (i.e., reactive coping method) often feigned by urban youth is conjured to "demand" respect and is assumed to be both "okay" and, in fact, principled behavior; youths may infer that the response style is the only method for obtaining "earned" or "owed" respect. Steinberg's view indicated that the strategy insures that beliefs become nested in youths' own values as opposed to becoming a system of values merely handed from parents, teachers, and other socializing adults (see Steinberg, 1999).

The previous suggests that, especially for many low-resource youth, the demand and demonstration of independence and responsibility occur early and are recognized in particular microsystems such as family, community, and church. However, if respect from the broader society, particularly school settings, is not generally forthcoming, the reactive or less constructive coping response may require the taking on of habitual right actions that are polar opposites to those generally valued by society, anticipated by schools, and associated with good school adjustment. For example, such gender-intensified behavior as hypermasculinity may be seen by youths as potentially more effective in generating respect, when, in fact, it may add to group stigma and further undermine school adjustment.

Accordingly, given the growth in autonomy and the unavoidable changes in the understanding of moral, political, and ideological issues, particularly those linked with social status, PVEST is helpful. As illustrated in Fig. 4.1, PVEST affords an opportunity for understanding value autonomy as a process that identifies competing coping methods and attendant moral and school-linked identities. Coping methods and identities may, in fact, represent the same shared values and beliefs generally valued across groups (e.g., academic achievement, good school adjustment, and school completion). However, they are often coupled with behaviors that suggest a significant need for respect as a consequence of early demonstrated independence and responsibility, which accompany human development processes originating in challenging settings. Negotiating roles and boundaries suggests challenges to autonomy that may result in quite different experiences for African American urban boys and adolescents. Although often psychologically fragile, many youths demonstrate resiliency and move forward across the life course and accomplish quite productive lives.

Resiliency expressions under conditions of risk: Socialization successes of African American parents. Parenting efficacy as a developmental task continues to be of primary importance throughout adolescence, although parental socialization supports are severely compromised by a lack of economic stability and neighborhood-level contextual risks. As we reviewed in Spencer, Swanson, and Glymph (1996), independent of ethnicity, social class, and race, middle adulthood is marked by particularly complex psychosocial tasks, of which the most important is the adolescent childrearing role. For visible minorities, developmental tasks are more difficult. Many midlife parenting adults are particularly challenged by structural racism and, in addition, frequently have problems and needs that are specific to low-resource families. Tasks are further exacerbated when attempting to rear youths who themselves are plagued with unique ethnicity-linked experiences generally unaddressed in the adolescent development literature.

The literature suggests that the community represents the critical context for socialization efforts by families and life course development for its members (see Spencer, Swanson, & Glymph, 1996). Although a *neighborhood emphasis* appears as a recent focus in the literature, an awareness that development does not occur in a vacuum but in a context of environmental influences has a long history in the ecological psychological literature (e.g., Barker & Wright, 1949, 1954; Bronfenbrenner, 1977, 1979; Garbarino, 1982). A neighborhood emphasis affords an important setting for exploring developmental processes, family functioning, and socialization efforts, and for investigating the mediating impact of stress and threat. Although economic threat has been frequently described, few studies have examined the intersect among gender, community-level threat, specific parental coping methods, and youths' responsive behavioral patterns as a function of developmental status (e.g., early adolescence vs. early adulthood). Given the varying developmental tasks associated with each stage, understanding the supportive and compromising roles of parents and neighborhoods is important.

As noted by Tienda (1991), the rise in urban underserviced neighborhoods, chronically impoverished communities, families under stress, and the common phenomenon of African American male joblessness continue to characterize the fragile infrastructure of many U.S. urban centers. Chestang (1972) was prescient in his basic premise that character formation for African American youth takes place in a hostile environment. Kochman (1992) suggested that African American communities are characterized by *environmental racism*—adverse environmental conditions that pose barriers to social, emotional, and health status. He suggested that because African American neighborhoods are beset with crowding problems, hazardous waste facilities, and other high-risk environmental conditions, these surroundings contribute to an increased level of stress and inadequate coping, a diminished sense of community and psychological mutuality, resulting behavior problems, and a "state of readiness" in its youth. Too frequently, behavior problems have represented the starting place for research (for example, the traditional "violence initiatives") as opposed to strategies that explore more interactive and transactional influences on untoward outcomes *and* resiliency. It is not enough to look at behavior. It is also essential to examine the manner in which people make meaning of their experiences.

One important setting in which meaning-making takes place is the home; meanings are worked out as parents and children interact with each other. Although seldom acknowledged, resiliency characterizes the urban experience for many lower income and minority parents and youth. Data patterns suggest that African American youth resiliency is associated with particularly patterned psychosocial characteristics (Spencer, 1983). Socialization efforts that include cultural identity features (e.g., ability to transmit cultural information concerning a group's history, strengths, and societal situation) are associated with parents who rear children who have Afrocentric or group-appreciating cultural values. Youth with group-accepting cultural values frequently demonstrate resiliency and intellectual competence (Spencer, 1983, 1990). Jarrett's (1995) observations concerning parenting stresses and strategies are unique and generally nontraditional in character. Of critical importance is her suggestion that despite the numerous research findings that associate negative developmental outcomes for African American adolescents from impoverished neighborhoods, a small proportion of youth do emerge from these same despondent neighborhoods achieving outcomes not usually associated with such neighborhoods, thus allowing opportunity for social mobility. In an effort to better understand potential resilience factors against the infamous detrimental effects of poverty, her research investigated the actual family strategies utilized by socially mobile African American youth. Jarrett reviewed 21 relevant research monographs and determined five characteristics associated with youth social mobility: supportive adult network structure, restricted family-community relations, stringent parental monitoring strategies, strategic alliances with mobility-enhancing institutions and organizations, and adult-sponsored development (Jarrett, 1995, p. 114).

As reported by Jarrett (1995), supportive adult networks refer to parents' ability to provide opportunities for youth through extended kinship networks. Many of the parents encouraged their children or youth to engage in relationships and activities with extended relatives who could provide better resources. For example, the mother of a female adolescent sent her daughter to an aunt, who resided in a more affluent neighborhood, on weekends in order to provide a "safer" play area. Many families of socially mobile youth restricted the children's family-community relationships. Adolescents were discouraged and even prohibited from engaging in relationships with neighbors whose family patterns and ideologies deviated from that of the socially mobile youth's family. Stringent monitoring techniques were also utilized by parents of socially mobile youth. A strategy of particular interest included having a sibling tag along on the adolescent's activities (see Jarrett, 1995, p. 123).

Also reported by Jarrett (1995) is that parents' support and/or alliance with institutions such as schools and churches serves as another source of opportunity for adolescents' social mobility via employment opportunities. In terms of schools, it was found that parents of socially mobile youth utilized "two strategies, collaborative and defensive, to ensure positive educational outcomes" (p. 125). Adult-sponsored youth development includes providing adolescents with the opportunity to engage in activities that entail learning new skills and competencies that allow for adult-oriented growth. Jarrett suggested that "early responsibility, when properly managed and channeled, has positive outcomes; it encourages mastery, enhances self-esteem, promotes positive gender role identity, and facilitates family cohesion" (p. 126). However, most important about Jarrett's analysis is its underscoring of the heterogeneity within neighborhoods and parental use of productive coping mechanisms. This is important given the generally static assumptions about familial responses to conditions of economic risk. Jarrett's (1995) review focused on family and youth resistence, and afforded a more enlightened perspective than other, more traditional analyses (e.g., Rosenbaum, 1989). Rosenbaum's (1989) approach, more similar to most research traditions, suggested assumed homogeneous outcomes and context associated behavioral patterns. Rosenbaum's (1989) focus on family dysfunction and female delinquency indicated several family-linked variables associated with youth delinquency. The variables of family violence, parent-child conflict, family size, structure, and stability were measured for 240 women who were committed to the California Youth Authority (CYA) as adolescents. Results showed that only a minute fraction (7%) of the women had come from intact families. As adolescents, many of these girls lived with their mothers and their mothers' boyfriends or relatives (e.g., aunts and uncles or grandparents). Even in the former living arrangements, there was little stability in the adults who circulated in the adolescents' world. Although family size varied, the mean was 4.3 children per family. Often times, the children were fathered by different men. Rosenbaum (1989) reported that a majority (76%) of the girls also had family members who had a criminal record. Self-reports and documented child abuse and/or neglect court records also showed that violence was present in many of the girls' homes. Family conflict was prevalent as well. Rosenbaum concluded that all of the variables noted resulted in weakened parent-child relationships. However, an important critique is the absence of information about the girls' perceptions of parental strategies to protect and support. As evidenced by Jarrett's review (1995), an understanding of productive practices employed and youths' reactive strategies as responses would be helpful in determining and understanding the range of conditions associated with parental strategies that succeed and those that fail or are associated with ultimate negative youth outcomes. Importantly, many families are further burdened with the implementation of parenting strategies under difficult conditions with youths who have special needs.

AN EMPIRICAL DEMONSTRATION OF THE ICE PERSPECTIVE

As indicated in the description and explanation of PVEST, it is not merely experience but one's *perception of experience* in culturally diverse contexts that influences how one evolves an identity and experiences a sense of self (e.g., as a learner, a girl, an athlete, or a boy). Our use of an ICE perspective, as noted, is theory-driven and serves as an abbreviated "handle" for the undergirding theory. ICE serves as a reminder that the theory's basic assumption is that identity, culture, and context influence perceptual processes and experiences as an individual's life unfolds across the life course. As described in Fig. 4.1 and Fig. 4.2, it aids our understanding of the links among life course risks, stressors and supports, coping strategies, coping responses as emergent identities, and stage-specific coping outcomes or products.

For middle childhood through adulthood males, the choice of an aggressive attitude as a maladaptive corrective problem-solving strategy, over time, may result in a stable hypermasculine identity. Importantly, at some points the hypermasculine style may be a coping strategy. For other youths, through patterned responses over time, hypermasculinity may serve as an emergent identity due to repetitive use, irrespective of context and evident stressors. Component 5 of PVEST (refer to Fig. 4.1) lists adverse and productive coping products. A productive life stage outcome might be academic persistence for a middle childhood youngster with a culturally pluralistic ethnic identity. Because of inferred negative teacher perceptions in high school, an adolescent male's hypermasculinity may be linked with a reactive Afrocentric identity; that is, one may have a superficial cultural identification and affinity (e.g., the wearing of a Malcolm X sweat shirt), albeit without the full benefit of cultural knowledge, traditions, and values that could serve as a source of cultural reaffirmation and ego strength.

The Study

Using data from the Promotion of Academic Competence (PAC) longitudinal project, qualitative data are described and three regression models are presented. The role of risks, stressors, and coping strategies are explored for the prediction of hypermasculinity, academic grade point average, and high school completion for a subsample of 204 male African American adolescents. The sample was comprised of 219 African American adolescent males from a southeastern metropolitan area who represented a subsample of youths participating in a longitudinal study, the PAC Project (Spencer, 1989). Findings reported are from the third year (1991-1992) of the longitudinal data set (1989-1994) when participants were generally in Grades 8, 9, and 10; however, due to the high retention rates of African Americans in the school districts from which these students were drawn (particularly for males), the participants' ages ranged from 14 to 17. The students either were enrolled in one of four middle schools in the same geographical area or had been promoted to one of approximately 40 metropolitan senior high schools. The student populations of three of the four middle schools where the students were originally sampled were more than 90% African American; more than 60% of the students in the fourth middle school were African American. From parent-reported family income information, it was determined that 58% of the subjects' families met federal poverty guidelines. As such, the high schools were similar in demographics: majority African American. Both qualitative and quantitative analyses were conducted. First, descriptive data were obtained from frequency distributions of the interview items. Second, consistent with the PVEST model of Fig. 4.1, quantitative analyses employed set-wise regression for the prediction of hypermasculinity; because of its redundant use, it is conceptualized as an emergent identity (i.e., component 4 of PVEST: stable coping responses/emergent identities). As listed and described, the predictors were three *stress* measures (component 2 of the PVEST model) and two *maladaptive coping* solutions (i.e., component 3 of PVEST; refer to Fig. 4.1).

Qualitative findings. Interview findings from adolescents suggest that the majority value school, attend church regularly, and report good parent-child relations. Parental reports displayed in Fig. 4.3 illustrate parental valuing of their sons' athletic prowess and diverse activities.

Figure 4.3
Year 3 - Parental Report of Youth Competency by Gender

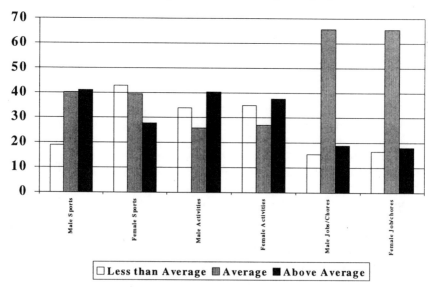

Quantitative findings. As indicated in other reports, African American male hypermasculinity is linked to the perceptions of environmental risk and challenge (e.g., see Cunningham, 1994; Glymph, 1994; Spencer, 1999). As both an unproductive coping method and an emergent (stable) identity, hypermasculinity is also linked to adverse academic experiences, negative learning attitude, and an aggressive attitude. Table 4.1 lists significant differences by school completion (i.e., graduation) for several stressors and coping methods measures used in the regression analyses. Table 4.2 presents the total intercorrelation matrix.

Table 4.1
Mean Scores on Selected Stress and Coping Methods
by High School Attainment
Boys Only
(N=204)

Measure	Graduated High School		Did Not Graduate High School		p
	Mean	(SD)	Mean	(SD)	
Stress/Support					
Negative teacher perception	49.3	(9.0)	50.2	(8.3)	NS
Perceived parental knowledge	49.5	(10.2)	43.3	(14.2)	*
Guardian hassles	40.1	(16.3)	49.4	(13.2)	**
Stressful events	54.4	(8.1)	50.5	(9.6)	**
Coping Methods					
Aggressive attitude	47.8	(10.6)	52.7	(9.6)	**
Hypermasculinity	48.3	(8.6)	52.5	(9.0)	**
Negative learning attitude	48.2	(9.5)	51.8	(9.7)	NS
Generally positive attitude	49.2	(10.3)	43.3	(12.5)	**
Help seeking	49.4	(9.5)	45.0	(9.1)	*

Note. $*p < .05$; $**p < .01$; $***p < .001$

Several predictor variables were used in the prediction of hypermasculinity. As noted in Fig. 4.4, two represent stressor variables (i.e., component 2 of the PVEST framework noted in Fig. 4.1) and two are unproductive or "reactive" coping variables (i.e., component 3 of the PVEST framework presented in Fig. 4.1).

The self-report measures were rescaled for an African American adolescent sample and obtained good alphas. Measures included the Abbott Adjective Checklist (AAC), an inferred negative teacher perception scale ($a = .87$); and the Student Perceived Parental Monitoring (SPPMS) measure which was designed to

Table 4.2

Intercorrelation Matrix for Stress, Coping, and Emergent Identity Variables (Boys Only)

Year 3 (N = 219)

	Parental (monitoring) Knowledge	Negative Learning Attitude	Aggressive Attitude	Help Seeking	Mother's Highest Grade	Parental Depression	Guardian General Hassles	Hyper Masculinity	General Positive Attitude	HS Degree	GPA	Stressful Life Events
Negative Teacher Perception	-.10	.34***	.28***	-.20**	-.02	-.08	.12	.29***	-.31***	-.04	-.24**	-.12
Parental (monitoring) Knowledge		-.17*	-.16*	.32***	.08	-.03	-.15	-.30***	.14	.24**	.25**	.08
Negative Learning Attitude			.23**	-.38***	-.04	-.12	.02	.32***	-.32***	-.16	-.18*	-.33***
Aggressive Attitude				-.17*	-.15*	.11	.19*	.39***	-.19**	-.21**	-.25**	-.10
Help Seeking					.07	.02	-.07	-.20***	.24***	.20*	.25**	.11
Mother's Highest Grade						-.10	-.11	-.13	.02	.09	.14	.07
Parental Depression							.29***	-.01	-.03	-.02	.09	-.04
Guardian General Hassles								-.03	-.14	-.25**	-.13	-.04
Hyper-Masculinity									-.19**	-.21*	-.29***	-.09
Generally Positive Attitude										.24**	.32***	.20**
HS Degree											.75***	.21*
GPA												.12

Note: *p < .05; **p < .01; ***p < .001

Figure 4.4

Regression of Hypermasculinity on Stress Supports (Negative Teacher Perception, Preceived Parental Knowledge), and Unproductive Coping Methods (Aggressive Attitude and Negative Learning Attitude)

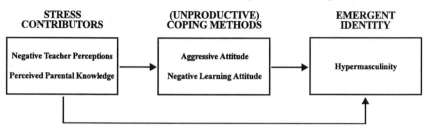

assess the adolescent's perception of parental supervision ($a = .90$). Coping measures included the rescaled Negative Learning Attitude scale ($a = .74$); the second coping measure was a scale of the Olweus Aggression Measure, aggressive attitudes ($a = .87$). Finally, the dependent measure, the Hypermasculinity Inventory, was rescaled for adolescents; the resultant measure, the *Adolescent Machismo Scale* (*AMS*), is a single scale instrument ($a = .71$).

In the three regression analyses modeled as Fig. 4.3, Fig. 4.4, and Fig. 4.5, parental variables (e.g., mother's educational attainment and parental [monitoring] knowledge) are used as mediators in the prediction of hypermasculinity, academic grade point average (GPA), and school completion, respectively. Findings from the intercorrelation matrix presented as Table 4.2 suggest that questions of mediation can be explored.

Figure 4.5

Regression of GPA on Risk (Mother's Education), Stresses and Supports (Negative Teacher Perception, Perceived Parental Knowledge) and Coping Methods (Agressive Attitude, Hypermasculinity, General Positive Attitude)

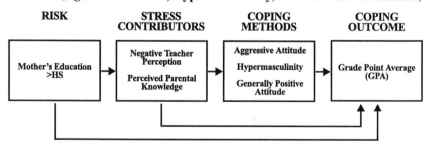

Table 4.3 indicates that although negative teacher perception is a potent predictor of hypermasculinity at the 0.01 level, when linked with the parenting variable, perceived parental (monitoring) knowledge, 13% of the variance is accounted for ($p < .001$). At step 2 following the addition of unproductive coping methods, the perceived parental (monitoring) knowledge variable remains significant (.05 level of significance). Parental knowledge is viewed as a stress buffer or source of support between the risk component and coping strategy evoked. Together, stress and unproductive coping methods predict 23% of the variance (.001 level of significance). The findings suggest that adolescents' negative teacher perceptions matter even when *positive* coping methods are also considered (see Table 4.6). What is more important is whether or not parents have knowledge (monitoring) about their youth. The findings have important implications for needed parental supports and resources because it is difficult to monitor when parents, themselves, are overburdened with their own adult tasks.

Table 4.3
Regression of Hypermasculinity on Stresses and Supports (Negative Teacher Perceptions, Perceived Parental Knowledge), and Unproductive Coping Methods (Aggressive Attitude, Negative Learning Attitude)
Boys Only
(N = 150)

Step/Predictor Variables	Cumulative Adjusted R^2	F	Beta	Standard Error
1. Stress	.13	11.11***		
Negative teacher perception		11.03**	.26	.08
Perceived parental knowledge		7.08*	-.18	.07
2. Stress, Unproductive Coping Methods	.23	12.26***		
Stress		3.96*		
Negative teacher perception		2.49	.12	.08
Perceived parental knowledge		4.53*	-.14	.06
Unproductive Coping Methods		11.78***		
Aggressive attitude		16.42***	.23	.06
Negative learning attitude		4.17 *	.14	.07

Note. *$p < .05$; **$p < .01$; ***$p < .001$

Table 4.4
**Regression of GPA on Risk (Mother's Education), Stresses and Supports
(Negative Teacher Perceptions, Perceived Parental Knowledge),
and Coping Methods (Aggressive Attitude, Hypermasculinity, Generally
Positive Attitude)
Boys Only
(N = 67)**

Step/Predictor Variables	Cumulative Adjusted R^2	F	Beta	Standard Error
1. Risk	.11	7.79**		
Mother's education: > HS			.58	.21
2. Risk, Stress	.20	6.70***		
Risk		6.63*		
Mother's education: > HS			.51	.20
Stress		5.62**		
Negative teacher perception		1.16	-.01	.01
Perceived parental knowledge		7.87**	.02	.01
3. Risk, Stress, Copin Methods	.21	3.93**		
Risk		4.22*		
Mother's education: > HS			.43	.21
Stress		3.39*		
Negative teacher perception		0.21	-0.005	.01
Perceived parental knowledge		5.93*	.02	.01
Coping Methods		1.13		
Aggressive attitude		0.06	-.002	.01
Hypermasculinity		0.31	-.01	.01
Generally positive attitude		2.69	.01	.01

Note. *p < .05; **p < .01; ***p < .001

Table 4.5
Logistic Regression of High School Attainment
on Selected Risk, Stress, and Coping Methods
Boys Only
(N = 80)

Variable	Parameter Estimate	Standard Error	Odds Ratio
Risk			
Mother's education> high schoo	2.475*	1.30	11.9
Stress/Support			
Perceived Parental Knowledge	0.072*	0.03	1.07
Coping Methods			
Aggressive attitude	-0.020	0.03	0.98
Hypermasculinity	-0.006	0.04	0.99
Generally positive attitude	0.027	0.03	1.03
Constant	-2.542	3.31	--------

Note. *$p < .05$

Figure 4.6
Regression of High School Attainment on Selected Risk, Stresses and
Supports and Mixed (Productive and Unproductive) Coping Methods

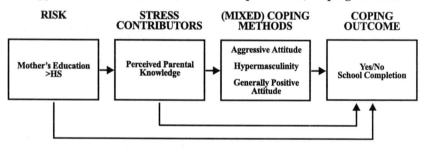

Similarly, as a demonstration of Fig. 4.5, Table 4.4 indicates that mother's education past secondary educational attainment is an important predictor of their youths' academic GPA (11% of the variance accounted for); it functions to offset risk (.01 level of significance). When the stress variables are added at Step 2 (i.e., negative teacher perception and perceived parental [monitoring] knowledge), 20% of the variance is accounted for (.001 level of significance), with the parenting relevant variables serving as significant mediators. Finally, when the youth coping strategies are added at Step 3, the variance remains significant (.01 level of

Table 4.6
Regression of Hypermasculinity on Stresses and Supports (Negative Teacher Perceptions, Perceived Parental Knowledge), and Coping Methods (Aggressive Attitude, Negative Learning Attitude, Generally Positive Attitude, Help Seeking)
Boys Only
(N = 150)

Step/Predictor Variables	Cumulative Adjusted R^2	F	Beta	Standard Error
1. Stress	.13	9.55***		
Negative Teacher Perception		7.91**	.24	.09
Perceived Parental Knowledge		7.00*	-.18	.07
2. Stress, Coping Methods	.22	7.00***		
Stress		3.18*		
Negative Teacher Perception		1.69	.12	.08
Perceived Parental Knowledge		4.03*	-.14	.07
Coping Methods		5.10***		
Aggressive Attitude		13.18***	.22	.06
Negative Learning Attitude		3.12	.14	.08
Generally Positive Attitude		0.14	-.02	.06
Help Seeking		0.02	-.01	.08

Note: *p<.05, **p<.01, ***p<.001

significance) with the parental variables remaining significant as predictors although the coping methods are not important; the *lack* of significance for the coping methods is important because each of the simple correlations is significant with GPA, as indicated in Table 4.2.

Table 4.5 presents a logistic regression of Fig. 4.6 that parallels multiple regression analysis. In this case, the dependent variable is the log odds of a dichotomy rather than a continuous measure. Findings from Table 4.5 indicate that, for the two variables that attained significance (at .05/2-tailed), having a mother with greater than a high school education makes the odds of the student attaining a high school degree 10.9 times greater (or increase by 1,090), holding all other variables constant. For each additional point increase on the parental (monitoring) knowledge scale, the odds of the student attaining a high school degree are 1.07 times greater (or increase by 7%).

DISCUSSION

When psychological research focuses on minorities, as has been the case for African American males, it often views them as pathological products of oppression (e.g., Kardiner & Ovesey, 1951). Little attention is paid to the positive, resilient as well as the field of developmental psychology have often failed to recognize and capitalize on these factors when considering the experiences of minorities. PVEST affords unique opportunities for identifying multiple points of appropriate supports and micro- and macrolevel structured interventions.

Psychological interventions emphasize changing individual behavior rather than promoting macrolevel societal changes. Although the latter is certainly a desirable goal, it also requires more resources and is more difficult to accomplish in light of financial and political obstacles. Moreover, macrolevel change may not be enough to produce positive outcomes, as individual behavior is guided not only by opportunities but by perceptions of those opportunities. Thus, resilient outcomes can be achieved in spite of barriers if one perceives that barriers can be surmounted. Alternative formulations are needed, such as an ICE perspective that considers perceptual processes that can enhance the identification of important mediators.

The qualitative findings suggest that urban male youth have productive values and warm relationships with parents, and participate in activities and sports highly valued by parents. It is not surprising that the quantitative data suggest a As society moves forward into the new millennium with added concerns about intergroup relations and the acquisition of more equitable opportunities for all its citizens, greater macrolevel improvements should be engineered. At the microlevel, added supports for overburdened parents should heighten their ability to monitor and accrue knowledge about their youths' activities: the quantitative findings sugespoused values to the desired outcomes. An ICE perspective affords numerous opportunities for specifying the needed contextual supports for the successful transitioning of fragile youth and coping, caring, and overburdened parents.

ACKNOWLEDGMENTS

This study was made possible by funding from the Ford and W. K. Kellogg Foundations, the Office of Educational Research and Improvement (OERI), and the National Institute of Mental Health (NIMH).

REFERENCES

Barker, R. G., & Wright, H. F. (1949). Psychological ecology and the problem of psychosocial development. *Child Development, 20*, 131–143.

Barker, R. G., & Wright, H. F. (1954). *Midwest and its children: The psychological ecology of an American town.* Evanston, IL: Row & Peterson.

Bonilla-Silva, E. (1996). Rethinking racism: Toward a structural interpretation. *American Sociological Review, 62*, 465–480.

Bronfenbrenner, U. (1975). The origins of alienation. In U. Bronfenbrenner & M. Mahoney (Eds.), *Influences on human development.* Hinsdale, IL: Dryden Press.

Bronfenbrenner, U. (1977). Toward an experimental ecology of human development. *American Psychologist, 32*, 513–531.

Bronfenbrenner, U. (1979). *The ecology of human development: Experiments by nature and design.* Cambridge, MA: Harvard University.

Chestang, L. W. (1972). *Character development in a hostile environment.* Occasional Paper No. 3 (Series) (pp. 1–12). Chicago, IL: University of Chicago.

Cunningham, M. (1993). African American adolescent males sex role development. *Journal of African American Males Studies, 1*(1), 30–37.

Cunningham, M. (1994). *Expressions of manhood: Predictors of educational achievement African American adolescent males.* Unpublished doctoral dissertation, Emory University, Atlanta, GA.

D'Souza, D. (1995). *The end of racism: Principles for a multiracial society.* New York: Free Press.

Eggers, M. L., & Massey, D. S. (1992). A longitudinal analysis of urban poverty: Blacks in U.S. metropolitan areas between 1970 and 1980. *Social Science Research, 21*, 175–203.

Ellenberger, H. F. (1958). A clinical introduction to psychiatric phenomenology and existential analysis. In R. May, E. Angel, & H. F. Ellenberger (Eds.), *Existence: A new dimension in psychiatry and psychology.* New York: Basic Books.

Fordham, S., & Ogbu, J.U. (1986). Black students' school success: Coping with the "burden of acting White." *Urban Review, 18*(3), 176–206.

Garbarino, J. (1982). *Children and families in the social environment.* New York: Aldine de Gruyter.

Glymph, A. (1994). *Assessing youths' perception of their neighborhood: Development of the student perception of neighborhood scales.* Unpublished master's thesis, Emory University, Atlanta, GA.

Harris, S. M., Gold, S. R., & Henderson, B. B. (1991). Relationships between achievement and affiliation needs and sex-role orientation of college women whose fathers were absent from home. *Perceptual and Motor Skills, 72*, 1307–1315.

Havighurst, R. J. (1953). *Human development and education.* New York: McKay.

Hill, J., & Lynch, M. (1983). The intensification of gender-related role expectations during early adolescence. In J. Brooks-Gunn & A. Peterson (Eds.), *Female puberty.* New York: Plenum Press.

Jarrett, R. L. (1995). Growing up poor: The family experiences of socially mobile youth in low income African-American neighborhoods. *Journal of Adolescent Research, 10*(1), 111–135.

Kardiner, A., & Ovesy, L. (1951). *The mark of oppression: Explorations in the personality of the American Negro.* New York: Norton.

Ketterlinus, R., & Lamb, M. E. (1994). *Adolescent problem behaviors.* Hillsdale, NJ: Lawrence Erlbaum.

Kochman, T. J. (1992). *The relationship between environmental characteristics and the psychological functioning of African American youth.* Unpublished honors thesis. Emory University, Atlanta, GA.

Ladner, J. A. (1972). *Tomorrow's tomorrow: The black woman.* New York: Doubleday Press.

Mincy, R. B. (1994). (Ed.). *Mentoring young Black males.* Washington, DC: Urban Institute Press.

Murray, C. (1984). *Losing ground: American social policy, 1950–1980.* New York: Basic Books.

Rosenbaum, J. L. (1989). Family dysfunction and female delinquency. *Crime and Delinquency, 25*(1), 31–44.

Ruble, D. N. (1988). Sex-role development. In M. H. Bornstein & M. E. Lamb (Eds.), *Developmental psychology: An advanced textbook* (2nd ed., pp. 411–459). Hillsdale, NJ: Lawrence Erlbaum.

Spencer, M. B. (1982a). Preschool children's social cognition and cultural cognition: A cognitive developmental interpretation of race dissonance findings. *Journal of Psychology, 112*, 275–286.

Spencer, M. B. (1982b). Personal and group identity of Black children: An alternative synthesis. *Genetic Psychology Monographs, 106*, 59–84.

Spencer, M. B. (1983). Children's cultural values and parental child rearing strategies. *Developmental Review, 3*, 351–370.

Spencer, M. B. (1985). Cultural cognition and social cognition as identity factors in Black children's growth. In M. B. Spencer, G. K. Brookins, & W. R. Allen (Eds.), *Beginnings: The social and affective development of Black children* (pp. 215–230). Hillsdale, NJ: Lawrence Erlbaum.

Spencer, M. B. (1989). *Cognition, identity and social development as correlates of African American children's academic skills.* Discussion paper series #1: The preschool and early childhood years. Ann Arbor, MI: University of Michigan Center for African and African American Studies (CAAS).

Spencer, M. B. (1990). Parental values transmission: Implications for Black child development. In J. B. Stewart & H. Cheathan (Eds.), *Interdisciplinary perspectives on Black families* (pp. 111–130). New Brunswick, NJ: Transaction Books.

Spencer, M. B. (1995). Old issues and new theorizing about African American youth: A phenomenological variant of ecological systems theory. In R. L. Taylor (Ed.), *Black youth: Perspectives on their status in the United States* (pp. 37–69). Westport, CT: Praeger.

Spencer, M. B. (1999). Social and cultural influences on school adjustment: The application of an identity-focused cultural ecological perspective. *Educational Psychologist, 34*(1), 43-57.

Spencer, M. B., & Dornbush, S. (1990). Challenges in studying minority youth. In S. Feldman & G. Elliott (Eds.), *At the threshold: The developing adolescent* (pp. 123–146). Cambridge. MA: Harvard University Press.

Spencer, M. B., Dupree, D., & Hartmann, T. (1997). A phenomenological variant of ecological system (PVEST): A self-organization perspective in context. *Development and Psychopathology, 9*, 817–833.

Spencer, M. B., Kim, S., & Marshall, S. (1987). Double stratisfaction and psychological risk: Adaptational processes and school experiences of Black children. *Journal of Negro Education, 56*(1), 77–86.

Spencer, M. B., & Markstrom-Adams, C. (1990). Identity processes among racial and ethnic minority children in America. *Child Development, 61*(2), 290–310.

Spencer, M. B., Swanson, D. P., & Glymph, A. (1996). The prediction of parental psychological functioning: Influences of African American adolescent perceptions and experiences of context. In C. D. Ryff & M. M. Seltzer (Eds.), *The parental experience in midlife* (pp. 337–380). Chicago: University of Chicago Press.

Spencer, M. B., Swanson, D. P., & Cunningham, M. (1991). Ethnicity, ethnic identity and competence formation: Adolescent transition and identity transformation. *Journal of Negro Education, 60*(3), 366–387.

Steinberg, L. (1987). Impact of puberty on family relations: Effects of pubertal status and pubertal timing. *Developmental Psychology, 23*(3), 451–460.

Steinberg, L. (1988). Reciprocal relation between parent-child distance and pubertal maturation. *Developmental Psychology, 24*(1), 122–128.

Steinberg, L. (1999). *Adolescence.* New York: McGraw-Hill.

Swanson, D. P., & Spencer, M. B. (1997). Developmental considerations of gender-linked attributes during adolescence. In R. D. Taylor & M. C. Wang (Eds.), *Social and emotional adjustment and family relations in ethnic minority families* (pp. 181–199). Mahwah, NJ: Lawrence Erlbaum.

Swanson, D. P., Spencer, M. B., & Petersen, A. (1998). Identity formation in adolescence. In K. Borman & B. Schneider (Eds.), *The adolescent years: Social influences and educational challenges*, Ninety-seventh Yearbook of the National Society for the Study of Education, Part 1 (pp. 18–41). Chicago: University of Chicago Press.

Tienda, M. (1991). Poor people and poor places: Deciphering neighborhood effects on poverty outcomes. In J. Huber (Ed.), *Macro-micro linkages in sociology* (pp. 244–262). Newberry, CA: Russell Sage Foundation.

Wellman, D. (1993). *Portraits of White racism.* Cambridge, England: Cambridge University Press.

Wilson, W. J. (1987). *The truly disadvantaged: The inner city, the underclass, and social policy.* Chicago, IL: University of Chicago Press.

Wilson, W. J. (1991). Studying inner city dislocations: The challenge of public agenda research. *American Sociology Review, 56,* 1–14.

5

Context and Meaning in Neighborhood Studies of Children and Families

Jill E. Korbin
Case Western Reserve University

This chapter is a response to Dr. Spencer's excellent and thought-provoking chapter on African American urban male youth and her model for examining the role of individuals in context. I draw on some of our neighborhood research in Cleveland, Ohio, with respect to three points in Dr. Spencer's chapter. First, her emphasis on individual resilience points toward the importance of better understanding the interrelationships among individual, family, and contextual neighborhood factors. This is more than identifying the strengths and weaknesses inherent in individuals and in neighborhoods; it is understanding the transactions among these factors. Second, Dr. Spencer's discussion of individual resilience also indicates the importance of the heterogeneity of both individuals and neighborhoods. Third, her chapter also points to the importance of individual perceptions in understanding the relationship between person and context. Dr. Spencer demonstrates the important consideration of both meaning and context in understanding neighborhood effects on children and families.

"It Takes a Village" has worked its way into the U.S. vernacular and conventional wisdom about the role of the neighborhood and community as an important, but often overlooked, force in the well-being of the nation's children. Reported to be an African proverb, this saying, "It takes a village to raise a child," could well have come from many places around the world. Indeed, in the cross-cultural literature on smaller scale societies, studied primarily by anthropologists, this is virtually a given, but with some caveats that have relevance to current neighborhood studies and efforts to address social problems at the neighborhood level. First, the societies in which this saying rings most true are those in which most people know one another and have a congruence around child rearing goals as well as parental and wider adult responsibility for children, with responsibility for monitoring and enforcing rules and standards of good behavior more diffuse than one or two parents. Second, even in societies with a strong "village," some children, and categories of children, fall outside the purview of this adult village and are less well cared for than others. The cross-cultural record tells us that a village will not protect or care for all of its children equally well (e.g., Korbin, 1981). In our own society, there are distinct categories of children, as Dr. Spencer points out, who are left out of what the village has to offer in terms of protection and opportunity.

Third, the village itself must have, or be able to call on, a sufficient level of resources to enable it to support its families and children.

Following Bronfenbrenner's (1979) ecology of human development (and subsequent elaborations of this model, including that of Dr. Spencer and colleagues), context and the meanings that individuals take from that context are integral parts of understanding human development and behavior. However, understanding precisely how neighborhood context shapes development and behavior has been a challenge. There has been increasing interest in the role of the neighborhood as context, perhaps as the "village" for child development and well-being (e.g., Brooks-Gunn, Duncan, & Aber, 1997). This increased research interest has had mixed results, and the precise mechanisms and processes by which the neighborhood impacts on children and families remain somewhat elusive. The sometimes relatively small amount of variance attributable to neighborhoods, however, must be kept in perspective. Research on neighborhood, although reflecting long-standing interests in social organization, is relatively recent as compared with concerted efforts to understand and measure parenting, for example. Multimethod, multilevel, and multicity studies are badly needed. Individual risk factors may have different effects in neighborhoods with different patterns of risk (Coulton, Korbin, & Su, 1999; O'Campo, Xue, Wang, & Caughy, 1997). Segregation and the concentration of both poverty and affluence restrict the range of neighborhoods available for research, and patterns of concentrated poverty and affluence vary among cities and regions (Coulton, Chow, Wang, & Su, 1996).

Our research in Cleveland sought to link neighborhood factors and conditions with child well-being, specifically child maltreatment. In this work, we used a coordinated combination of an aggregate/epidemiological approach and a qualitative/ethnographic-like approach. In keeping with social organization theory (Sampson & Groves, 1989; Shaw & McKay, 1942) and prior research linking an ecological model with child maltreatment (Belsky, 1980; Garbarino & Crouter, 1978), we found that four factors explained approximately half the variance in neighborhood rates of child maltreatment reports (Coulton, Korbin, Su, & Chow, 1995):

- Impoverishment (poverty rate; unemployment rate; vacant housing; population loss; female-headed households; percent African American population)
- Child-Care Burden (ratio of children to adults; ratio of adult males to adult females; percent of population that is elderly)
- Instability (proportion of residents who moved to or from a different house in the past previous 5 years; proportion of households in their current home for less than 10 years; percent of households that have lived in their current home less than 1 year)
- Contiguous to Concentrated Poverty (if the census tract was bordered by one or more census tracts with greater than 40% poverty rate)

These structural factors are similar to those associated with a myriad of social problems in urban areas. Combined with this structural analysis, we employed an ethnographic or ethnographic-like approach to assist in understanding the processes that connect aspects of neighborhood to individuals, and vice versa. A summary of some of our findings follows.

Adult Intervention

In the ethnographic interviews, we sought to elaborate on the meaning and impact of a high ratio of children to adults from the perspective of neighborhood adults. This domain was of particular interest to us because of Coleman's (1988) concept of social capital, Sampson and colleagues' conceptualization of collective efficacy (Sampson, Raudenbush, & Earls, 1997), Wilson's (1987, 1991) "reciprocal guardian behavior," and Furstenberg's (1993) analysis of differences in parenting strategies in response to neighborhood conditions. Connections among adults and the perceived abilities of adults to have an impact on the behavior of neighborhood children quickly emerged as an important theme in ethnographic interviews. Residents of neighborhoods with higher rates of child maltreatment reports and other adverse conditions and outcomes for children and families (violent crime, drug trafficking, juvenile delinquency, teen pregnancy, and low birthweight births) perceived their neighborhoods as settings in which they and their neighbors were the least able to intervene in or control the behavior of neighborhood children.

Neighborhood residents we interviewed believed that they were living in vastly changed circumstances from their own childhoods. Whereas almost 90% said that someone would have made them behave as children if their parents were not present, less than one third reported that someone would intervene nowadays if a child was misbehaving. A number of themes emerged as residents explained why they would not intervene in child misbehavior in their neighborhoods. First, residents expressed the belief that parents would take the child's side. Some residents expressed bewilderment as to why parents would believe a misbehaving child over a responsible adult. Second, residents alluded to a situation in which parents have very different standards about child care and child behavior. Third, residents were concerned that the child's parents would be angry with them for becoming involved at all with the child, disrupting relationships among neighborhood adults. Residents expressed the ethic of neighbors minding their own business and of childrearing being a family matter. Fourth, residents expressed frustration that past intervention had not only been unsuccessful at resolving problems, but also could exacerbate the situation. Fifth, and perhaps most importantly for our purposes in this volume, residents were concerned about retaliation from parents and children. Residents commented that parents would yell or swear at them, or come after them with knives or guns. Disturbingly, a degree of their hesitancy to intervene was tied to fear that children and adolescents also would verbally assault or physically retaliate. Not only were adults missing the network of other adults who had common goals and standards, and the power to scrutinize and enforce those standards, but they were also fearful of children themselves (Korbin & Coulton, 1996). Residents in the highest risk neighborhoods (highest rates of child maltreatment reports) were most likely to express concerns that children or adolescents would verbally or physically retaliate against them. Neighborhood adults believe that they and their neighbors have great difficulty in controlling child behavior. A high ratio of children to adults, to males, and to elders identified in the aggregate analysis, then, was coupled with hesitancy and fear about intervening in the children's behavior identified in the ethnographic component of our study, diminishing the social capital or collective efficacy available to parents in rearing their own children. The meaning of child misbehavior, and the inability to do anything much about it, was potent. This dilemma is illustrated in the example of one woman's comments:

> Before, neighbors treated all children like their own. Now no one would step in. People don't want to step on other people's toes. And if they do step in sometimes the kids, or even the parents get nasty. Just a few days ago, there was a woman walking down the sidewalk by our house. She had a little boy with her who was throwing rocks at our dogs. I told the boy to stop it, and the mother turned around and said all kinds of words I can't repeat. Then the little kid repeated exactly what she said.

Neighborhood Resources

The aggregate analysis identified proximity or contiguousness to other poverty areas, suggesting that residents of poor neighborhoods are even further compromised if they live near other poor areas, presumably with equally diminished resources and facilities. The presence of more affluent neighbors has been shown to be related to more positive outcomes for children (Brooks-Gunn, Duncan, Klebanov, & Sealand, 1993). The ethnographic interviews also suggested the importance of neighborhood resources, but neighborhood resources were a mixed bag. Caution is needed, for example, in placing a liquor store that also sells necessities squarely in the neighborhood deficit column because this store might have both positive and negative effects on the neighborhood. Similarly, simply counting churches in the neighborhood strengths column may be misleading because some churches may have only a minimal involvement with the neighborhood

In keeping with Dr. Spencer's emphasis on perceptions, objective and subjective impressions of neighborhood resources did not consistently match. For example, an objective measure of neighborhood quality for children and families might be the presence of a playground with modern play equipment in good repair. One would expect parents and young children to cluster at this resource, becoming acquainted, forming play groups, and sharing information. However, residents in neighborhoods with perceived high crime, delinquency, and drug trafficking extended their vision beyond the state of repair and quality of playground equipment. In one neighborhood, parents avoided a playground that had among the nicest facilities in the area because they regarded it as dangerous due to crime, drugs, and gangs. Whether or not groups of teens represented actual gangs, parents perceived danger. This overlaps with the perceived inability to control the behavior of other children and teens previously discussed. Conversely, a dead-end alleyway or a vacant lot within sight of a well-regarded adult might be classified as an eyesore by an objective measure but be viewed as a neighborhood asset by caregivers of young children.

Along similar lines, small food and convenience stores in some neighborhoods are a mixed blessing. On the one hand, prices are generally higher than in larger grocery or discount stores, draining household resources. On the other hand, these small stores provide a number of advantages to residents including accessibility and responsiveness to short-term (weekly and monthly) economic fluctuations through the giving of credit for the purchase of items and breaking down of packages into smaller units that residents could afford (unfortunately, this often involved cigarettes). The absence of neighborhood resources had important meaning for residents. Neighborhood residents in some high rate African American communities took it as a substantial insult, not merely an inconvenience, that there were no banks in the vicinity. They acutely felt racism that they attributed to banks' fears of crime and skepticism that they could make a profit in their neighborhoods. Similarly, the lack of other amenities, such as postal drop boxes, indicated a larger societal antipathy toward and neglect of them beyond the inconvenience of having nowhere nearby to mail bills and letters.

Residential Mobility and Neighborhood Stability

Ethnographic interviews also elaborated on the meaning of residential mobility. It is not movement alone, but the composition of that movement that was salient to residents. There was a difference in whether instability reflected an increase in renters or an increase in homeowners and known individuals. Renters were viewed as a detriment, as individuals who were uncommitted to the neighborhood and, therefore, unpredictable and unreliable. Turnover of renters also meant that neighbors had diminished opportunities to get to know one another. On the other hand, homeowners and known individuals moving back into the neighborhood signaled individuals who would be invested in the community. Individuals in neighborhoods that were quite impoverished, but in which new homes were being built, clearly saw this as an important positive feature of their surroundings. Anecdotal data suggested that in some impoverished African American neighborhoods, adult children of current residents were moving back into the neighborhood with their families. These returning new residents, then, were known to long-time residents, who knew them when they were growing up and who saw them visiting their parents. This is evidence to residents that the neighborhood is on a positive trajectory if children of current residents, who could choose to live elsewhere instead are moving back "home."

Intra-group Analyses

Dr. Spencer's chapter points to the strengths of African American families and neighborhoods and points out the need for greater attention to within-group differences (see also Duncan & Aber, 1997; Sampson, Raudenbush, & Earls, 1997). In aggregate analyses, measures of social disorganization are typically correlated with ethnic minority status. It may be helpful to undertake within-group analyses of factors that have typically been compared across racial categories. Previously, we found that the impoverishment factor described here had a significantly weaker effect on maltreatment rates in African American than in EuroAmerican census tracts. Focused ethnographies in four selected block groups with child maltreatment report rates in the highest and lowest quartiles suggested that this was because of stronger social fabric in the African American tracts as well as racial segregation that restricted movement and kept stronger neighbors in the community. It would be an error, then, to conclude that African American neighborhoods pose a greater risk for children merely because they have higher scores on traditional indicators of impoverishment than European American neighborhoods. These primarily economic factors may be insufficient indicators of community capacity when applied to neighborhoods with residents who have been restricted in their economic and social mobility by external forces. The fact that some impoverished African American neighborhoods provide a supportive social environment for families, however, should not be taken as an excuse to ignore the serious economic disadvantage within these communities (Korbin, Coulton, Chard, Platt-Houston, & Su, 1998).

Definitions of Neighborhood

I also would like to comment on what a neighborhood is in light of Dr. Spencer's comments on the importance of perceived neighborhood. We used both census tracts and block groups as our units of analyses. These units may not conform to resident perceptions of their neighborhoods. In a recent study, we asked residents to draw the maps of their neighborhood boundaries. Residents drew areas larger than a block group, about the size of a census tract, but not necessarily overlapping with their own census tract. However, social indicators calculated for census tracts and residents' common areas were often similar (Coulton, Korbin, Chan, & Su, 1999). Neighborhood research, then, must take into account what entity individuals are reporting on when they discuss aspects of their neighborhoods.

In our research in Cleveland's neighborhoods, we combined an interest in both meaning and context, both of which Spencer points to in her chapter. We took advantage of the complimentary nature of qualitative and quantitative methods in understanding both associations among factors and processes underlying those associations (Korbin & Coulton, 1997; Sullivan, 1996). Aggregate findings would have been difficult to interpret without the ethnographic sources of information. Yet, we would have been hesitant to draw inferences about the effects of community structure from just a few ethnographies. This approach has facilitated consideration of the balance of risk and protective factors (Cicchetti & Lynch, 1993; Garbarino, 1977) as well as incorporating Bronfenbrenner's expansion of an ecological model to encompass neighborhood both as subjectively experienced (Bronfenbrenner, 1979) and as objectively measured (Bronfenbrenner, 1988).

Dr. Spencer's emphasis on resilience and on the need to accommodate diversity in models of context and development can encompass a variety of approaches to neighborhood work. Neighborhoods that appear structurally weak have strengths that allow at least some parents and some children to have more positive outcomes than might be expected. This is not a justification for continued lack of investment in impoverished neighborhoods, but a challenge to better understand and disentangle the interrelationships among individual, family, neighborhood, and larger sociocultural influences.

ACKNOWLEDGMENTS

This research was supported by the National Center on Child Abuse and Neglect, Administration for Children, Youth and Families, Department of Health and Human Services, and by the Foundation for Child Development.

REFERENCES

Belsky, J. (1980). Child maltreatment: An ecological integration. *American Psychologist, 35*, 320–335.

Bronfenbrenner, U. (1979). *The ecology of human development.* Cambridge, MA: Harvard University Press.

Bronfenbrenner, U. (1988). Foreword. In A. Pence (Ed.), *Ecological research with children and families. From concepts to methodology* (pp. ix–xix). New York & London: Teachers College Press.

Brooks-Gunn, J., Duncan, G., & Aber, J. L. (Eds.). (1997) *Neighborhood poverty: Context and consequences for children* (pp.132–144). New York: Russell Sage Foundation.

Brooks-Gunn, J., Duncan, G., Klebanov, P., & Sealand, N. (1993). Do neighborhoods influence child and adolescent development? *American Journal of Sociology, 99*, 353–395.

Cicchetti, D., & Lynch, M. (1993). Towards an ecological/transactional model of community violence and child maltreatment. *Psychiatry, 56*, 96–118.

Coleman, J. (1988). Social capital in the creation of human capital. *American Journal of Sociology, 94*, S95–S120.

Coulton, C., Chow, J., Wang, E., & Su, M. (1996). Geographic concentration of affluence and poverty in 100 metropolitan areas, 1990. *Urban Affairs Review, 32*, 186–216 (formerly the *Urban Affairs Quarterly*).

Coulton, C., Korbin, J., Chan, T., & Su, M. (1999) *Mapping residents' perceptions of neighborhood boundaries. A methodological note.* Manuscript submitted for review.

Coulton, C., Korbin, J., & Su, M. (1999 in press). Neighborhoods and child maltreatment: A multi-level study. *Child Abuse & Neglect: The International Journal.*

Coulton, C., Korbin, J., Su, M., & Chow, J. (1995). Community level factors and child maltreatment rates. *Child Development, 66,* 1262–1276.

Duncan, G. J., & Aber, L. (1997). Neighborhood models and measures. In J. Brooks-Gunn, G. J. Duncan, & J. L. Aber (Eds.), *Neighborhood poverty: Context and consequences for children* (pp. 62–78). New York: Russell Sage Foundation.

Furstenberg, F. F. (1993). How families manage risk and opportunity in dangerous neighborhoods. In W. J. Wilson (Ed.), *Sociology and the public agenda* (pp. 231–258). Newbury Park, CA: Sage.

Garbarino, J. (1977). The human ecology of child maltreatment: A conceptual model for research. *Journal of Marriage and the Family, 39,* 721–735.

Garbarino, J., & Crouter, A. (1978). Defining the community context for parent-child relations: The correlates of child maltreatment. *Child Development, 49,* 604–616.

Korbin, J. (Ed.). (1981). *Child abuse and neglect: Cross-cultural perspectives.* Berkeley & Los Angeles: University of California Press.

Korbin, J., & Coulton, C. (1996). The role of neighbors and the government in neighborhood-based child protection. *Journal of Social Issues, 52,* 163–176.

Korbin, J., & Coulton, C. (1997). Understanding the neighborhood context for children and families: Epidemiological and ethnographic approaches. In J. Brooks-Gunn, G. Duncan, & L. Aber (Eds.), *Neighborhood poverty: Context and consequences for children* (pp. 77–91). New York: Russell Sage Foundation.

Korbin, J., Coulton, C., Chard, S., Platt-Houston, C., & Su, M. (1998). Impoverishment and child maltreatment in African-American and European-American neighborhoods. *Development and Psychopathology, 10,* 215–233.

O'Campo, P., Xue, X., Wang, M. C., & Caughy, M. O. (1997). Neighborhood risk factors and low birthweight in Baltimore: A mulitlevel analysis. *American Journal of Public Health, 87,* 1113–1118.

Sampson, R. J., & Groves, W. B. (1989). Community structure and crime: Testing social disorganization theory. *American Journal of Sociology, 94,* 775–802.

Sampson, R., Raudenbush, S., & Earls, F. (1997) Neighborhoods and violent crime: A multilevel study of collective efficacy. *Science, 277,* 918–924.

Shaw, C., & McKay, D. (1942). *Juvenile delinquency and urban areas.* Chicago: University of Chicago Press.

Sullivan, M. (1996). Neighborhood social organization. A forgotten object of ethnographic study? In R. Jessor, A. Colby, & R. Shweder (Eds.), *Ethnography and human development. Context and meaning in social inquiry* (pp. 205–224). Chicago: University of Chicago Press.

Wilson, W. J. (1987). *The truly disadvantaged: The inner-city, the underclass, and public policy.* Chicago: University of Chicago Press.

Wilson, W. J. (1991). Studying inner-city social dislocations: The challenge of public agenda research. *American Sociological Review, 56,* 1–14.

6

Issues in the Analysis of Neighborhoods, Families, and Children

Scott J. South

State University of New York at Albany

Professor Spencer's chapter covers a wide terrain and raises a number of important issues regarding how neighborhoods affect the ability of families to raise children. I am not by training a developmental psychologist, so I learned a considerable amount from the remarkably thorough literature review. The grand heuristic model developed and described in this chapter may help to organize and synthesize the many strands of research currently being done in this area. At the same time, however, the ultimate test of such models must rest not on the pithiness of the acronyms used to label them, but on their ability to generate testable—and falsifiable—propositions. I fear that the sheer complexity and grandiosity of some of these theoretical models frequently renders them less useful than their originators intended. In particular, unraveling causal relations among the various identity formation processes is certainly a Herculean task. I suspect that it is considerably easier to sketch out such grandiloquent models, having myriad interrelated concepts and multiple feedback loops, than it is to subject these models to rigorous empirical tests.

Here I focus on the two aspects of Professor Spencer's chapter that, to my mind at least, raise some of the most important issues regarding neighborhood effects on families and children.

THE VARIABLE SALIENCE OF NEIGHBORHOODS

Although touched on relatively briefly in Professor Spencer's chapter, the question of whether neighborhood characteristics affect all social and demographic groups in the same way is an important, but largely unresolved, issue. Professor Spencer—quite correctly, I think—suggests that residence in disadvantaged neighborhoods may have different effects for younger versus older children, and different effects for boys and young men than for girls and young women. Implicit in her analysis as well is that neighborhood characteristics have different effects for African American youth than for White adolescents. It might be worth pushing this idea even further to consider in greater detail under what conditions and for what types of people neighborhood conditions might make a difference.

In reading the contemporary literature on neighborhood effects, I was struck by its tendency to overlook a venerable theoretical tradition, rooted primarily in the field of community studies, that addresses this issue. Urban and community sociologists such as Fischer (1984), Greer (1962), Hunter (1974), Keller (1968), and Wellman (1977), among others, all claimed that neighborhoods matter more for some people than for others, and many claimed that, for most people, the influence of neighborhoods on social behavior has declined markedly over time and perhaps disappeared entirely. It is, I think, somewhat ironic that the burgeoning concern with neighborhood effects over the past decade—spurred largely by Wilson's influential (1987, 1996) treatises—comes at a time well after community sociologists have roundly proclaimed the *unimportance* of neighborhoods in social life. In general, these theorists argue that increasing geographic mobility and technological advances in transportation and communication have caused social networks to become de-spatialized, liberated from the local, territorial community. As these networks expand beyond the immediate neighborhood, the impact of neighborhood-based peer groups and other sources of influence that might conceivably transmit neighborhood effects presumably dissipates.

Theorists in this tradition also point to other factors that might moderate or condition the impact of neighborhood characteristics on behavioral outcomes. For example, Fischer (1995) has long contended that neighborhoods matter less in large, densely populated metropolitan areas than in small towns because the size and heterogeneity of big cities allows residents to choose friends and intimates on the basis of common interests rather than spatial propinquity. Even in large metropolitan areas, however, neighborhoods matter more for immigrant and minority groups, where a shared ethnic identity reinforces the effects of residential propinquity, creating the "urban villages" described by Gans (1962), among others. Moreover, because community attachment and neighborhood involvement increase with duration of residence in the local area (Kasarda & Janowitz, 1974; Sampson, 1988), neighborhood characteristics should presumably have a stronger influence on long-term residents than on short-term residents.

Neighborhood effects might also vary by age and sex. Children and adolescents, whose social worlds seldom extend beyond the immediate neighborhood, are most likely to be influenced by neighborhood conditions. The transition to young adulthood involves a broadening of the social world and an expansion of social contacts and experiences outside of the local area. And, as Professor Spencer's chapter suggests, neighborhood conditions might matter more for young women than for young men. One possibility is that stricter parental supervision of daughters than of sons might constrain the daily routines of girls more than boys to the immediate neighborhood, where they would presumably be influenced by whatever mechanisms transmit neighborhood effects. Alternatively, if parents supervise their daughters more strictly than their sons, perhaps girls are less exposed than boys to the noxious effects of dangerous neighborhood environments.

A colleague and I recently attempted to test some of these hypotheses regarding the variable effects of neighborhoods using geocoded data from the Panel Study of Income Dynamics for the 25-year period between 1968 and 1993 (South & Crowder, 1998, 1999). We focused on family formation patterns, particularly the timing of the transition to first marriage, and how they are influenced by the level of socioeconomic disadvantage of the neighborhood. Admittedly, delaying marriage (or eschewing it altogether) is only one of the many behavioral outcomes that might be influenced by neighborhood characteristics, but it is an outcome that is strongly implicated in Wilson's (1987) theory, and it is closely allied with other social dislocations such as nonmarital childbearing and the growth of single-parent families.

Findings from this project buttress the view that neighborhood effects operate differently for different social groups. One quite robust finding is that neighborhood socioeconomic disadvantage hastens entry into first marriage among Whites, but delays first marriage among African Americans. We also found, as have others (Brooks-Gunn, Duncan, Klebanov, & Sealand, 1993), that neighborhood poverty has a stronger impact on out-of-wedlock childbearing among White women than among Black women. More relevant to Professor Spencer's chapter, we found that, at least among Whites, the effect of neighborhood socioeconomic status on the transition to first marriage declines significantly with age, implying that neighborhood conditions become less relevant at later stages in the life course. Also, for White males, we found that the impact of neighborhood SES has indeed declined significantly over time, is weaker in metropolitan than in nonmetropolitan areas, and increases with the length of time spent in the neighborhood (South & Crowder, 1998).

Perhaps one factor that helps to explain differential effects of neighborhood characteristics across sociodemographic groups and over time is the degree to which children and adolescents are actually exposed, through their routine activities, to neighborhood conditions. Whatever mechanisms transmit neighborhood effects—whether it is peer group behavior and norms, exposure to conventional role models, collective monitoring and supervision, attitudes such as hypermasculinity, or some other cause—presumably affect only those individuals who spend time outside of their residence milling about in the neighborhood. Theoretically, neighborhood conditions should have little impact on children (and others) who rarely venture out into the local area. Personally, I doubt very much that our neighborhood has much influence on the behavior of my eight-year-old son; I can rarely get him to play in our backyard, much less roam the neighborhood. Although time-use studies tell us a great deal about *how* individuals spend their time, they unfortunately tell us very little about *where* children spend their time (Robinson & Godbey, 1997). As others have noted (Furstenberg, 1993; Jarrett, 1997), parental strategies for coping with dangerous neighborhoods frequently include limiting children's exposure to the neighborhood itself, by focusing activities within the household or in structured environments outside of the neighborhood altogether. Variations in the use of these strategies, and, more generally, variations in the extent of exposure to the neighborhood environment might help us to explain the differential effects of neighborhood conditions. To my knowledge, however, few if any data sets commonly used to explore neighborhood effects contain adequate measures of exposure to the neighborhood. Measures of the amount of time children spend in the neighborhood, and the degree to which their peer groups and social networks are concentrated in the neighborhood, would seem to be plausible candidates for measuring this concept.

In sum, not only might the effects of neighborhoods vary by individual's developmental stage (as Professor Spencer suggests) and by family management practices (as Duncan & Raudenbush, chap. 8, this volume, suggest), but neighborhood effects might also be contingent on both other individual characteristics and the broader environment, including both historical time and place. Although prior research has given some attention to the potentially variable nature of neighborhood effects, I think that there is much more that can and should be done in this area.

HOW NEIGHBORHOOD EFFECTS OPERATE

A second issue addressed in Professor Spencer's chapter that I would like to elaborate on deals more directly with the mechanisms through which neighborhood effects operate. Indeed, this may well be the most important unresolved issue in this area of research. Professor Spencer makes a useful contribution here by suggesting that behavioral adaptations to high-risk neighborhood environments that are beneficial for some outcomes might prove detrimental for other outcomes. Adopting a hypermasculine persona, suffused with bravado and swagger, might well be a valuable mechanism for coping with the "code of the streets" in violent neighborhoods, while at the same time serving to inhibit relations with teachers and parents that contribute to success in other arenas, particularly academic and occupational spheres. Yet, my reading of the theoretical literature suggests no shortage of plausible candidates that might transmit neighborhood effects. Even an abbreviated list would include the behavior and attitudes of peer groups, exposure to mainstream and economically successful role models, perceived opportunity costs to an early transition to adulthood (including early school exits and unmarried parenthood), educational and occupational aspirations, access to social capital, and the monitoring and supervision of adolescents by parents, neighbors, and other social control agencies. Adding the coping mechanisms suggested by Professor Spencer, such as hypermasculine behaviors and aggressive attitudes, gives us even more possibilities.

However, if we are to make real progress in this area, I doubt it will come from assembling an even longer list of potential intervening mechanisms, but rather in the careful and rigorous testing of those mechanisms that have already been proposed. Moreover, identifying these mechanisms is surely vital if our research is to inform parents how best to cope with raising children in disadvantaged neighborhoods. Professor Spencer's empirical analysis is useful in this regard because it shows that hypermasculinity and aggressive attitudes are in fact *not* important conduits of neighborhood effects on young Black men's educational attainment. Although Professor Spencer's models lack measures of neighborhood conditions, the absence of significant net effects of the hypothesized coping methods means that these variables cannot explain whatever neighborhood effects may exist. Admittedly, this is a very small sample, and variation in the key variables may be too truncated to observe the expected intervening effects. However, I think this general approach to identifying intervening mechanisms in the right way to go, and at this stage in our collective research, disconfirming hypothesized mechanisms is no less important than identifying the correct ones.

One of the barriers to progress in this area is that the data sets that have proven most valuable in *documenting* neighborhood effects—the PSID, the National Survey of Family Growth (NSFG), the Infant Health and Development Program (IHDP)—rarely contain good (if any) measures of the potentially intervening mechanisms. I am currently analyzing neighborhood-geocoded data from the National Survey of Children (NSC), a longitudinal, nationally representative survey that contains measures, albeit imperfect, of many of these hypothesized mechanisms. I will not go into the intricacies of the findings here, but my very preliminary work (with Eric Baumer) looking at neighborhood effects on various dimensions of adolescent sexual activity shows that, compared to adolescents in more advantaged neighborhoods, adolescents in disadvantaged neighborhoods have first intercourse earlier and intercourse more often, are less likely to use contraception, and have more sex partners. More to the point, of the various hypothetical intervening mechanisms that we can measure, what seems to matter most for interpreting the effects of neighborhood disadvantage are the attitudes and behaviors of peers. Parental supervision, perceived opportunity costs, various aspects of social capital, and the attitudes of parents, neighbors, and the respondents themselves frequently have significant effects on these outcomes, but in general do little to explain the influence of neighborhood socioeconomic disadvantage on these dimensions of adolescent sexual activity.

As both Duncan and Raudenbush (chap. 8, this volume) and Sampson (chap. 1, this volume) make clear, the search for the mechanisms through which neighborhood effects operate presents many challenges. One potential complexity is that neighborhood effects might be transmitted differently for different social behaviors. For example, neighborhood disadvantage might raise the risk of early intercourse by influencing peer group norms increase delinquency because of lower levels of adult supervision and social control of adolescents in distressed communities, and raise the risk of dropping out of school because neighborhood poverty fosters the hypermasculine and aggressive attitudes and behaviors suggested by Professor Spencer. Another challenge—one posed by the title of this volume—is how best to incorporate parenting behaviors into models of neighborhood effects. Professor Spencer is right to emphasize the reciprocal nature of children's and parent's behaviors, but it is unclear to me precisely how this observation should inform and guide our empirical models. Are parenting strategies a direct reaction to neighborhood conditions, or are they a reaction to children's behavior that, in turn, is partly a function of neighborhood attributes? Are certain parenting strategies more effective in some neighborhood environments than others? I suspect that answering important questions such as these is likely to require more complicated models than we ordinarily estimate when examining neighborhood effects on social behavior.

ACKNOWLEDGMENTS

The research described here was supported by grants from the National Science Foundation (SBR-9511732, SBR-9729797) and the National Institute of Child Health and Human Development (R01 HD35560).

REFERENCES

Brooks-Gunn, J., Duncan, G. J., Klebanov, P. K., & Sealand, N. (1993). Do neighborhoods influence child and adolescent development? *American Journal of Sociology, 99*, 353–395.

Fischer, C. S. (1984). *The urban experience*. New York: Harcourt, Brace, Jovanovich.

Fischer, C. S. (1995). The subcultural theory of urbanism: A twentieth-year assessment. *American Journal of Sociology, 101*, 543–577.

Furstenberg, F. F. Jr. (1993). How families manage risk and opportunity in dangerous neighborhoods. In W. J. Wilson (Ed.), *Sociology and the public agenda* (pp. 231–238). Newbury Park, CA: Sage.

Gans, H. J. (1962). *The urban villagers*. New York: The Free Press.

Greer, S. (1962). *The emerging city: Myth and reality*. New York: The Free Press of Glencoe.

Hunter, A. (1974). *Symbolic communities: The persistence and change of Chicago's local communities*. Chicago: University of Chicago Press.

Jarrett, R. L. (1997). Bringing families back in: Neighborhood effects on child development. In J. Brooks-Gunn, G. J. Duncan, & J. L. Aber (Eds.), *Neighborhood poverty, Volume II: Policy implications in studying neighborhoods* (pp. 48–64). New York: Russell Sage Foundation.

Kasarda, J., & Janowitz, M. (1974). Community attachment in mass society. *American Sociological Review, 39*, 328–339.

Keller, S. (1968). *The urban neighborhood*. New York: Random House.

Robinson, J. P., & Godbey, G. (1997). *Time for life: The surprising ways Americans use their time*. University Park, PA: Pennsylvania State University Press.

Sampson, R. J. (1988). Local friendship ties and community attachment in mass society: A multilevel systemic model. *American Sociological Review, 53*, 766–779.

South, S. J., & Crowder, K. D. (1998). The declining significance of neighborhoods? Marital transitions in community context. Unpublished paper. Department of Sociology, State University of New York at Albany.

South, S. J., & Crowder, K. D. (1999). Neighborhood effects on family formation: Concentrated poverty and beyond. *American Sociological Review, 64,* 113–132.

Wellman, B. (1977). Who needs neighborhoods? In R. L. Warren (Ed.), *New perspectives on the American community* (pp. 218–223). Chicago: Rand McNally.

Wilson, W. J. (1987). *The truly disadvantaged.* Chicago: University of Chicago Press.

Wilson, W. J. (1996). *When work disappears: The world of the new urban poor.* New York: Random House.

7
Hyperghettos and Hypermasculinity: The Phenomenology of Exclusion

Mercer L. Sullivan
Rutgers University

The concentration of health and behavior problems among children and adolescents living in inner city neighborhoods in the United States has been the subject of more than a decade of intensive research dedicated to identifying and explaining the *neighborhood effects* stemming from the residential concentration of poverty posited in Wilson's (1987) seminal formulations of this problem. As noted elsewhere in this volume, these posited neighborhood effects have proved notoriously difficult to isolate. What once seemed a relatively straightforward scientific undertaking, that of demonstrating additive effects of neighborhood disadvantage over and above those of family and individual disadvantage, has proved an extraordinary challenge. If nothing else, we now know that concepts such as *neighborhood* and *community* are vastly more complex than we used to think and require considerable theoretical work and sophistication of measurement in order to be operationalized in scientific research.

There are certainly those who maintain that the failure to identify powerful and easily measured neighborhood effects thus far is simply a demonstration that these effects are not there. I am pleased to note in the papers the opinions of eminent social scientists that this conclusion is premature. The spatial concentrations of delinquency, mental health, and other problems continue to defy this conclusion, while sober scientific scrutiny continues to suggest many reasons why so much research to date has not been more conclusive.

The issues raised by Spencer (chapter 4, this volume) concerning the ways in which neighborhoods affect families' abilities to raise and nurture children bring to the surface an important and generally neglected aspect of the problem of neighborhood effects, namely, that of the connection between ecology and phenomenology. In the long chain of effects from the structural aspects of neighborhood context to individual human development, the proximal level of the lived experience of children growing up in these environments is perhaps the least examined link in recent research.

My comments here first reprise what I see as the main points raised by Spencer. I then address those points from the perspective of my own research and of others in research traditions that feed directly into my work. Specifically, I concentrate on the notion of hypermasculinity among young, African American males, drawing primarily on qualitative research by sociologists and anthropologists such as myself. Methodologically, I feel that the important questions of phenomenology raised by Spencer cannot be addressed without drawing on narrative data that reflect lived experience in natural settings. As Sampson (chap. 1, this volume) observed earlier, something ecological is happening here, even if we don't know what it is. Unless we pay close attention to the phenomological viewpoint of those to whom it is happening, we probably never will.

The main points raised by Spencer seem to me to be the following:

1. Developmental processes need to be situated in ecological context and interpreted in a phenomenological framework.
2. Young African American males in inner city neighborhoods grow up in contexts that are especially precarious and confusing.
3. Attitudes and identities that can be designated with the term *hypermasculinity* are one result of their precarious ecological position.
4. Hypermasculine identities in these circumstances can be adaptive in the short term but are almost always maladaptive in the longer term.
5. Finally, we can identify some protective factors, such as high levels of maternal education, that help to mitigate these maladaptive developmental processes.

I am in substantial agreement with all of these propositions. My principal criticisms of the paper are that the qualitative data referred to are not presented in much detail. More of these data would certainly help to advance the methodological agenda advocated here, by illuminating how young males perceive and represent their own situations. In addition, I would be very interested to see the actual survey items used to measure hypermasculinity, given the centrality of that concept to the overall argument.

Let me now turn to my own reflections on these issues by suggesting some theoretical perspectives and bodies of research both old and new that I find helpful in thinking about the social and cultural factors shaping definitions of masculinity. At a minimum, I would suggest that in order to think about what it means to be male, we need to address three domains of social life: work, sexuality, and violence. Men's roles with respect to these domains vary, as do the interconnections among these roles.

A recent work that provides a convenient place to begin this discussion is with the recent book, *Masculinities* (Connell, 1995). Drawing on the traditions of psychoanalysis and sociology, Connell compared qualitative data drawn from four groups of men in different structural positions to argue a point embodied in his title. By referring to masculinity in the plural, he emphasized that there is not just one. Rather, definitions of what it is to be male in society vary. Groups of men in similar circumstances interact with one another to produce culturally constructed definitions of masculinity appropriate to those circumstances.

The criminologist Messerschmidt (1997) drew on this idea to provide an explanation for the vastly skewed gender differences in crime and violence that is sociologically based rather than appealing to simplistic biological determinism. Drawing on my own work and that of other ethnographers, he explicitly argued that being of low status in society interacts with universal expectatations equating manliness with power to produce criminality.

So far, these ideas are perfectly congruent with the ecological-phenomenological perspective advocated by Spencer, but we have not yet discussed race. In order to gain some perspective on the particularly precarious social position of young, African American males, I think it is useful to move backwards in the criminological and sociological literature because the ideas raised by Spencer have a long heritage. They deal with the phenomenological perspectives of juvenile delinquents, both White and non-White, in different times and places and thus allow us to think about how the precariousness of the ecological position of young African American inner city males at present is both similar to and different from the positions of other low-status males.

I could go back to the 1940s and the young Italian American males depicted in Whyte's *Street Corner Society* (Whyte, 1943) or even farther back to Shaw's young Polish American jack-roller (1966), but let me begin with Cohen's 1955 book, *Delinquent Boys*, an early attempt to relate gender identity to delinquency. Cohen's argument resonates strongly with Spencer's depiction of the hostile encounter between the masculine self-concept of lower class boys and the culturally feminized (from their point of view) norms of the school environment. The resulting phenomenological dissonance crystallizes for the boy who, throwing a spitball in class, sees other boys crack up and suddenly realizes that *he is not alone* in his discomfort. At this point, a subculture is born. The resistance of working-class boys to middle class gender norms becomes collective.

A more recent work—widely influential in education, sociology, anthropology, and cultural studies—that repackages Cohen's ideas in the terminology of structural Marxism is Willis' 1977 book *Learning to Labour*, subtitled *How working-class kids get working-class jobs*. This study of English boys in secondary school built on Cohen to present a more finely grained account of how the particular correlates of the boys' structural position, in terms of gender, generation, neighborhood, and work, produced a culturally patterned process of school-to-work transition. His "lads" engage in minor deliquency and precocious sexual activity, despise their more studious peers, scrape by in school, and move directly into dead-end manual jobs. His conclusions also resonate strongly with the ideas in Spencer's paper, up to a point. Willis found that the oppositional behaviors of the "lads" are adaptive in the short run. They have more fun and sex and they start making money sooner. In the longer term, however, these short-term adaptations "bind them back" into the social structure they thought they were escaping by limiting their occupational mobility.

The point where similarities to African American, inner city youth break down, of course, is that at which the "lads" move into the labor force. Willis noted this explicitly and asked what will be different from the new immigrants to Britain during this time, persons of color from Asia and the Caribbean who face unemployment rather than merely low level, but relatively stable positions in the labor market.

These were precisely the questions I engaged in my comparative ethnography of work and crime, *Getting Paid: Youth Crime and Work in the Inner City* (1989a). I compared a group of White, working-class youths who appeared quite similar to Willis' "lads" to two groups of minority youths (one African American, the other Latino and Puerto Rican) and found exactly the kinds of differences that Willis implied. The youths of color, facing much different labor market prospects based on differences in neighborhood context and informal labor market networks, were more likely to progress from minor delinquency to sustained criminal activity and to enter prison rather than stable employment.

At this point, new terms become useful. Wacquant and Wilson (1989) referred to these new environments of extreme racial segregation and concentrated poverty as *hyperghettos*. Massey and Denton (1993) have referred to the processes generating these environments as *hyper-ghettos*. It is in these distinctive environments that Spencer locates the social constructions of maleness designated as *hypermasculinity*. The progression of the terminology over time has a definite coherence. What was once discussed with respect to White boys in working-class neighborhoods in terms of "masculinity" has now changed to a discussion of "hypermasculinity" for boys of color in neighborhoods with extraordinarily high rates of un- and underemployment.

What is hypermasculinity, though, and how, if at all, does it differ from regular masculinity? This is not an easy question. In my remaining remarks, I engage this concept critically, for although I think it points to an important connection between processes of social exclusion and cultural constructions of gender among the excluded, I also think it is a loaded and possibly dangerous term, with the potential for reinforcing certain stereotypes that need to be criticized rather than reified.

Let me begin by referring to a critique of representations of African American male sexuality advanced in a work of the protest literature of the late 1960s, Eldridge Cleaver's *Soul on Ice*. In this excoriating work of personal confession and social criticism, Cleaver ridiculed the idea of the "super-masculine menial." He argued that the notion that African American men possessed extraordinary sexual powers, a notion he confessed to having internalized at one point, was in fact a projection by White Americans that had been used historically to justify lynching and other, lesser forms of oppression.

Of course, *super-masculine* and *hypermasculine* are not the same term, but they are similar enough to call our attention to the need to distinguish between representations of African American manhood, whether by African American men themselves or by others, and their actual experiences as physical and social beings. I can point to some areas in which critical evaluation of these issues is needed. I think it important in discussing such matters to pay careful attention to three things: intracommunity differences, intraindividual differences, and self-conscious critiques of what it means to be a man with African American communities.

Existing research, both classic and more recent, suggests that we need to be attentive to both the diversity of male roles within African American communities and the extraordinary complexity of the multiple roles that individual African American men enact in different situations and over time. From this perspective, *hypermasculinity* comes to look less like a defining personality trait and more like one role in a broad repertoire developed by a group for whom the very precariousness of their circumstances requires flexibility.

Research, for example, points to the existence of male roles in the inner cities that do not conform to stereotypes of violent and sexually exploitative behavior. My reading of the neighborhood effects literature to date indicates that one of the main reasons these effects have been elusive is the heterogeneity of attitudes and behavior within even the most disadantaged neighborhoods. There is also compelling ethnographic evidence. Burton's fascinating work (1995) identified a social role of male caregiving that flew in the face of many representations of these environments. My own work on the male role in teenage pregnancy and parenting (Sullivan, 1989b) showed that so-called "absent fathers" in these communities are not necessarily so absent as they appear to the authorities who officially count such things.

I think the evidence is also compelling that men who express ostensibly hypermasculine attitudes are far more complex in their actual social relationships. This ground was charted a generation ago in Liebow's 1967 classic, *Tally's Corner.* Liebow portrayed the sexual bravado of the men he studied in unflinching detail, with sympathy but without romanticizing it. He characterized the attitudes they expressed to each other as a "shadow" system of values. He then elucidated this brilliant concept by explaining that these streetcorner values—of sexual predation and dereliction of responsibility for children—were ephemeral and contradictory. Even in the minds of the men who proclaimed them, these values were inseparable from the mainstream values they appeared to contradict, just as shadows are inseparable from the objects that cast them. These shadow values were ultimately rooted in labor market failures and then extended into personal and familial relationships. Streetcorner bravado was a way of rationalizing these failures in the company of men like themselves.

Yet, this bravado hardly corresponded to their actual relationships with women and children. Liebow gave the ironic title of "Ruthless Exploiters of Women" to these attitudes and then proceeded to show that the men maintained a much wider range of relationships. These relationships included relationships of mutual support and being exploited along with sometimes doing the exploiting. Not only are there many male roles in the hyperghettos, different roles can be played by the same man in various situations.

Finally, I think it important to acknowledge that it is not just social scientists who talk about what it means to be Black and male in the inner city. This discussion takes place there also. I believe it has been going on in a significant way recently. One kind of evidence for this comes from the social programs that were initiated in recent years to provide support for young fathers in these areas. I served in an advisory capacity to programs of this type operated by Public-Private Ventures and the Manpower Demonstration Research Corporation.

One unanticipated finding of these programs was the degree to which the young men become engaged in support groups. The initial expectation was that the promise of employment would be the strongest draw. Although employment was often what brought them in, the support groups seem to have kept them there, even when the employment programs were less useful than anticipated. Recently released research on the Manpower Research Demonstration Corporation (MDRC) program, for example, reports that the program increased child support even though it failed to increase employment. Another example of community-level critique of what it means to be male is the Million Man March, an event that I think has had effects that are still unfolding.

Masculinity is a social construction. It takes many guises in various circumstances. The processes of exclusion that generated the hyperghettos may well have generated a set of attitudes that can usefully be referred to as masculinity. I would hope, however, that we can be careful to situate these attitudes and identities carefully within these complex environments, alongside the other kinds of attitudes and identities with which they coexist.

REFERENCES

Burton, L. M. (1995). Intergenerational patterns of providing care in African-American families with teenage childbearers: Emergent patterns in an ethnographic study. In V. L. Bengston, W. Schaie, & L. M. Barton, (Eds.), *Adult intergenerational relations.* New York: Springer Publishing Company.

Cleaver, E. (1968). *Soul on ice.* New York: McGraw-Hill.

Cohen, A. (1955). *Delinquent boys.* New York: Free Press.

Connell, R. W. (1995). *Masculinities.* Berkeley, CA: University of California Press.

Liebow, E. (1967). *Tally's corner: a study of Negro street corner men.* Boston: Little, Brown.

Massey, D. M., & Denton, N. A. (1993). *American apartheid: Segregation and the making of the underclass.* Cambridge, MA: Harvard University Press.

Messerschmidt, J. W. (1997). *Crime as structured action: Gender, race, class and crime in the making.* Thousand Oaks, CA: Sage.

Shaw, C. R. (1966). *The Jack-Roller: a delinquent boy's own story* (pp. v-xiii). Chicago: University of Chicago Press. (Original work published in 1930.)

Sullivan, M. L. (1989a). *Getting paid: Youth crime and work in the inner city.* Ithaca, NY: Cornell University Press.

Sullivan, M. L. (1989b, Jan.). "Absent fathers in the inner city." *The Annals of the American Academy of Political and Social Science, 501,* 48–58.

Wacquant, L. J., & Wilson, J. (1989, Jan.). The cost of racial and class exclusion in the inner city. *The Annals of the American Academy of Political and Social Science, 501,* 8–26.

Whyte, W. F. (1943). *Street corner society.* Chicago: University of Chicago Press.

Willis, P. (1977). *Learning to labor*. Farnborough, England: Saxon House.

Wilson, W. J. (1987). *The truly disadvantaged: The inner city, the underclass, and public policy*. Chicago: University of Chicago Press.

III

How do Neighborhoods Affect the Development of Adolescent Problem Behavior?

8

Neighborhoods and Adolescent Development: How Can We Determine the Links?

Greg J. Duncan
Northwestern University

Stephen W. Raudenbush
University of Michigan

Despite ample theoretical reasons to suspect that neighborhood conditions influence adolescent development and behavior, the task of securing precise, robust, and unbiased estimates of neighborhood effects has proved remarkably difficult. This chapter provides an assessment of the conceptual and, especially, methodological issues involved, as well as guidance on the most promising research designs for obtaining an unbiased understanding of the nature of neighborhood effects.

Key methodological issues include (a) obtaining neighborhood-level measures that approximate the theoretical constructs of interest; (b) allowing for the possibility of simultaneous influences between youth and their contexts; (c) avoiding bias from unobservable characteristics of parents that influence both choice of neighborhood and child outcomes; (d) consideration of ways in which families mediate and moderate neighborhood influences; and (e) using samples with sufficient variability in neighborhood conditions.

We argue that (a) studies that draw their samples from only a handful of different neighborhoods have little chance of distinguishing among the many theoretical ways in which neighborhoods may influence youth; (b) neighborhood-effects estimates from studies that measure neighborhood characteristics from youth or parental self-reports or by aggregating responses of youth or their parents are likely to be biased, especially when the youth outcomes themselves are based on youth or parent reports; (c) neighborhood data drawn from independent samples of residents or by more economical systematic social observation methods are more promising for addressing some of the hypotheses of interest; (d) a simple but informative method of estimating upper bounds on the scope of potential neighborhood effects is to estimate outcome correlations for pairs of youth who live close to one another; and (e) quasi- and random-assignment experimental studies represent our best hope for discovering the scope, if not nature, of neighborhood influences.

WHY NEIGHBORHOOD CONDITIONS MIGHT MATTER

Why might extrafamilial contexts—neighborhoods, communities, schools, and peers—affect an adolescent's behavior? The literature is filled with answers to this question, some but not all of which argue that higher socioeconomic status (SES) environments are better for children. Because this literature is reviewed more completely in other chapters in this volume, we provide in this section an exceedingly brief and selective review of theories of contextual—especially neighborhood—effects, with an eye toward motivating our methodological discussion.

Jencks and Mayer (1990) developed a taxonomy of theoretical ways in which neighborhoods may affect child development. They distinguished:

- *epidemic* theories, based primarily on the power of peer influences to spread problem behavior;
- theories of *collective socialization*, in which neighborhood role models and monitoring are important ingredients in a child's socialization;
- *institutional* models, in which the neighborhood's institutions (e.g., schools, police protection) rather than neighbors per se make the difference;
- *competition* models, in which neighbors (including classmates) compete for scarce neighborhood resources; and
- models of *relative deprivation*, in which individuals evaluate their situation or relative standing vis-à-vis their neighbors (or classmates).

The first three of these explanations predict that "better" environments promote positive development. The last two predict that some youth may be negatively affected by exposure to higher SES environments.

Because adolescents typically spend a good deal of time away from their homes, explanations of neighborhood influences based on peers, role models, schools, and other neighborhood-based resources would appear to be more relevant for them than for younger children. However, it is possible that neighborhood influences begin long before adolescence. A substantial minority of 3- and 4-year-olds are enrolled in center-based daycare or preschool (Hofferth & Chaplin, 1994). Physically dangerous neighborhoods may force mothers to be isolated in their homes and thus restrict opportunities for their children's interactions with peers and adults (Furstenberg, 1993). Parks, libraries, and children's programs provide more enriching opportunities in relatively affluent neighborhoods than are available in resource-poor neighborhoods. Parents of high socioeconomic status may be observed to resort less frequently to corporal punishment and to engage more frequently in learning-related play. Thus, there are many ways in which neighborhood conditions might affect both children and adolescents (Chase-Lansdale, Gordon, Brooks-Gunn, & Klebanov, 1997).

Social disorganization theory identifies key elements of collective socialization and institutional forces likely to influence child and adolescent development. Following Shaw and McKay (1942), Sampson and his colleagues argued that a high degree of ethnic heterogeneity and residential instability leads to an erosion of adult friendship networks and undermines a values consensus in the neighborhood (Sampson & Lauritsen, 1994), which in turn means that problem behavior among young people is not controlled as effectively as in more socially organized neighborhoods.

Sampson, Raudenbush, and Earls(1997) argued for the importance of the concept of *collective efficacy*, which combines social cohesion (the extent to which neighbors trust each other and share common values) with informal social control (the extent to which neighbors can count on each other to monitor and supervise youth and protect public order). Thus it represents the capacity for collective action by neighbors. Sampson et al. (1997) found that collective efficacy so defined relates strongly to neighborhood levels of violence, personal victimization, and homicide in Chicago, after controlling for prior crime and for social composition as measured by census variables.

Wilson's (1987) explanation of inner city poverty in Chicago relied on a more complicated model in which massive changes in the economic structure, when combined with residential mobility among more advantaged Blacks, results in homogeneously impoverished neighborhoods that provide neither resources nor positive role models for their children and adolescents.

Furstenberg (1993) and Furstenberg, Cook, Eccles, Elder, and Sameroff (1998) argued for the importance of family-management practices in understanding neighborhood effects. Basing their work on both ethnographic and survey-based studies, they pointed out that families formulate different strategies for raising children in high-risk neighborhoods, ranging from extreme protection and insulation to an active role in developing community-based *social capital* networks that can help children at key points in their academic or labor-market careers. This work highlights the need to consider family-neighbor interaction effects in neighborhood research.

METHODOLOGICAL CHALLENGES TO "GETTING CONTEXT RIGHT"

Distinguishing empirically among these complementary and, in some cases, competing theories is not an easy task. Collectively, the theories suggest many possible mechanisms, most of which are not easily measured. However, measurement issues are only part of a collection of conceptual problems that await the aspiring neighborhood-effects researcher.

Building on Manski (1993), Moffitt's very useful review paper (1998) distinguishes among (a) the simultaneity problem; (b) the omitted-context-variables problem; and (c) the endogenous membership problem. To this list we would add (d) consideration of ways in which families mediate and moderate neighborhood influences, and (e) the more practical problem of selecting samples with sufficient contextual variability.

To frame the methodological issues, consider a model in which adolescent i's achievement or problem behavior (y) is an additive function of i's family (FAM) and extra-familial contextual (CON) influences:

$$y_i = A' \ FAM_i + B' \ CON_i + e_i \qquad (1)$$

For the moment, we assume one child per family. Our interest is in obtaining unbiased estimates of B', the effect of context on the youth outcome. Interactions between FAM and CON (i.e., the possibility that the effect of CON on y depends on FAM conditions) are considered next and do not invalidate our discussion based on equation 1.[1]

The Simultaneity Problem

A first possible problem is that of simultaneous causation—that contextual conditions themselves may be caused by y's behavior. In this case, we have a two-equation system:

$$y_i = A' \ FAM_i + B' \ CON_i + e_i \qquad (2)$$

$$CON_i = C' \ y_i + D' \ Z + w_i \qquad (3)$$

where Z is a vector of other determinants of contextual conditions that might include the behavior of other individuals who are part of the context, as well as structural and political factors.

The idea that children are not only shaped by, but also shape, their family environments is a familiar one to developmentalists and a key element of *transactional* models of development (Sameroff & Chandler, 1975). That two-way *transactions* may play a role in extrafamilial contexts is best seen in the case of best friends or peer groups. In the case of best friends, CON_i might be the behavior of i's best friend. Equation 2 then reflects the assumption that i's behavior is causally linked to the behavior of his or her best friend, but Equation 3 then reflects the assumption that i's best friend's behavior is also causally dependent on i's own behavior. Identification of the Bs and Cs in a two-equation system such as 2 and 3 is a difficult task.

Less obvious but not implausible are simultaneity problems involving adolescents and their neighborhood-based contexts. Suppose, as did Sampson et al. (1997),

---

[1] Also of note is the potential for a nonlinear relationship between context and outcomes. Jencks and Mayer (1990) discussed the policy importance of nonlinearities, pointing out that the net impact of redistributing contextual resources from the rich to the poor could produce a net gain or loss depending on the relative sizes of gains and losses to poor and rich adolescents affected by the policies. Typically, nonlinearities can be readily handled in the context of equation 1.

that the *collective efficacy* of the adults in a neighborhood is a forceful deterrent to the problem behavior of the neighborhood's youth. It is possible that a neighborhood's collective sense of efficacy is itself determined by youth behavior, and that misbehavior of even one youth, if sufficiently serious, could affect the context (in this case the collective efficacy in the neighborhood) of that youth.

Addressing the simultaneity problem for peer contexts is particularly difficult because it is virtually impossible to find Z-type determinants of the behavior of peers that are not also determinants of i's own behavior. Moffitt (1998) and Manski (1993) provided a more complete analysis of the peer case, assuming that i's choice of group members (e.g., i's best friend) is exogenous and distinguishing between the effects on i's behavior of i's best friend's behavior and demographic characteristics. They termed the former, behavioral effects *endogenous social interactions* and the latter, demographic-characteristic effects *exogenous social interactions*.

These distinctions have important policy implications. If contextual effects on, say, delinquency operate through peer behavior, then public policymakers might be able to stem local epidemics of teen problem behavior by focusing on prevention among a key set of high-risk adolescents. But if it is the neighbor or peer characteristics rather than behavior that matter, then more costly (in terms of resources and political capital) programs such as school and residential mobility programs become more important.

Estimating the reduced-form version of Equations 2 and 3 in which i's behavior is regressed on FAM and i's best friend's demographic characteristics (but not behavior), identifies the existence of social interactions but does not provide distinct estimates of exogenous and endogenous social interactions. Identifying the distinct role of endogenous and exogenous effects of peers is all but impossible, even in this simplistic framework in which they have assumed that i's choice of group members (e.g., i's best friend) is exogenous.

The identification problem is somewhat less serious in the case of neighborhood contexts because there is some hope for finding Z-type determinants of neighborhood structure (e.g., regional changes in economic conditions) that are not also determinants of i's own behavior.

The Omitted-Context Variables Problem

Distinct from the simultaneity problem is the more conventional problem of omitted variables—in this case context-level variables.[2] Regressing i's achievement or behavior on his or her family and contextual characteristics will bias estimates of B' if important characteristics of i's context are omitted from the regression. To illustrate this, we can add to Equation 1 a component of the error term (c_i) that reflects the collection of unmeasured influences of i's context:

---

[2] Moffitt (1998) presents a more general discussion of these problems under the heading "correlated unobservables."

$$y_i = A' \ FAM_i + B' \ CON_i + c_i + e_i \quad (4)$$

This model leads to the familiar omitted-variables problem and a biased estimation of B' (the effect of CON on y) if contextual conditions—represented in Equation 4 by c_i—are omitted from the estimation of Equation 4, affect y, and are correlated with CON. Attempts to measure key contextual constructs generally adopt administrative-data approaches, which, we argue, are limited in scope, or survey-based approaches, which often suffer from substantial measurement error. Another measurement approach, explained in a subsequent section, is that of *systematic social observation* (SSO).

Administrative-data approaches. It is easy to argue that many existing studies of neighborhood context suffer from omitted-variables bias. Most draw their data from the decennial census. Every 10 years, the census bureau collects information that can be used to construct demographic-based neighborhood measures such as the fraction of individuals who are poor, the fraction of adults with a college degree, and the fraction of adult men without jobs. Subsets of such data are available for census blocks and block groups; complete census data are available for "tracts" (geographic areas encompassing 4,000 to 6,000 individuals with boundaries drawn to approximate neighborhood areas), zip codes, cities, counties, metropolitan areas, labor market areas, and states. Other administrative databases can be used for measuring certain physical characteristics of neighborhoods and schools as well as certain ecological risk factors (such as crime and infant mortality rates of neighborhoods), although these data are often not uniformly measured across contexts nor available for geographic areas as small as tracts.

There are two problems with studies that rely on census-based sources. Some use only a single neighborhood measure such as poverty or the welfare receipt rate in the census tract of residence or a single (often factor-analysis-derived) index of such measures. Significant coefficients on the census-based measure are taken as evidence of neighborhood effects. In some cases where only one census variable is used (e.g., tract poverty or welfare rate), the interpretation is further extended (erroneously in most cases) to suggest that it is neighborhood poverty or welfare dependence as such, as opposed to many other dimensions of neighborhoods correlated with rates of poverty or welfare receipt, that is behind the neighborhood effect.

The multitude of theoretical ways in which neighborhood processes operate suggest that many different kinds of measures, even if all of them can be derived from census-based sources, are needed to capture the different kinds of neighborhood effects. For example, epidemic models focus on the presence of "problematic" peers and have often been implemented with measures of neighborhood poverty or low-SES job structure (Clark, 1992; Crane, 1991). In contrast, social control and institutional models focus more on the presence of higher SES neighbors than the presence or absence of low-SES neighbors. This distinction is subtle, but easily conceived if SES is thought to have at least three strata—say, low, medium, and high levels of SES.

The diversity of U.S. neighborhoods produces different combinations of these three strata, which enables researchers to distinguish empirically among their effects on developmental outcomes. Brooks-Gunn, Duncan, Klebanov, and Sealand (1993) and authors of several chapters in Brooks-Gunn, Duncan, and Aber (1997) found that it is the presence or absence of affluent, high-SES neighbors, rather than the presence or absence of poor neighbors, that relates most strongly to child and adolescent outcomes. Wilson's (1987) focus on male joblessness adds yet another correlated but theoretically distinct dimension of neighborhood structure. Given the relatively high correlation among neighborhood joblessness, poverty, and race, geographically diverse samples are crucial to distinguish empirically between Wilson's and other models.

Much more problematic from an omitted-variables point of view are tests of theoretical approaches based on neighborhood influences not well captured by administrative data. Institutional, social disorganization, and family-process models are examples because the required measures are not readily available from census-based sources. Absent from census forms, and either absent from or inconsistently measured in other administrative sources, are data about schools (e.g., number, type, and quality of schools in the area), law enforcement (e.g., number of police, number and type of crimes, percent of crimes reported that are cleared by arrest, various characteristics of local police practices), access to transportation (e.g., distance to freeway entrances and public transportation), drugs and gang activity, neighborhood collective efficacy, intergenerational ties, and churches and other community institutions.

Survey-based approaches. In attempting to go beyond the constraints imposed by census- or administrative-based sources, some studies sought to use youth or their parents as informants about the characteristics of their neighborhoods or schools. A major problem with this strategy is that measurement errors in these assessments are likely to be correlated with the measurement errors in the youth-based outcomes. For example, a depressed mother may give overly pessimistic assessments of both neighborhood conditions and her children's social behavior. If the mother's mental health is not controlled in the regression analysis, then the estimated relationship between neighborhood conditions and child behavior will be overstated. Another example of bias induced by self-reports is when an adolescent's report of his or her peers' attitudes is spuriously correlated with his or her self-reports of attitudes and behavior. This correlated-errors problem can be eliminated if the youth outcomes are based on administrative (e.g., test scores, school attendance, arrest records) rather than survey data (e.g., Cook et al., 1998), although possible problems from measurement error in the youth self-reports remain.

There is less reason to suspect measurement-error-driven bias from context measures formed by aggregating demographic characteristics such as ethnicity, sex, or social class to construct segregation indices or other measures of social composition. For example, Lee and Bryk (1989) constructed measures of the social and ethnic composition of U.S. high schools from student survey data and used those measures to predict the same students' academic achievement. There is a small risk that a student's report of demographic background is influenced by his or her achievement. In contrast, an aggregated measure of perceived instructional quality would quite plausibly reflect the achievement of the student reporters, and it would therefore be inadvisable to use such a measure of instructional quality as a predictor of student achievement.

A more satisfying, if expensive, strategy is to obtain an independent sample of capable informants about a context and pool their reports to create context-level measures. This approach has been successfully used in national data on school climate (c.f., Raudenbush, Rowan, & Kang, 1991), with multiple teachers surveyed about their degree of control, collaboration, and supportive administrative leadership, and in data assessing the social cohesion, informal social control, and collective efficacy of neighbors in Chicago (Sampson et al., 1997). In both cases, 15 to 30 informants per context were required to obtain reliable contextual-level measures. Clearly, the expense of this measurement strategy grows rapidly with the number of contexts sampled, and it increases during the course of a longitudinal study as mobility creates greater dispersion of participants across contexts and, hence, produces more contexts to be assessed.

Endogenous Membership

The contexts in which children develop are not allocated by a random process, which leads to the third problem—endogenous membership. This is most clearly seen in the case of selection of best friends and peer groups, where decisions rest almost entirely with the adolescent.[3] A youth's immediate neighborhood and, to a somewhat smaller extent, school also have an element of choice, in this case on the part of the parent. The propensity of children to live in better or worse neighborhoods or attend better or worse schools depends on parental background characteristics and current circumstances, not all of which can be easily measured.

As with the omitted-context-variables problem, the endogenous membership problem involves omitted variables, but in this case at the level of the individual (in the case of youth i's choice of best friends or peers) or family (in the case of youth i's parent's choice of neighborhood or school). Presuming the latter, family-based, source of endogenous membership bias, we can illustrate the problem and potential solutions by adding to our model an error component (f_i) denoting unmeasured family-specific influences on choice of context:

$$y_i = A' \ FAM_i + B' \ CON_i + f_i + c_i + e_i \quad (5)$$

---

[3] We emphasize that the possible endogeneity of group membership is distinct from the possible endogeneity of the social interactions themselves. As noted in our section on simultaneity, the problem of determining whether youth j's behavior affects youth i's behavior is distinct from the problem of determining why i and j choose to become best friends.

Here the omission of explicit measures of f_i will bias B' to the joint extent that f_i is an important determinant of y, and f_i is correlated with CON. A parallel argument holds for omitted individual-level influences on choice of context.

The direction of endogenous-membership bias in estimates of Equation 5 is uncertain. Suppose parents choose between holding two jobs and using the extra income to buy a better neighborhood or having a single earner and living in a poorer neighborhood. Suppose further that parents who live in poorer neighborhoods and/or send their children to worse schools make up for the deficiencies of the neighborhood or school through the additional time that parents spend with their children. Neighborhood or school conditions matter in this scenario, but an empirical analysis will show this to be the case only if it adjusts for differences in parental time use. Failure to adjust for parental employment will cause conventional regression-based approaches to understate neighborhood or school effects. In terms of Equation 5, failure to include parental employment as part of FAM will likely bias the estimate of B' toward zero.

Another scenario, also leading to an understatement of neighborhood or school effects, is one in which parents well equipped to resist the effects of bad neighborhoods choose to live in them to take advantage of cheaper housing or perhaps shorter commuting times. Unless measures of parental competence are included in the model, the estimated effects of bad neighborhoods or schools on youth outcomes will be smaller than if parents were randomly allocated across neighborhoods.

It is perhaps more likely that parents especially *ill*-equipped to handle bad neighborhoods or schools are most likely to live in them, because these parents lack the (partly unmeasured) wherewithal to move to better neighborhoods. In this case, the coincidence of a poor neighborhood or school and the poor developmental outcomes of their children results from their inability to avoid either, thus leading to an overestimation of the effects of current neighborhood conditions. Conversely, parents who are effective in promoting the developmental success of their children may find their neighborhood choices dominated by considerations of developmental consequences. If this parental capacity is not captured in measured parental characteristics, then the coincidence of positive developmental outcomes for their children and living in a better neighborhood would be misattributed to current neighborhood conditions and thus lead to an overestimation of neighborhood effects. Here again, in terms of regression model 5, the omitted f_i factors are unobserved characteristics of the parents (e.g., concern for their children's development) that affect developmental outcomes. Regressions of contextual effects that do not control for all relevant parenting variables will produce biased estimates of the effects of those contextual factors.

Random assignment. There are three approaches for addressing the endogenous membership problem. The best is to rely on data in which families are randomly assigned to neighborhood contexts. In terms of Equation 5, the random assignment of CON effectively eliminates the correlation between family-specific omitted factors (f_i) and context (CON), and thus eliminates the possibility of omitted-variables bias. As described later, HUD's Moving to Opportunity program contains such experimental data on neighborhood context. Second-best solutions to the nonrandom context selection problem are to rely on quasiexperimental data such as those generated by the Gautreaux program, analyses of which are also summarized later.

Measure the unmeasured. The best nonexperimental approach to the endogenous membership problem is to locate data that measure the crucial family- and individual-level omitted variables. For example, some child-development data sets contain fairly sophisticated measures of parenting characteristics and parental mental health. Controls for such measures in regression-based analyses can help reduce the endogenous-membership bias to the extent that those measures capture the determinants of the process of contextual choice. Of course, it is impossible to demonstrate that all relevant variables have been included in a model, which suggests that this measurement-based strategy for the omitted variables problem should be accompanied by others.

Instrumental variables. Another nonexperimental approach to the bias problem is to replace the contextual measure (CON) in Equation 5 with a predicted value of CON that is purged of CON's spurious correlation with unobserved parenting or other family or individual-level measures. The instrumental variables approach is often implemented as a two-step procedure (Greene, 1993). In the first step, the contextual measure (CON) is the dependent variable and is predicted by other variables in Equation 5 plus exogenous variables that are not themselves determinants of y.[4] In the second stage, Equation 5 is estimated, replacing CON with the predicted value of CON obtained in the first stage.

Evans, Oates, and Schwab (1992) adopted this strategy to adjust for endogenous membership problems in a school-based study, although they relied on dubious instrumental variables. Their dependent variables of interest were high-school completion and out-of-wedlock teen childbearing. Their contextual variable was the SES of the student body. When they ignored endogeneity issues and regressed their outcomes on student-body SES and family-level controls, they found highly significant, beneficial effects of high student-body SES. However, when they estimated a two-equation model, with the first equation regressing student-body SES on characteristics of the metropolitan area in which the student resides and the second regressing the developmental outcomes on predicted student-body SES and family-level controls, the effects of student-body SES disappeared.

Dubious in the procedures of Evans et al. (1992) is the assumption that metropolitan-level characteristics do not influence youth outcomes such as high-school completion or fertility. It is easy to imagine that both labor-market conditions and metropolitan-specific norms might well influence the cost-benefit calculus behind these decisions, which would invalidate their approach. A more promising approach for identifying an instrumental-variables model is to rely on data from true or quasirandomized residential mobility designs.

---

[4] More formally, the identifying variable must be uncorrelated with the error term(s) in (5).

Sibling models. Yet another approach to the endogenous membership prob-lem is to use sibling-based, fixed-effects models to eliminate the biasing influence of omitted persistent, unmeasured parental characteristics.

In fixed-effects models, each sibling's score on the dependent and independent variables is subtracted from the average value of all siblings in the family. In the special case of two siblings per family, the deviation-from-means model becomes a sibling difference model. If we replace the subscript i in Equation 5 with 1 (for sibling 1) and 2 (for sibling 2), and assume that there is sufficient cross-sibling variability in family and contextual conditions to reference FAM and CON with the sibling subscripts, the sibling difference model takes the following form:

$$y_2 - y_1 = A' (FAM_2 - FAM_1) + B' (CON_2 - CON_1) + (f_2 - f_1) + (c_2 - c_1) + (e_2 - e_1) \quad (6)$$

In terms of measured variables, this amounts to estimating a regression in which sibling differences in the outcome of interest are regressed on sibling differences in observed family and contextual characteristics. Observed (FAM) and unob-served (f_i) family factors affecting choice of context that are constant across sib-lings are differenced out of Equation 6, thus eliminating the omitted-variable bias caused by family-determined endogenous group membership. Even if unobserved family factors differ across siblings, it is often reasonable to assume a low correla-tion between sibling differences in those family factors and sibling differences in context, in which case even unmeasured sibling-specific family factors will not impart much bias to estimates of neighborhood effects (B').

The sibling difference model thus "automatically" eliminates bias from all permanent family factors, observable and not, that do not differ between siblings. Time-varying family factors, especially those that might be correlated with neigh-borhood conditions (e.g., divorce, income changes), are a potential source of bias and should be controlled explicitly in the regression if possible. However, note that they will bias estimates only to the extent that they are correlated with the neighborhood differences. If uncorrelated with them, the unmeasured family dif-ferences between siblings will contribute to the lack of explanatory power of a sibling difference model, but will not bias the neighborhood parameter estimates.

Aaronson (1997) demonstrated the feasibility of this approach using data on Panel Study of Income Dynamics (PSID) adolescents. He used family residential changes as a source of neighborhood background variation within families to esti-mate sibling-based neighborhood effects that are substantially free of family-specific heterogeneity biases associated with neighborhood selection. Using a sample of multi-ple-child PSID families where the adolescent siblings are separated in age by at least 3 years, he estimated sibling-difference models of children's educational outcomes and found evidence of neighborhood effects. In fact, his family fixed-effect regres-sions using the neighborhood poverty rate as the measure of neighborhood condi-tions showed even larger neighborhood effects on high school graduation and grades completed than did conventional Ordinary Least Square (OLS) models.

Sibling models are not without problems, however. They require multiple-child families, which introduces a potential source of sample selection bias. Griliches (1979) pointed out that differencing between siblings reduces but does not eliminate endogenous variation in neighborhood regressors, since parental decisions to change neighborhoods may be motivated in part by their child-specific developmental consequences. At the same time, sibling-difference models filter out much of the exogenous variation in contextual conditions. And finally, family moves are often motivated by events that may themselves affect youth development.

Families as Mediators and Moderators of Neighborhood Effects

Thus far, our discussion of family influences on youth outcomes has assumed that they play a confounding role in attempts to gauge neighborhood influences. We have concluded that researchers who fail to measure them (especially the part of them that determines neighborhood choice) risk bias in their assessments of neighborhood influences. It is important to recognize the possibility of two other, more substantial, roles for families in neighborhood studies: mediators that help account for the "reduced form" effects of neighborhood conditions on youth outcomes, and moderators in which families and neighborhoods jointly influence youth outcomes.

Families as mediators. Models presented thus far assume that neighborhood conditions affect children directly. It is also likely that characteristics of families such as income, living arrangements, parenting and decision-making, and parental mental health are shaped by social and physical contexts like neighborhoods (Duncan, Connell, & Klebanov, 1997). If neighborhoods affect parents in ways that in turn affect children, then mere adjustments for family differences, as in Equation 1, will understate the total effects of neighborhoods on children. Better to conceive of these relationships recursively, with family conditions playing the role of mediators.

It is easy to imagine how neighborhoods might affect parents, especially low-SES parents. Persistent residence in a neighborhood with high levels of crime, low levels of economic opportunity, weak marriage pools, and poor transportation can erode and eventually dissipate the competence and commitment of single mothers to seek employment in that neighborhood, to marry, or to move to a neighborhood where they can work and provide safe activities outside the home for their children (Korbin & Coulton, 1997).

Assessments of neighborhood influences on families face many of the same methodological problems as studies of neighborhood influences on children. Particularly vexing is the endogenous membership problem—how much of an association between, say, bad neighborhood conditions and low parental income reflects neighborhood conditions causing employment problems and how much is the spurious result of omitted factors (e.g., mental health) causing both employment problems and residence in a bad neighborhood? An important area for future research is to secure unbiased estimates of the links between neighborhood characteristics and family conditions.

Families as moderators. Cook, Kim, Chan, and Settersten (1998) argued for interactions between family- and neighborhood-level conditions. Their Philadelphia-based analysis (as well as more general ones presented in other chapters of Furstenberg, Cook, Eccles, and Sameroff [1998]) illustrated the subtlety of the relationships among neighborhood conditions, family management practices, and youth outcomes.

Surprisingly, they found only modest differences in family management practices across their diverse sample of neighborhoods. Management styles were more restrictive in disadvantaged neighborhoods, but the relationship was not a very strong one. Families' institutional connections mattered for youth academic outcomes, but only in more disadvantaged neighborhoods. Parental restrictiveness reduced the involvement of children in potentially beneficial activities, but only in higher risk neighborhoods.

Variability in Contextual Characteristics

Estimating models of how neighborhood characteristics affect youth achievement and behavior with survey-based, nonexperimental data requires youth samples that are dispersed across a variety of contexts. If the researcher hopes to go beyond assessments of a single "good" versus "bad" neighborhood dimension and begin to distinguish among competing neighborhood-effects theories (e.g., based on male joblessness vs. resources vs. collective socialization), then the needed sample dispersion across different kinds of neighborhoods is considerable. However, since costs increase at least linearly with the number of sampled neighborhoods, it may be impossible to conduct worthy studies of neighborhood effects with small research budgets.

A discussion of the tradeoffs and options rests on the nature of the contextual data to be analyzed. One option is with administrative (e.g., census-based) data collected by geographic area and associated with sampled youth through address matching or some similar procedure. A second is by aggregating characteristics or survey responses of sampled youth or their parents. Our earlier discussion warned of instances when aggregation procedures are likely to bias estimates of contextual effects.

Is it desirable to cluster sample observations by context? To save costs, most surveys *cluster* their samples by selecting multiple households within a limited number of neighborhoods or multiple students within a limited number of classrooms. Whether this clustering hinders or helps attempts to model context effects depends on the source of the contextual data.

Suppose that administrative data are to be used to measure context. Suppose further that neither the costs of collecting administrative data (as is often the case) nor the costs of collecting survey data (as is rarely the case) depend on the number of sampled contexts. Under these conditions, clustering samples by context would be undesirable. Such clustering creates a (statistically) inefficient dependence across observations. In the absence of cost savings in collecting interview or contextual information, the optimal design would sample one subject per context.[5]

In most instances, interviewing costs associated with additional subjects per context are substantially lower than costs associated with subjects drawn from different contexts. The tradeoff between interviewing costs and statistical efficiency has long been a concern of sampling statisticians and, in the case of typical household surveys, leads to designs with relatively modest (e.g., 4 to 10) subjects per cluster. Studies that measure context by aggregating characteristics, perceptions, or behavior of respondents provide an additional rationale for clustering. Careful consideration of the costs and benefits (e.g., as with the Chicago Neighborhood Study) leads to larger cluster sizes (i.e., between 15 and 30 subjects per cluster).

Contextual variability. The cost of such clustering is that there is less dispersion across contexts than if the same field budget were spent on a less clustered sample. How limiting is it to restrict the geographic variability of the sample? Unfortunately, the relatively limited variability in neighborhood conditions found in sections of cities or even in entire geographic areas of many cities poses difficult tradeoffs for study design. Duncan and Raudenbush (1999) illustrated the scope of the problem by drawing tract-based data from the 1980 decennial census. They formed subsets of tracts to approximate typical study designs: (a) all tracts in the United States (to approximate national samples); (b) all tracts in the city of Chicago (to approximate a large study in a single but diverse city); (c) all Chicago tracts with a 30% or higher poverty rate (to approximate an "underclass" study in a large city); (d) all tracts in the city of Atlanta (to approximate a large study in a less diverse large city); (e) all Atlanta tracts with a 30% or higher poverty rate (to approximate an "underclass" study in a less diverse large city); and (f) all tracts in the city of Rochester, NY (to approximate a study in a medium-sized city).

They drew from the census files seven tract-level demographic measures often used in neighborhood-based research, each of which is associated with a distinct neighborhood-level theoretical process: *race*—the percentage of individuals in the tract who are black; *female headship*—the percentage of households headed by women; *welfare*—the percentage of households receiving public assistance; *poverty*—the percentage of non-elderly individuals with below-poverty household incomes; *high educational level*—the percentage of adults with college de-

---

[5] While such a design would be optimal for estimating regression coefficients, it provides no information about variation within and between contexts. To the extent it is important to gauge the magnitude of unmeasured sources of variation within and between contexts, the unclustered sample design is problematic, even when costs are ignored. Clustering observations within contexts also enables analysts to use "fixed effects" regression techniques to estimate family models that are free from bias from neighborhood factors. In these models, all families in a neighborhood area are identified and the data are transformed by subtracting each adolescent's measure from neighborhood averages. In capitalizing on intra-neighborhood variance, fixed-effects models produce no explicit estimate of neighborhood effects, but they do purge family effect estimates of neighborhood-based bias.

grees; *neighborhood stability*—the percentage of households who had lived in the same dwelling 5 years before; and *joblessness*—the percentage of adult males who worked fewer than 26 weeks in 1979.

To assess potential multicollinearity problems using these measures, Duncan and Raudenbush (1999) took the various collections of tracts and regressed each of the neighborhood measures on the remaining six neighborhood measures. Not surprisingly, the resulting R^2s indicated a great deal more multicollinearity in the city-specific samples than for the national set of tracts. For example, only 29% of the variation in the fraction of college-graduate adults could be accounted for by the other six measures in the national sets of tracts. In the city-specific samples, the squared multiple correlations ranged from 0.31 to 0.75 and averaged 0.50— nearly twice the degree of multicollinearity in the national set of tracts. Overall, the average extent to which the city-based squared correlations exceeded those for all U.S. tracts ranged from 0.07 to 0.25 across the seven measures.

The experiences of the authors contributing chapters to Brooks-Gunn et al. (1997) illustrate the same point in a different way. All sought a coordinated analysis of neighborhood effects by matching census-tract-based neighborhood measures (of the kind listed before) to the addresses of children and youth from a variety of samples. In the case of data from two national samples—the PSID and Children of the National Longitudinal Survey of Youth—the sample dispersion provided ample degrees of freedom to support estimates of the effects of a number of theoretically distinct but empirically correlated neighborhood dimensions. This was also the case for data from the eight-city Infant Health and Development Program. However, data from samples of three more specialized studies—children from a single urban school district in upstate New York; youth from high-poverty neighborhoods in New York, Baltimore, and Washington, DC, and children from high-poverty neighborhoods in a large Southern city—only supported estimates of the effects of a single "good" versus "bad" neighborhood dimension. Research designs that support only one neighborhood dimension are obviously incapable of identifying the nature of neighborhood processes.

SOME PROMISING APPROACHES

Rather than conclude with this depressing list of problems facing analysts of contextual effects, we prefer to draw uplifting examples from recent work that solve at least some of these problems. Our examples include (a) the Project on Human Development in Chicago Neighborhoods, which incorporates a well-conceived design for obtaining measures of neighborhood constructs; (b) correlation-based approaches to estimating upper bounds on the influences of neighborhood effects; (c) findings from the quasiexperimental Gautreaux project; and (d) preliminary findings from one site in HUD's Moving to Opportunity random assignment experiment.

The Project on Human Development in Chicago Neighborhoods

Sampson et al. (1997) is a promising approach to measuring context in a way that corresponds closely to theoretical constructs. As part of a study of the delinquent behavior of youth in a sample of Chicago neighborhoods, they measure the collective efficacy of neighborhoods by conducting a survey of adult residents in sampled neighborhoods rather than relying exclusively on decennial census measures.

Few researchers have the resources to conduct independent surveys of neighborhood residents to obtain their contextual measures. The Chicago Project also incorporates systematic social observation (SSO; Reiss, 1988) as an alternative source of contextual information. Some of its measurement strategies (e.g., videotaping and coding) are cumbersome and expensive. However, in one strategy, trained observers can fairly quickly assess aspects of a neighborhood such as its degree of social and physical disorder. Interviewers dispatched to conduct interviews can also be used to conduct such observations at a cost far less than that of conducting an independent survey of residents.

The Chicago Project implemented its "deluxe" version of SSO by having a van drive 5 miles an hour down every street within 80 target neighborhood clusters. Videotape recorders on both sides of the van captured physical characteristics of the streets and buildings on each side of the street as well as visible aspects of social interaction. Trained observers then coded the videotapes, noting the status of buildings (residential vs. commercial, detached homes or apartments, whether vacant or burnt out, their general condition, presence of security precautions such as bars or grates, etc.), presence of garbage, litter, graffiti, drug paraphernalia, broken bottles, abandoned cars, and other aspects of the physical environment.

The driver and a second rider in the van, trained to observe social interactions, also recorded their observations via audiotape. Social interactions included, for example, adults drinking in public, drug sales, children playing in the street, and apparent gang activity. Scales tapping social and physical disorder, housing conditions, and other aspects of the neighborhood environment showed high internal consistency across face blocks within neighborhood clusters and reasonably high construct validity as indicated by correlations with theoretically linked constructs measured by an independent community survey, by the census, and by official crime data. Analyses now underway are estimating the value added by the videotapes, above the information gleaned from the audiotapes. Generally, the videotaped data are far more expensive than the audiotaped data. It is feasible to use the audiotape strategy even when samples are not highly clustered because data collection per blockface is comparatively inexpensive.

SSO has substantial promise for efficient collection of data on the social organization of neighborhoods—data not available from administrative records. However, some of the constructs that can be captured through interviews, such as collective efficacy in Sampson et al. (1997), are not accessible via observational methods. Given the expense of interviewing residents in unclustered samples, researchers interested in neighborhood effects face difficult tradeoffs, discussed later. Similar tradeoffs face school researchers, who might opt for observational measures (cf., Mortimore, Sammons, Stoll, Lewis, & Ecob, 1988) as an alternative to survey methods designed to capture school organization and climate.

Correlations as Upper-bound Estimates of the Influence of Context

An alternative approach to the problem of unobservable neighborhood variables relies on correlations between children who are neighbors or classmates or, equivalently, on the explained variance of neighborhoods, schools, or classmates to provide an upper bound on the possible effect of these contexts. To motivate the logic of this approach, we first note that many studies have used sibling correlations to estimate the importance of shared family and other environmental experiences. For example, sibling correlations for years of completed schooling are quite high— around 0.55—indicating that there are important elements of the genes, family environments, neighborhoods, schools, and other aspects of the shared environments of siblings that make siblings much more alike in terms of completed schooling than two individuals drawn at random from the population.

Solon, Page, and Duncan (1999) argued that an analogous correlation for children growing up in the same neighborhood but not in the same family indicates how much of what is important in the shared environments of siblings lies outside the immediate family. A high completed-schooling correlation for unrelated neighbor children, for example, is consistent with a strong neighborhood effect and would imply that shared neighborhood conditions are an important component of the sibling correlations. (An alternative interpretation is that the extrafamilial correlations are driven by the often similar family backgrounds of children in neighboring families.) Neighbor correlations close to zero would suggest that the scope for pure (i.e., extrafamilial) neighborhood effects is quite small.

The beauty of sibling and neighbor correlations is that they provide an upper bound on the estimated impact of both measurable *and unmeasurable* aspects of the environments shared by siblings and neighbors. In particular, neighbor correlations address the omitted-context-variables problem because the strength of the correlations does not depend on whether the contextual factors driving them can be measured. Of course, a limitation of these correlations is that they reveal nothing about the process by which familial and extrafamilial influences operate to make siblings and neighbors more alike than two individuals drawn at random from the population. Nor do the neighborhood correlations address either the simultaneity or endogenous-membership problem.

Solon et al. (1999) formalized these arguments in terms of the same kind of additive model given in Equation 1:

$$y_{sfc} = A'FAM_{fc} + B'CON_c + e_{sfc.} \qquad (7)$$

In this case, c references the extrafamilial context (e.g., school class, neighborhood, peer group) and f references families. Siblings within families are referenced with s. FAM_{fc} is a vector of shared family influences for all siblings within the same family, CON_c is a vector of extrafamilial contextual influences (henceforth called *neighborhood* but applicable to other contexts) shared by all siblings and neighboring children, and e_{sfc} is an error term.

Solon et al. (1999) showed that the sibling covariance in y_{sfc} can be expressed as:

$$Cov(y_{sfc}, y_{sfc'}) = Var(A'FAM_{fc}) + Var(B'CON_c) + 2Cov(A'FAM_{fc}, B'CON_c), \quad (8)$$

that is, the sum of shared family variance, shared neighborhood variance, and twice the covariance between family and neighborhood factors.

The covariance between neighboring children from different families is:

$$Cov(y_{sfc}, y_{s'fc'}) = Var(B'CON_c) + 2Cov(A'FAM_{fc}, B'CON_c) + 2Cov(A'FAM_{fc}, A'FAM_{fc'}), \quad (9)$$

that is, the sum of the shared neighborhood variance and twice the covariance between family and neighborhood factors plus twice the covariance in family backgrounds among neighboring children. In comparing sibling (in Equation 8) and neighbor (in Equation 9) covariances, it can be seen that shared neighborhood variance and covariance between family and neighborhood factors are common to both. The shared family variance is obviously missing from the nonfamily neighbor covariance, whereas the family-background covariance of neighboring children is missing from the sibling covariance but is a part of the nonfamily neighbor covariance.

National surveys such as the PSID and the National Longitudinal Survey of Youth (NLSY) draw their samples from a set of tightly clustered neighborhood areas that often encompass only one or two blocks. Thus these clusters approximate neighborhood areas and, using anonymous cluster identification, it is possible to calculate both sibling and neighbor correlations for various outcomes of interest. Solon et al. (1999) calculated such sibling and neighbor correlations with a representative PSID sample consisting of individuals age 8 to 16 in 1968. For their outcome measure—years of completed schooling—the sibling correlation (0.54) is much higher than the estimated neighbor correlation (0.19), suggesting a rather limited scope for the effects of extrafamilial contexts. After removing effects of easily observed socioeconomic characteristics of families (race, family income, family structure, and maternal schooling) shared by children living in the same neighborhood, the neighbor correlation dropped further (to 0.10), suggesting an even more limited scope for unique neighborhood influences. All in all, the results suggest that neighborhood influences are much more limited than family influences in accounting for individual differences in completed schooling.

Correlations from Add Health. Duncan, Boisjoly, and Harris (1998) drew data from the National Longitudinal Survey of Adolescent Health (Add Health) to generalize this approach.[6] They used correlations between siblings within a family, between grademates within a school, between schoolmates residing in the same Census block group, and between peers as defined by a set of "best friend" nominations as respective upper-bound estimates of the potential influence of family, school, neighbors, and peers.[7] Add Health is a nationally representative study of adolescents in grades 7 through 12 in the U.S. in 1995, the vast majority of whom responded to an in-school, self-administered questionnaire, and a systematically chosen subset of whom responded to two waves of at-home personal interviews.

The data are uniquely able to characterize sibling, neighborhood, peer, and school environments of sample members. The sample itself is clustered within 134 schools drawn from a school-based sampling frame. In-home interviews administered to a random subset of students from each school provide representative samples of schoolmates that can be used to generate schoolmate-based correlations. The in-school questionnaires administered to all students asked each adolescent respondent to name his or her five best male friends and five best female friends, providing data for best-friend correlations. We distinguish instances where best friend nominations are and are not mutual. In-home data can also be aggregated across schoolmates residing in the same neighborhood, with neighborhood residence established through address matching to Census block group.[8] The design provides data on friendship and neighbor pairs that can span school grades, but must be from sampled schools. All twin pairs found in the schools were included in the in-home interviewing, providing substantial sample sizes for monozygotic twin, dizygotic twin, and non-twin siblings.

Two key outcomes available in the data are the Add Health Picture Vocabulary Test (PVT), an achievement-ability measure based on receptive vocabulary, and a delinquency scale. Both are continuous measures, the first with a nearly normal distribution. The delinquency scale consists of items on painting graffiti, damaging property, shoplifting, getting into a serious physical fight, stealing a car, stealing something worth less than $50, stealing something worth $50 or more, burglarizing a building, and selling drugs.

Table 8.1 presents correlations in age-adjusted PVT and delinquency scores for various groups of male siblings, friends, neighborhoods, and grademates. Brothers are divided into MZ and DZ twins, non-twin full siblings close and not close in age, and half-siblings. Best-friend, neighbor, and grademate correlations are computed both on scores that incorporate a simple age adjustment and on scores that

---

[6] The cited paper uses data from Add Health's in-school survey. The data presented here are preliminary and are taken from the in-home survey but follow the same procedures.

[7] Behavioral geneticists have used correlations in this way for nearly a century in studying family influences (Plomin et al., 1990), as have sociologists for the last quarter century when examining school effects (e.g., Coleman, 1966; Jencks & Brown, 1975) and peer effects (e.g., Billy & Udry, 1985; Kandel, 1978).

[8] We are grateful to John Billy for supplying us with the necessary anonymized block-group identifiers.

Table 8.1
Correlations in Age-adjusted PVT and Delinquency Scores
Within Various Groups of Adolescent Males

	PVT achievement test score	Delinquency score	Number of pairs
Family-based			
Monozygotic twin boys	.80	.45	141
Dizygotic twin boys	.56	.30	123
Non-twin full brothers <2 years apart	.55	.23	168
Non-twin full brothers >2 years apart	.64	.13	160
Half brothers	.44	.14	107
Mutual best friends			
Not family-SES adjusted	.46	.28	282
Family-SES adjusted	.33	.28	282
Nonmutual best friends			
Not family-SES adjusted	.33	.16	672
Family-SES adjusted	.12	.15	672
Neighbors			
Not family-SES adjusted	.18	.02	153,110
Family-SES adjusted	.04	.02	153,110
7th- and 8th-grade grademates			
Not family-SES adjusted	.14	.04	16,822
Family-SES adjusted	.05	.03	16,822
10th- through 12th-grade grademates			
Not family-SES adjusted	.19	.00	166,165
Family-SES adjusted	.05	.00	166,165

Source: Calculations by Johanne Boisjoly using data from the National Longitudinal
Survey of Adolescent Health.

also adjust for a handful of readily observed measures of family SES—income, parental education, and family structure. Furthermore, grademate correlations are computed separately for middle- and high-school grademates to test the hypothesis that context-driven correlations strengthen as children move from early to later adolescence.

PVT correlations across family groups have a similar pattern to those found in the voluminous literature on full-scale IQ correlations.[9] MZ twin correlations (0.80) are considerably higher than DZ twin correlations (0.56). Simple behavioral genetics models produce 48% and 32% estimates of heritability and shared environmental influences, respectively. [9] As with the Solon et al. (1997), neighbor correlations of completed schooling, grademate and neighbor correlations are much smaller than sibling correlations and drop even more in the presence of adjustments for family SES. The results imply an upper-bound explained variance of 4% for neighborhoods effects and 5% for school effects on achievement. At 0.46 (and, SES-adjusted, 0.33), mutual best-friend correlations are closer to sibling correlations. Correlations for non-mutual best friends (i.e., where person A named B as best friend but B named as best friend someone other than A) are considerably lower. Unfortunately, it is impossible with correlation-based method to determine upper bounds on either the exogenous or endogenous component of peer effects.

Correlations for delinquency are not as high as those for the test scores and are much less affected by adjustments for family SES. In this case, simple behavioral genetics models imply 30% and 15% estimates of heredity and shared environmental influences on delinquency.[11] As with test scores, the delinquency correlations among neighbors (0.02) and grademates (0.00 to 0.04) suggest at most a very modest scope for neighborhood and school effects. That grademate correlations are smaller for older as compared with younger adolescents is surprising and indicates that school-based contextual influences may be stronger at the earlier ages. At 0.28, best friend correlations are higher than all but the twin correlations.

Caveats regarding correlations. There are a number of important qualifications for using correlations among classmates, peers, and neighbors as upper-bound estimates of the importance of extrafamilial contexts. First, the transitory nature of neighborhoods, schools, and, especially, peer groups (Urberg, Digermencioglu, & Tolson, 1995) in the lives of children may impart a measurement-error-induced downward bias to the correlations. For example, because residential mobility is quite common in the United States, especially among younger children, children sharing a neighborhood at any given point may have quite different residential

---

[9] Bouchard and McGue (1981) conducted a meta-analysis of 212 IQ correlation studies and report the following weighted average correlations for pairs reared together: .86 for MZ twins; .60 for DZ twins; .47 for non-twin siblings; and .31 for half-siblings. In the case of twin studies of verbal comprehension, Nichols (1978) reported average correlations for identical and fraternal twins of .78 and .59.

[10] Behavioral geneticists use the pattern of correlations among siblings and parent-child pairs with varying degrees of genetic relatedness and co-residence during childhood to estimate the role of genes and shared and unshared environmental influences (Falconer, 1981). Roughly speaking, a personality trait with a mixture of purely genetic and unshared environmental causes should produce outcome correlations twice as high in monozygotic (MZ, i.e., one-egg) twins as in either dizygotic (DZ, i.e., two-egg) twins or siblings born at different times, since MZ twins have 100% genetic relatedness while DZ and other full siblings share only 50% genetic relatedness. Under these assumptions, the extent to which the MZ correlation is less than perfect reflects the importance of a combination of unshared environmental causes and measurement error. Allowing for the potential importance of the environments shared by twin and non-twin siblings (e.g., unchanging parenting practices, permanent family resources and, for twins, in-utero conditions) complicates inferences from these correlations. If genes were unimportant and environments similar then one would expect similar MZ, DZ, and non-twin sibling correlations. Simple behavioral genetics models suggest that the heritability of a trait equals twice the difference between MZ and DZ correlations and that the role of shared environment can be expressed as twice the DZ correlation minus the MZ correlation.

[11] These MZ and DZ twin correlations are considerably smaller than the .71 and .47 correlations reported in Rowe (1983).

histories. However, this bias may not be large because residential moves typically occur between similar neighborhoods (Solon et al., 1997). Peer mobility also typically occurs among individuals with similar characteristics (Urberg et al., 1995).

Second, the endogenous nature of context, particularly peer groups, will cause best-friend correlations to overstate, perhaps dramatically, the causal role played by peer contexts. Third, the differential reliability of our various outcome measures will impart correspondingly differential bias to our correlations.

Fourth, there is no easy way with the correlation method of allowing for non-linear neighborhood effects, so this technique says little about how living in an extremely disadvantaged (or, for that matter, advantaged) neighborhood might affect outcomes.

Finally, and perhaps most important from a policy perspective, effect sizes that program evaluators commonly view as moderate or even large translate into small proportions of variance in individual outcomes "explained" by neighborhood membership (Cain & Watts, 1972; Duncan & Raudenbush, 1999; Rosenthal & Rubin, 1982) and into small intra-neighborhood correlations. Duncan and Raudenbush (forthcoming) consider standardized effect sizes—that is, standardized mean differences between a set of experimental neighborhoods and an equal number of control neighborhoods, commonly viewed as small ($d = .2$ of a standard deviations, medium ($d = .4$), large ($d = .6$) or very large ($d = .8$). These effect sizes would give rise to the intraneighborhood correlations given below[12]:

Standardized mean difference	Approximate intra-neighborhood correlation (ICC)
$d = .20$	ICC = .01
$d = .40$	ICC = .04
$d = .60$	ICC = .08
$d = .80$	ICC = .14

---

[12] Suppose we have two "treatment" groups and we compute the standardized mean difference, d, between those two groups. The proportion of variance explained by "treatment" is then R^2, which in this case is:

$$R^2 = d^2/(d^2 + 1/(p*q))$$

that is, the square of the effect size divided by the sum of that squared effect size and the reciprocal of p times q where p is the proportion of subjects in treatment group 1 and q = 1-p is the proportion in treatment group 2. This relation is commonly used in meta-analysis. Setting p = q = .50 (a balanced design) gives

$$R^2 = d^2/(d^2+4)$$

which is the formula used in the table. We note that the intra-cluster correlation (ICC) is the ratio of the between-cluster variance to the total variance (Bryk & Raudenbush, 1992, Chapter 4). In our hypothetical example, all between-cluster variance is created by the "treatment." Hence, R^2 is equivalent to the ICC. In non-experimental settings, we do not have treatment groups but rather risk groups defined by neighborhood characteristics (that is, we have a "high-" and a "low-" risk set of neighborhoods.) If the risk groups are not equal in size, the R^2s for each d will be lower than those in our table. Thus, those in our table set an upper bound on R^2 for any given d, because the maximum p*q occurs at p = q = .5 given p + q = 1.

Thus, even very large effect sizes translate into correlations generally regarded as small. A small correlation between neighbors does not rule out a large effect size associated with a measured difference between neighborhoods.[13]

Gautreaux as a Quasiexperimental Design

Rosenbaum (1991) was able to circumvent endogenous membership bias by using data from an unusual quasiexperiment involving low income Black families from public housing projects in Chicago. As part of the Gautreaux court case, nearly 4,000 families volunteered to participate in a subsidized program that arranged for private housing, much of it in predominantly White Chicago suburbs, but some of it in predominantly White sections of the city of Chicago itself.

The program's procedures create a quasiexperimental design with respect to the initial neighborhoods in which participants are placed. Although all participants come from the same low-income Black city neighborhoods (usually public housing projects), some move to middle-income White suburbs and others move to White and Black city neighborhoods. Until 1990, participants were assigned to city or suburb locations in a quasirandom manner. Apartment availability was determined by housing agents who do not deal directly with clients, and availability was unrelated to client interest. Counselors offered clients units as they became available according to their position on the waiting list, regardless of clients' locational preference. Until 1990, counselors did not honor clients' preferences because it was feared that others would demand similar treatment, creating bottlenecks and conflicts. Although clients can refuse an offer, very few have done so, since they risk not getting another in the 6-month period of their eligibility. Consequently, participants' preferences for city or suburbs have virtually nothing to do with where they end up moving.

The quasirandom assignment of Gautreaux families to their (in this case new) contexts provides statistical leverage against the endogenous membership problems by all but eliminating the correlation between family characteristics (both measurable and not) and context. A disadvantage is that inferences regarding neighborhood effects from these data are limited to low-SES families willing to volunteer for such programs.

Rosenbaum and his colleagues analyzed Gautreaux youth outcomes using data from interviews conducted with these children and their mothers in 1989, at which point the age of the children averaged 18 (Kaufman & Rosenbaum, 1992). Among their findings:

- More city movers dropped out of high school than did suburban movers (20% in the city vs. less than 5% in the suburbs).

---

[13] Nor does this imply that interventions producing even very small effects (e.g., $d = .10$) are ill-advised. Cost-effectiveness depends upon effect sizes relative to cost, and it is quite possible for there to be socially profitable intervention policies in the context of a small effect size.

- Although test scores were not available for individual respondents, they found that suburban movers had virtually the same grades as city movers (a C+ average in city and suburbs). Because suburban students usually get about a half-grade lower than city students with the same achievement test scores, the grade parity of the two samples implies a higher achievement level of suburban movers.
- Although research finds that Blacks are underrepresented in college tracks in racially integrated schools (Coleman, 1966; Rosenbaum & Presser, 1978), the Gautreaux results showed that suburban movers were more often in college tracks than were city movers (40% vs. 23%).
- Although the higher suburban standards might be a barrier to college attendance by these youths, we found that suburban movers had significantly higher college enrollment than city movers (54% vs. 21%).
- Among the Gautreaux youth attending college, almost 50% of the suburban movers were in 4-year institutions, whereas only 20% of the city movers were. Of those not attending 4-year institutions, two thirds of the suburban movers were working toward an associate's degree, whereas just half of the city movers were.
- For youth not attending college, a significantly higher proportion of the suburban youth had full-time jobs than did city youth (75% vs. 41%). Suburban youth were also four times as likely to earn over $6.50 an hour as were city youth (21% vs. 5%). The suburban jobs were significantly more likely to offer benefits than were city jobs (55% vs. 23%).

Crucial questions for reconciling the large effects found by Rosenbaum with the more modest ones found in the nonexperimental literature are: to what extent his use of quasi-experimental data better addresses the endogenous membership problem; whether large neighborhood effects exist for underclass Blacks but not for other population groups; and whether the volunteer nature of his sample produces larger effects than would be the case for a more general sample of low income, inner city Blacks.

It is also important to note that quasiexperiments such as Gautreaux can help avoid bias problems in assessing the effects of neighborhood conditions on family conditions—the "family as mediator" issue raised earlier. Popkin, Rosenbaum, and Meaden (1993) compared city versus suburban movers on employment outcomes for mothers and found substantially greater employment (but not higher wage rates) for mothers assigned to suburban as opposed to city locations.

The Moving to Opportunity Experiment

With funding for 10 years, MTO is randomly assigning housing project residents in five of the nation's largest cities to one of three groups: (a) a group receiving housing subsidies to move into low poverty neighborhoods (called here the *experimental group*); (b) a comparison group receiving conventional Section 8 housing assistance but not constrained in their locations (the *Section 8 group*); and (c) a second comparison group receiving no special assistance (the *control group*).

Ludwig, Duncan, and Hirschfield (1998) used the experimental data from the Baltimore site to evaluate the effects of the two program components on the frequency of criminal activity among adolescents, as reflected in the Maryland Department of Juvenile Justice's criminal-offender records and used the experimental variation as part of an instrumental-variables procedure to estimate a model of the effects of neighborhood poverty on such criminal activity.

By way of background, eligibility for the Baltimore MTO program was limited to families with children who lived in the five poorest census tracts (average poverty rate of 67% in the 1990 Census) in the city of Baltimore. Virtually all of the families who volunteered for the program were African American and headed by females. As with families at all other MTO sites, baseline surveys in Baltimore reveal that escaping from gangs and drugs was the most important stated reason for participating in the MTO program.

Not all families randomly assigned to experimental and Section 8 groups relocated during their 6-month eligibility periods. Indeed, only about half of the experimentals moved, with 90% of this group moving to census tracts with poverty rates under 10%. Three quarters of the Section 8 families moved, with 16%, 27%, and 19% of these moving to census tracts with poverty rates under 10%, 10 to 20%, and 20 to 30%, respectively. Thus, the program's randomization applies to the "intention to treat" volunteer families with the three treatments, but not to the actual neighborhood conditions chosen by those families.

Ludwig et al.'s (1998) analysis sample is restricted to 358 13- to 17-year-old children who continued to live in the state of Maryland for at least 1 year following baseline random assignment to the experimental ($n = 157$), Section 8 ($n = 94$), and control ($n = 107$) groups. Juvenile justice records reveal that 15% of the 358 had been arrested for a violent offense (rape, robbery, or assault) prior to baseline randomization, 12% had been arrested for a property offense (burglary, auto theft, or theft/larceny), and 11% had been arrested for a collection of "other" offenses (e.g., disorderly conduct, weapons, drugs).

Table 8.2 shows key results from a comparison of the experimental and Section 8 program groups relative to the controls on pre- to postprogram changes in violent, property, and other crime arrests for the 358 MTO children who were ages 13 to 17 for at least 1 year during the post-program.[14] For girls, there are no significant differences in crime rates across either of the program groups.

---

[14] The estimates are of the effects on juvenile crime of assignment into a particular MTO treatment group, known as the "intent-to-treat" effect (Manski, 1996). The form of the regression is a so-called "difference-in-difference" model following Hausman and Wise (1979), since comparisons of pre- to post-baseline changes across treatment groups produce sharper estimates of program impacts than comparing outcomes across treatment groups in the post-program period. Difference-in-difference estimates also help adjust for the fact that the prevalence of criminal activity for the experimental group was somewhat higher in the pre-program period.

Table 8.2
Experimental and Section 8 vs. Control Regression Coefficients and Standard Errors of the Effects of MTO Program on Fraction Arrested for Juvenile Crime

	% Arrested	
	Experimental vs. Controls	Section 8 vs. Controls
Males		
Violent offenses	-17.3	-5.7
	(7.1)*	(10.6)
Property offenses	-9.5	-9.5
	(7.5)	(8.9)
Other offenses	-13.2	-14.5
	(6.2)*	(5.9)*
Females		
Violent offenses	2.9	-7.5
	(8.6)	(4.2)
Property offenses	1.5	5.7
	(5.2)	(10.1)
Other offenses	-3.9	0.6
	(5.8)	(9.0)

Note. These prevalence estimates of the change in arrest probabilities are derived from a "difference in difference" probit model. Data come from the Baltimore Moving to Opportunity site. *$p < .10$

For boys, the data reveal a number of interesting differences. First comparing experimentals and controls, there is a sizable and statistically significant reduction in the proportion who are arrested for violent (17 percentage points) and "other" (13 points) offenses. The point estimate of program effects on property crime was negative but not statistically significant. Effect sizes for the Section 8 versus control group comparison were smaller for violent crime but similar for the property and "other" crime categories.

These "intention to treat" estimates of the effects of the MTO program offer follow directly from the random-assignment nature of the program. However, it is also possible to go beyond direct program assessments and use random assign-

Table 8.3
Instrumental Variables Coefficient and Standard Error Estimates for
Effects of Neighborhood Poverty on Juvenile Crime

		% Arrested	
		Residence in < 10% vs. > 40% Poverty Tract	Residence in 10%–39% vs. > 40% Poverty Tract
Males			
	Violent offenses	-36.3	-3.6
		(18.8)*	(22.7)
	Property offenses	-17.5	-30.2
		(16.2)	(22.0)
	Other offenses	-40.7	-49.2
		(16.3)*	(23.4)*
Females			
	Violent offenses	-2.3	-9.4
		(13.3)	(15.7)
	Property offenses	8.4	25.5
		(10.0)	(13.3)*
	Other offenses	-1.6	7.1
		(12.1)	(19.9)

Note. These prevalence estimates of the change in arrest probabilities are derived from a "difference in difference" probit model. Data come from the Baltimore Moving to Opportunity site. *$p < .10$

ment to identify more general models of the relationship between neighborhood characteristics and juvenile crime. Simply comparing experimental relocators with control families produces biased estimates of the effects of neighborhood poverty on juvenile crime because families are randomized with respect to treatment groups rather than their actual residential locations. However, the MTO random assignment can be used as an instrumental variable in a model of neighborhood effects because treatment assignments influence relocation outcomes by changing the "price" of relocation, yet by construction are uncorrelated with the unobservable determinants of juvenile crime.

Ludwig et al. (1998) used random assignment to instrument neighborhood poverty rates as part of a model of the effects of neighborhood poverty on juvenile criminal outcomes. It is important to note that the analysis does not identify the specific attributes of the neighborhoods that are responsible for these effects, so they could not distinguish between the effect of neighborhood poverty itself from dimensions of neighborhood quality that are correlated with poverty.

The first stage of the instrumental-variables estimation strategy consists of estimating the likelihood of residence in a very low- or medium-poverty neighborhood during the postprogram period. With these predicted values, one can estimate a model of crime prevalence. Not surprisingly, first-stage estimates showed that treatment group assignments are powerful predictors of families' postprogram neighborhood poverty rates. The results of estimating second-stage, crime equations are presented in Table 8.3. For males, living in a low (<10%) rather than high (> 40%) poverty neighborhood is estimated to have large effects on the prevalence of arrests for violent (-36 percentage points) and "other" (-41 percentage points) crimes. Both of these effects are statistically significant at conventional levels, although the rather large standard errors associated with these estimates show that they are not estimated very precisely. Compared with high poverty areas, living in a neighborhood with moderate poverty rates (10% to 39%) has no clear effect on violent crimes, but may, for males, have some effects on participation in "other" crimes. For females, in all but one case (an anomolous positive effect of residence in moderate poverty neighborhoods on property offenses), the results show no effects of neighborhood conditions on crime.

All in all, Ludwig et al. (1998) found that the experimental MTO treatment in particular, and neighborhood poverty (and/or its correlates) more generally, appear to have sizable effects on juvenile arrests. Not surprisingly, these effects are concentrated among the subgroup of teens who tend to be most criminally active— males—and those in the highest crime years of 13 to 17.

CONCLUSION

Correlational studies based on youth from general population samples indicate that the family (and possibly the genetic component of the family) accounts for much more of the variation in youth achievement and behavior than do neighborhood and school contexts. Although small in size, the degree of neighborhood-based "action" may still large enough to be consistent with cost-effective, neighborhood-based interventions. Unaddressed in these correlational studies are assessments of why context matters and whether context matters much more for disadvantaged than for general population youth.

We have argued that regression-based approaches to estimating models of contextual effects on youth outcomes face three daunting methodological challenges: simultaneous causation, omitted (contextual) variables, and endogenous membership. In the case of neighborhood context, the second and third of these are particularly problematic. Also problematic in these kinds of efforts are modeling the role of the family and ensuring adequate variability in contextual conditions across the youth sample.

We conclude that convincing quantitative assessments of the effects of neighborhood conditions on youth achievement and behavior require either (a) nonexperimental data, drawn from geographically dispersed samples, containing theoretically motivated contextual measures, and estimated with models that address problems of simultaneity, omitted context variables, and endogenous membership; or (b) experimental or quasiexperimental data, based on theoretically interesting samples and experimental conditions, that are estimated with models that address problems of simultaneity and omitted-context variables.

Very few existing studies are in a position to provide the needed data. In the case of nonexperimental data, we have argued that the design of the Project on Human Development in Chicago Neighborhoods is an important advancement toward developing measures of context that correspond closely to theoretical constructs. Neighborhood studies conducted with representative youth samples in Philadelphia, Prince Georges County (MD), and Chicago by the MacArthur Network on Youth in High-Risk Settings may also solve this problem. It remains to be seen whether analyses of these data can address simultaneity and endogenous membership problems.

It is conceivable that data from national sample studies such as the PSID, NLSY, and Add Health could support convincing studies of neighborhood effects, but only if such studies address our list of model-based concerns through innovative statistical modeling. PSID- and NLSY-based assessments of measured neighborhood characteristics are confined to information available in administrative data sources—an important constraint. Context measurement is not as problematic in the Add Health design, which provides a wealth of interview-based assessments about youth, parents, and schools from a highly clustered yet geographically dispersed sample. Here again, it remains to be seen whether analyses of these data can address the simultaneity and endogenous membership problems as well as avoid the correlated-error problem endemic to studies that construct context measures by aggregating respondent characteristics.

Data from quasi- and randomized experimental studies such as Gautreaux and, especially, Moving to Opportunity provide convincing "intention to treat" assessments of their respective mobility programs as well as crucial leverage for implementing an instrumental variables-based strategy against the vexing endogenous membership problem. An added advantage from a policy perspective is that these assessments are drawn for samples of disadvantaged, inner city youth. Disadvantages include the facts that they do little to identify exactly what aspect of context matters most, and that they are often based on samples of families that volunteer for the programs.

Unless they aspire to very expensive "big science" data collections, researchers interested in generating yet more sources of data to assess neighborhood effects should avoid nonexperimental studies that, given resource constraints, are confined to local samples. Secondary analyses of the emerging underanalyzed studies mentioned in this chapter (especially Add Health), using statistically innovative methods, are one potentially fruitful avenue for their efforts.

Researchers intent on new data collections are advised to consider clever ways of taking advantage of Gautreaux-type "natural experiments" that provide exogenous sources of contextual variation. One example is of the public housing relocations associated with the court-ordered desegregation of public housing in Yonkers. Brooks-Gunn is leading an effort to compare families moving to the new integrated public housing site with families who applied for the new housing but, by losing the housing lottery, did not have the opportunity to move.

At a more microlevel, studies of peer interactions might be able to circumvent the endogenous membership problem by taking advantage of some natural experiments such as universities' random assignment of freshman roommates in some dormitories.[15] Comparisons of attitudes, behavior, and achievement between randomly assigned and self-selected roommates provide an indication of the size of the endogeneity problem.

At a more macrolevel, there is value in before-after comparisons of the effects of a beneficial economic "shock" on neighborhoods and families from natural experiments such as legalized gambling. Sites such as Tupelo, MS, are especially interesting because a riverboat gambling industry appeared there almost overnight and restrictive laws in neighboring states have maintained Tupelo's monopoly on the industry.

Natural experiments such as these have their limitations. But the quasiexperimental variation in context they offer researchers enriches their analytic value to a point far beyond that of most nonexperimental studies.

ACKNOWLEDGMENTS

Portions of this chapter are drawn from Duncan and Raudenbush's "Assessing the effects of context in studies of child and youth development," *Educational Psychologist*, 1999. It benefited from discussions with fellow members of the MacArthur Foundation Methodology Working Group—Robert Sampson, Helena Kraemer, Ron Kessler, John Nesselroade, and, especially, Tom Cook—as well as comments from Johanne Boisjoly, Dorothy Duncan, Rachel Dunifon, Kathleen Harris, Lori Kowaleski-Jones, Dan Levy, Jens Ludwig, Sheila Murray, Marianne Page, and Gary Solon. We are grateful to the Family and Child Well-being Research Network of the National Institute of Child Health and Human Development (U01 HD30947-06) for supporting this research.

---

[15] Daniel Levy, Michael Kremer, and Richard Freeman are currently engaged in a research project based on this idea.

REFERENCES

Aaronson, D. *(1997)*. Sibling estimates of neighborhood effects. In J. Brooks-Gunn, G. J. Duncan, & L. Aber (Eds.), *Neighborhood poverty: Policy implications in studying neighborhoods* (Vol. 2, pp. 80-93). New York: Russell Sage Foundation.

Billy, J., & Udry, J. (1985). Patterns of adolescent friendship and effects on sexual behavior. *Social Psychology Quarterly, 48*, 27-41.

Bouchard, T., & McGue, M. (1981). Familial studies of intelligence: A review. *Science, 212*, 1055-1059.

Brooks-Gunn, J., Duncan, G., & Aber, J. L. (1997). *Neighborhood poverty: Context and consequences for children.* New York: Russell Sage Foundation.

Brooks-Gunn, J., Duncan, G., Klebanov, P., & Sealand, N. (1993). Do neighborhoods affect child and adolescent development? *American Journal of Sociology, 99*(2), 353-395.

Bryk, A., & Raudenbush, S. W. (1992). *Hierarchical linear models for social and behavioral research: Applications and data analysis methods.* Newbury Park, CA: Sage.

Cain, G., & Watts, H. (1972). Problems in making policy inferences from the Coleman Report. *American Sociological Review, 35*(2), 228-252.

Chase-Lansdale, L., Gordon, R., Brooks-Gunn, J., & Klebanov, P. (1997). Neighborhood and family influences on the intellectual and behavioral competence of preschool and early school-age children. In J. Brooks-Gunn, G. Duncan, & J. L. Aber (Eds.), *Neighborhood poverty: Context and consequences for children.* New York: Russell Sage Foundation.

Clark, R. (1992). *Neighborhood effects on dropping out of school among teenage boys.* Mimeo. Washington, DC: Urban Institute.

Coleman, J. (1966). *Equality of educational opportunity.* Washington, DC: Government Printing Office.

Cook, T., Kim, J.-R., Chan, W.-S., & Settersten, R. (1998). How do neighborhoods matter? In F. Furstenberg, Jr., T. Cook, J. Eccles, G. Elder, & A. Sameroff (Eds.), *Managing to make it: Urban families in high risk neighborhoods.* Chicago: University of Chicago Press.

Crane, J. (1991). The epidemic theory of ghettos and eighborhood effects on dropping out and teenage childbearing. *American Journal of Sociology, 96*(5), 1126-1159.

Duncan, G., & Raudenbush, S. (1999). Assessing the effects of context in studies of child and youth development. *Educational Psychology, 34*(1), 29-41.

Duncan, G., Boisjoly, J., & Harris, K. (1998, Feb.). *Sibling, peer and schoolmate correlations as indicators of the importance of context for adolescent development.* Paper presented at the biennial meetings of the Society for Research on Adolescence, San Diego, CA.

Duncan, G., Connell, J., & Klebanov, P. (1997). Conceptual and methodological issues in estimating causal effects of neighborhoods and family conditions on individual development. In J. Brooks-Gunn, G. Duncan, & J. L. Aber (Eds.), *Neighborhood poverty: Context and consequences for children* (Vol. I, pp. 219-250). New York: Russell Sage Foundation.

Evans, W. N., Oates, W. E., & Schwab, R. M. (1992). Measuring peer group effects: A study of teenage behavior. *Journal of Political Economy, 100*, 966-991.

Falconer, D. (1981). *Introduction to quantitative genetics.* New York: Longman.

Furstenberg, F., Jr. (1993). How families manage risk and opportunity in dangerous neighborhoods. In W. J. Wilson (Ed.), *Sociology and the public agenda.* Newbury Park, CA: Sage.

Furstenberg, F. Jr., Cook, T., Eccles, J., Elder, G., & Sameroff, A. (1998). *Managing to make it: Urban families in high risk neighborhoods.* Chicago: University of Chicago Press.

Greene, W. (1993). *Econometric analysis.* 2nd edition. New York: Macmillan.

Griliches, Z. (1979). Sibling models and data in economics: Beginnings of a survey. *Journal of Political Economy, 87*, S37-S64.

Hausman, J., & Wise, D. (1979). Attrition bias in experimental and panel data: The Gary Income Maintenance Experiment. *Econometrica, 47*(2), 455-473.

Hofferth, S., & Chaplin, D. (1994). *Caring for young children while parents work: Public policies and private strategies.* Washington, DC: The Urban Institute.

Jencks, C., & Brown, M. D. (1975). Effects of high schools on their students. *Harvard Education Review, 45*, 273-324.

136   DUNCAN AND RAUDENBUSH

Jencks, C., & Mayer, S. (1990). The social consequences of growing up in a poor neighborhood. In L. Lynn & M. McGeary (Eds.), *Inner-city poverty in the United States* (pp. 111-186). Washington, DC: National Academy Press.

Kandel, D. B. (1978). Homophily, selection, and socialization in adolescent friendships. *American Journal of Sociology 84*, 427-436.

Kaufman, J., & Rosenbaum, J. (1992). The education and employment of low-income Black youth in White suburbs. *Educational Evaluation and Policy Analysis, 14*(3), 229-240.

Korbin, J., & Coulton, C. (1997). Understanding the neighborhood context for children and families: Combining epidemiological and ethnographic approaches. In J. Brooks-Gunn, G. Duncan, & J. L. Aber (Eds.). *Neighborhood poverty: Policy implications in studying neighborhoods* (Vol. 2, pp. 65-79). New York: Russell Sage Foundation.

Lee, V., & Bryk, A. (1989). A multilevel model of the social distribution of educational achievement. *Sociology of Education, 62*, 172-192.

Ludwig, J., Duncan, G., & Hirschfield, P. (1998). *Urban poverty and juvenile crime: Evidence from a randomized housing-mobility experiment*. Mimeo. Northwestern University.

Manski, C. F. (1993). Identification of endogenous social effects: The reflection problem. *Review of Economic Studies, 60*, 531-542.

Manski, C. F. (1996). Learning about treatment effects from experiments with random assignment of treatments. *The Journal of Human Resources, 31*, 709-733.

Moffitt, R. (1998). Policy interventions, low-level equilibria, and social interactions. Baltimore, MD: Johns Hopkins University. Working Paper.

Mortimore, P., Sammons, P., Stoll, L., Lewis, D., & Ecob, R. (1988). *School matters*. Los Angeles: University of California Press.

Nichols, R. C. (1978). Twin studies of ability, personality and interests. *Homo, 29*, 158–173.

Plomin, R., DeFries, J. C., & McClearn, G. E. (1990). *Behavioral genetics: A primer* (2nd ed.). New York: W. H. Freeman.

Popkin, S., Rosenbaum, J., & Meaden, P. (1993). Labor market experiences of low-income black women in middle-class suburbs: evidence from a survey of Gautreaux program participants. *Journal of Policy Analysis and Management, 12*, 556–573.

Raudenbush, S., Rowan, B., & Kang, S. (1991). A multilevel, multivariate model for studying school climate in secondary schools with estimation via the EM algorithm. *Journal of Educational Statistics, 16*(4), 295–330.

Reiss, A. J., Jr. (1988). Systematic observation surveys of natural social phenomena. In *Perspectives on attitude assessment: Surveys and their alternatives*. (pp. 132–150). Proceedings of a Conference Held at the Bishop's Lodge, Santa Fe, New Mexico. Prepared for the Office of Naval Research.

Rosenbaum, J. (1991). Black pioneers—do their moves to the suburbs increase economic opportunity for mothers and children? *Housing Policy Debate, 2*(4), 1179–1213.

Rosenbaum, J. E., & Presser, S. (1978). Voluntary racial integration in a magnet school. *School Review, 86*(2), 156–186.

Rosenthal, R., & Rubin, D. (1982). Comparing effect sizes of independent studies. *Psychology Bulletin, 92*, 500–504.

Rowe, D. (1983). Biometrical genetic models of self-reported delinquent behavior: Twin studies. *Behavioral Genetics, 13*, 473–489.

Sameroff, A., & Chandler, M. (1975). Reproductive risk and the continuum of caretaking causalty. In F. D. Horowitz (Ed.), *Review of child development research* (Vol. 4, pp. 187-244). Chicago: University of Chicago Press.

Sampson, R., & Lauritsen, J. L. (1994). Violent victimization and offending: Individual, situational and community-level risk factors. In A.J. Reiss & J. Roth (Eds.), *Understanding and preventing violence: Social influences* (Vol. 3, pp. 1–114). Washington, DC: National Academy Press.

Sampson, R., Raudenbush, S., & Earls, F. (1997). Neighborhoods and violent crime: A multilevel study of collective efficacy. *Science, 277*, 918–924.

Shaw, C., & McKay, H. (1942). *Juvenile delinquency and urban areas*. Chicago: University of Chicago Press.

Solon, G., Page, M., & Duncan, G. (1999). *Correlations between neighboring children in their socioeconomic status as adults*. Mimeo. Ann Arbor, MI: University of Michigan.

Urberg, K., Degirmencioglu, S., & Tolson, J. (1995). The structure of adolescent peer networks. *Developmental Psychology, 31*, 540–547.

Wilson, W. J. (1987). *The truly disadvantaged: The inner city, the underclass and public policy*. Chicago: University of Chicago Press.

9
Better Ways to do Contextual Analysis: Lessons From Duncan and Raudenbush

John O. G. Billy
Battelle Centers for Public Health Research and Evaluation

In 1982, when Mason and Entwisle introduced hierarchical linear modeling to demographers and members of other disciplines at the Population Association of America meetings, they titled their paper *A Better Way to do Contextual Analysis* (Mason & Entwisle, 1982). The Duncan and Raudenbush chapter could equally be titled *Better Ways to do Contextual Analysis*, perhaps more appropriately so than the name they gave it. In the first half of their chapter, the authors very clearly articulate the "methodological challenges of getting context right." Many of these challenges are not new to researchers. Clearly, the *omitted variables problem* is an issue that we all need to address, whether we are modeling contextual effects or not. Nor is the *endogenous membership problem* new to contextual effects researchers. It is something that we all have been pondering for some time. For example, in a 1993 article by Brooks-Gunn and her colleagues that examined neighborhood influences on child and adolescent outcomes, the authors commented about the selection into context issue as follows: "We are not very sanguine about the likelihood that standard adjustments for selection bias would liberate us from these problems . . . As do other authors of empirical work on neighborhood effects . . . we leave the task of modeling selection bias on the agenda of important future research" (Brooks-Gunn, Duncan, Klebanov, & Sealand, 1993, p. 358). What the Duncan and Raudenbush chapter (chap. 8, this volume) is telling us is that in order to obtain, in the authors' words, "precise, robust, and unbiased estimates of neighborhood effects," the time has come for us to give greater consideration to these problems and make every attempt to deal with them. What this chapter offers us is an agenda, guidelines, and tools for doing contextual analysis better.

At its most basic level, the chapter provides aspiring contextual effects researchers with just about everything they need to know, to consider, and to worry about before engaging in this line of inquiry. Unlike many previous attempts, the methodological problems and possible solutions are presented in a manner that is easily understandable even to those who are not methodologists. It also covers a tremendous amount of ground in a brief number of pages, with appropriate discussions of not only the neighborhood but other relevant contexts like schools and peers as well. As such, the chapter is certain to become an educational tool that "teaches" contextual effects. For a more experienced researcher, the methodological issues developed in this chapter provide a convenient checklist against which to evaluate one's research design in terms of its ability to overcome the many problems that beset contextual analyses.

At a higher level, the chapter is stimulating in two respects. First, by proposing a number of promising research designs, it tells us what we should be doing (and what we should not be doing) in order to advance contextual effects research, not only in the area of adolescent problem behavior but also more generally. The recommendations are right on the mark. Second, unlike some other critiques of the methodology of the neighborhood effects literature, a careful reading of the chapter should not lead one to despair that contextual analyses cannot be conducted or provide rewarding insights into fundamental social processes that shape individuals' lives. What is clear from the chapter, however, is that the "methodological challenges to getting context right" are substantial and will require innovative research designs and modeling techniques. It is also clear that no single design or technique will provide the "magic bullet" that solves every problem. It is very important to note that *every* research design recommended in the chapter has some drawbacks, and no single design effectively addresses each of the five methodological issues that Duncan and Raudenbush discuss. As in other areas of social science research, proof of the existence and nature of contextual effects will gradually evolve from the set of the best theory-driven empirical works. The Duncan and Raudenbush chapter provides us a picture of what these studies will need to look like.

It is hard to disagree with any of the conclusions reached in the chapter, or with any of the discussion leading up to the conclusions. Indeed, the paper is so thorough and convincing in terms of the direction in which contextual effects research needs to move that there are few new things to add. The following comments, then, should be interpreted as a way of further developing some of the points made in the chapter. These generally follow the structure of the chapter and the major methodological issues that it addresses.

THE SIMULTANEITY PROBLEM

The first comment touches on the *simultaneity issue* and the plausibility that an adolescent's behavior can affect the community or neighborhood context. The chapter provides the example of *collective efficacy*. The issue also seems relevant in the case of contextual policy variables that are not randomly distributed among communities, but instead are often located on the basis of need. Consider, for example, family planning clinics that may be more likely to be placed in areas of need as indicated by higher nonmarital births rates. Under this scenario, aggregate-level nonmarital birth rates would *positively* affect clinic availability, and this reciprocal causation, if left unaccounted for, would then tend to understate the hypothesized negative effect of clinic availability on birth rates. From a multi-level perspective, one might expect the same reduced effect of clinic availability on an adolescent's risk of a nonmarital birth if for no other reason than the fact that an adolescent sampled from a community with a high nonmarital birth rate has a higher likelihood herself of having had a birth outside of marriage.

A recent article by Angeles, Guilkey, and Mroz (1998) demonstrates the simultaneity problem in the case of family planning program effects in Tanzania. A standard recursive analysis underestimates the impact of family planning service provision on a woman's fertility. When corrected for the endogenous placement of family planning services, the negative effect of these services on fertility is much larger than obtained from the standard analysis.

THE OMITTED-CONTEXT VARIABLES PROBLEM

With regard to the chapter's discussion of the omitted-context variables problem, an administrative data approach to measuring contextual constructs is limited in scope for all of the reasons given in the chapter. At the same time, the benefits of this approach should not be overlooked. Researchers often have an interest in examining contextual effects on the behaviors of members of a more generalized population (e.g., a representative sample of adolescents in the United States). In this case, assembling data from the census and other administrative data sources is the only practical alternative to what would be a prohibitively expensive task of collecting contextual data by systematic social observation in each sampled respondent's community. As is evident throughout the Duncan and Raudenbush chapter, there is always some type of trade-off among possible approaches. Here, the trade-off is greater representativeness at the sacrifice of "thicker, richer" contextual data that might better measure the social ties and interactions that are implicit in the concept of neighborhood.

The size of the trade-off depends on the nature and uses of administrative data, as well as on a researcher's ability to effectively use systematic social observation to create measures of neighborhood processes. Add Health, for example, has a huge amount of administrative data attached to it, including census data down to the block group level and extensive community information drawn from 15 other administrative sources. In addition, the whole purpose of Add Health was to allow the investigation of how social context structures adolescents' lives. As such, Add Health also has detailed characteristics of the family, peer, and school contexts. It, therefore, may provide the best opportunity to study the behavior of a generalized population of adolescents, while at the same time minimizing the omitted-context variables problem.

There is another point to be made about the use of administrative data, even if only census data are available. Although some neighborhood influences may not be well captured by census and other external data sources, many are. Consider two basic reasons for modeling contextual variables. The first is when the question is, "How does context affect behavior X?," and there is a primary focus on the contextual predictor variables in an effort to show that communities and neighborhoods do matter in shaping adolescent development and behavior. Here, it may make more sense to concentrate on a localized population where measurement can be made more detailed and precise through systematic social observation. The second reason is to answer the question, "In accounting for behavior X, are there contextual factors that need to be considered?" Here, the focus is more on the behavior itself and trying to better explain it by considering an array of theoretically relevant factors at multiple levels, some of which are at the community or neighborhood level. In this case, it is appropriate to use well-defined measures derived from the census that adequately capture the desired concept. For example, in studying relationship formation, it would be desirable to include some measure of the opportunity structure that is afforded by a favorable or unfavorable sex ratio in a person's community. As another example, when examining a young woman's risk of a nonmarital birth, it is desirable to test for an effect of female labor force opportunities in the community. Census data can provide adequate measures of these opportunities.

An important point made in chapter 8 in connection with the omitted variables problem is the inclusion of a single contextual variable and subsequent false attribution of its effect, when in reality other neighborhood characteristics are at play. Contextual dispersion of the sample, combined with proper measurement of *theoretically* distinct aspects of neighborhood context, can help avoid this problem. Even with these procedures, however, it may often be difficult to *empirically* distinguish among a set of variables. Neighborhood conditions do not evolve in isolation of one another. They tend to come in "bundles." For some studies, it may be appropriate to conduct preliminary analyses that permit identification of separate, theoretically relevant bundles, and then model these underlying constructs rather than their individual components. As another strategy, it may be possible to select a unique sample of communities or develop a unique research design that permits estimation of the effects of two or more theoretically distinct but highly correlated neighborhood characteristics. This approach was adopted in the Add Health study at the individual level. By oversampling a large number of Black adolescents whose parents are highly educated, the Add Health data will permit researchers to better distinguish between the effects of race and the effects of SES.

THE ENDOGENOUS MEMBERSHIP PROBLEM

One of the key methodological issues discussed in chapter 8 is the *endogenous membership problem*. As they note, individuals are not randomly distributed across contextual units. Rather, residential location is the result of a decision-making process in which choices are based on the observed characteristics of the various locations being considered. This is problematic for contextual analyses to the extent that those residential choices are influenced by decisions about the behavior being examined. If individuals tend to select residential characteristics because of their impact on the costs of engaging in the behavior being studied, unbiased estimates of the effects of such characteristics cannot be obtained. Although adolescents typically select neither their residence nor their school, parental choices about an adolescent's context may still pose a threat to obtaining unbiased estimates of contextual effects on the adolescent's development and behavior if parents make choices about their child's context based on their own characteristics and if those characteristics also influence the behavior of their child.

Sometimes, appropriate measures of parental characteristics are available and can be included in the model to control for any spurious relationship between context and the adolescent's behavior. It is only when important parental characteristics remain unobserved that they pose a threat to obtaining unbiased estimates of the effects of contextual characteristics. Duncan and Raudenbush (chap. 8, this volume) provide an excellent example of a difficult to measure or otherwise typically unavailable parental characteristic—namely, concern for their child's development. The potential for introducing bias into a model occurs when parents' residential choices are affected by their concerns or expectations about how those contexts will impact their child's behavior or development. Importantly, the magnitude of the bias is related to the importance of these expectations relative to other factors considered when selecting a community or neighborhood. Given the considerable monetary and psychic costs associated with moving, one might imagine that compared to other concerns such as housing costs or the availability of employment, concern for the child's development is only modestly important in selecting a community or neighborhood. A very basic question, then, is the extent to which neighborhood choices are dominated by parental concerns for their child's behavior and development. By extension, the answer to this question provides information on the extent to which one should worry about the endogenous membership problem.

Data from the Add Health study help to answer this question. Parents (mostly mothers) of adolescents who participated in the in-home survey also completed an extensive questionnaire. They were presented with 10 possible reasons for living in a particular neighborhood and asked to indicate whether each was part of their decision to live in their current neighborhood. These reasons can roughly, but not unambiguously, be divided into nonchild-related reasons and child-related reasons. Table 9.1 presents the percentage of parents who, for each of the reasons, replied that it was important in their selection of where they currently live.

Half of all parents reported that affordable housing was important in their

Table 9.1
Add Health Parents' Reasons for Living in Their Neighborhoods

Nonchild-related	
Respondent (or spouse/partner) was born in neighborhood	18.2%
Had outgrown previous housing	37.7%
Neighborhood is close to where respondent (or spouse/partner) used to work	23.7%
Neighborhood is close to where respondent (or spouse/partner) now works	37.3%
Neighborhood offers better housing than affordable in other neighborhoods	49.8%
Neighborhood is close to friends or relatives	44.0%
Child-related	
Less crime in this neighborhood than in other neighborhoods	61.1%
Less drug use and other illegal activity by adolescents in this neighborhood	56.8%
Children in this neighborhood the same ages as children in household	30.8%
Schools better in this neighborhood than in other neighborhoods	49.2%
Any child-related reason	75.3%

Note. Sample Ns = ~17,300; percentages based on weighted data.

residential choice, and more than one third reported that being close to where they currently work is a significant factor. Most importantly, a large percentage of parents indicated that child-related concerns were important. Less crime was cited by 61%, 57% indicated less drug use and other illegal activity by adolescents, and 49% reported that better schools were at least partially responsible for their decision to live where they do. At least one of the four child-related reasons was cited by 75% as a factor affecting their residential choice.

Table 9.2 shows the single most important reason for parents living in their neighborhoods. Although affordable housing is cited as the primary reason by more parents than any other factor (19.2%), it is followed closely by the child-related reason of "better schools" (18.2%). Another child-related factor, "less crime," is also among the most frequently cited reasons for choosing a neighborhood (12.6%).

Although these results are no doubt subject to some amount of social desirability bias in reporting, post hoc rationalization of residential choice decisions, and other types of measurement error, they nevertheless provide ample evidence that concerns about their child's development motivate a large percentage of parents when deciding where to live. As such, the *residence selection problem* looms large in contextual effects research. Indeed, among the five methodological issues discussed in chapter 8, when examining the effects of *neighborhood* context on adolescent behaviors, it is probably the single most important issue that contextual

Table 9.2
Add Health Parents' Most Important Reason
for Living in Their Neighborhoods

Nonchild-related	
Respondent (or spouse/partner) was born in neighborhood	7.0%
Had outgrown previous housing	10.6%
Neighborhood is close to where respondent (or spouse/partner) used to work	1.5%
Neighborhood is close to where respondent (or spouse/partner) now works	10.7%
Neighborhood offers better housing than affordable in other neighborhoods	19.2%
Neighborhood is close to friends or relatives	14.5%
Child-related	
Less crime in this neighborhood than in other neighborhoods	12.6%
Less drug use and other illegal activity by adolescents in this neighborhood	4.3%
Children in this neighborhood the same ages as children in household	1.4%
Schools better in this neighborhood than in other neighborhoods	18.2%
Total	100.0%
	(16,324)

Note. Sample N in parentheses; percentages based on weighted data.

effects researchers need to be mindful of and develop strategies to address.

Duncan and Raudenbush (chap. 8, this volume) suggest a number of possible solutions to the endogenous membership problem. Clearly, the two programs they describe that provide for random assignment are unique and offer exciting opportunities to explore the nature of neighborhood effects under experimental conditions, albeit for limited groups. Researchers should always be on the lookout for such rare opportunities. A more standard statistical approach is an instrumental variables procedure, which has a number of problems. Chief among these is that no one ever likes another person's choice of instruments, and if a lot of potentially endogenous contextual variables are to be modeled, then a lot of instruments are needed to identify the model. Good instruments are hard to find; a lot of good instruments are virtually impossible to come up with. Nevertheless, progress is being made in developing useful approaches for handling endogeneity. The paper discusses fixed-effects models as one. Another promising strategy is the *discrete factor approximations* (factor models) approach developed by Mroz and Guilkey (1992). This is a simultaneous equation estimation procedure that, unlike an instrumental variables approach, does not require that a large number of instruments be used when the effects of a large number of potentially endogenous contextual variables are being estimated. That is, the model is identified through other statistical procedures.

MUDDYING THE WATERS

At the risk of muddying the waters, this discussion concludes with some brief comments about a conceptual, methodological issue that does not receive a great deal of attention in the Duncan and Raudenbush chapter. Researchers are often interested in modeling adolescent behaviors as dynamic processes, whereby adolescents experience important life course events and transitions to adult statuses. For example, there may be interest in examining the transition to first intercourse, the initiation of any given problem behavior, continuation of schooling, and so forth. During later adolescence, researchers might want to examine entry into the labor force or the risk of nonmarital childbearing.

Obviously, for any given sample of adolescents, the observation period over which these transition behaviors can occur will be relatively long. Because they will occur at different times for different adolescents, the question is, "How much contextual data are needed to properly conceptualize and model the influence of community and neighborhood characteristics on the risk of experiencing these events?" In many data sets containing both individual-level and contextual data, information about context is fixed at a single point in time, usually according to residence at interview. In those cases, when modeling contextual influences, it must be assumed that these contexts are invariant over the period when the behaviors of interest are being observed. In other data sets, it is possible to determine some prior contexts, as is the case for the Panel Study of Income Dynamics (PSID) and Add Health. However, it is seldom, if ever, the case that complete residence histories are available that permit researchers to define each of an adolescent's previous contexts.

Whether complete information is needed on all previous and current contexts in order to properly understand the effects of neighborhood characteristics on an adolescent's risks of making important transitions depends on the extent to which adolescents actually change *contexts*. Clearly, they change *residences*. Based on geographical mobility data from the Current Population Survey (CPS), it is estimated that Add Health respondents will have moved (changed house or apartment) on average two times, from the time they were age 12 to the time when they all will be between ages 18 to 24 in the upcoming year 2000 Wave III interview. What is not known at present is the extent to which these residential changes actually represent changes in critical community and neighborhood characteristics that may be hypothesized to affect their behaviors. Duncan and Raudenbush reported some limited evidence that residential moves typically occur between similar neighborhoods (see Solon, Page, & Duncan, 1997). Still, this is an empirical question that requires careful additional analysis.

If the contexts of many adolescents do change along critical dimensions, then the data needs and difficulty of modeling contextual effects on transition behaviors escalate dramatically. In terms of data needs, residential histories and the geocoding of those previous residences would be required. Obtaining past addresses, especially from adolescents, is obviously no easy task. Further, it would be extremely difficult to collect information about past contexts using systematic social observation. Administrative data would almost certainly need to be used. Even this approach might be problematic because it is hard to obtain data on community characteristics that are specific to the time period when the adolescent resided in that area.

Assuming that all information was available so that adolescents could be properly assigned to their relevant contexts when at risk of making a transition, there is the additional complexity of the potential need to take both past and present contexts into account in statistical models. It might be expected that community characteristics that operate by increasing or decreasing opportunities for engaging in a behavior would have rather instantaneous effects. That is, some community characteristics may rather immediately channel or constrain the opportunities for an adolescent to engage in the behavior being examined. In that event, it would be important to know only the context in which the behavior did (or did not) take place. However, community and neighborhood characteristics might also influence behavior by engendering social norms that influence the psychic costs and tastes for engaging in particular behaviors. In this case, it might be critical to know the past community and neighborhood environments to which the adolescent has been exposed because their effects on perceived costs and tastes may outlast the adolescent's tenure in those contexts. In other words, failure to take past contexts into account requires the perhaps untenable assumption that the past contexts in which individuals lived have no continuing influence on their behaviors.

To summarize, an accurate and complete understanding of the influences of community and neighborhood characteristics on behavior may require an ability to identify and differentiate the separate effects of current and past contexts. This is yet another conceptual and methodological issue with which contextual effects researchers have barely begun to deal.

CONCLUSION

This discussion was not intended to create a greater sense of despair and hopelessness in terms of researchers' abilities to conduct contextual effects analyses. Rather, it was to reaffirm what should be a major conclusion to be drawn from chapter 8 of this volume—namely, that the challenges to "getting context right" are substantial and will require greater conceptual and methodological development. The authors are to be commended for stimulating readers' thinking, and for producing what is certain to be a major contribution to improving efforts to identify community and neighborhood effects.

ACKNOWLEDGMENTS

The author is grateful to William R. Grady, Daniel H. Klepinger, and Charles E. Slusher for their helpful advice and suggestions during the preparation of this comment. The views expressed in this chapter are those of the author and do not necessarily reflect the opinions or policies of the Battelle Memorial Institute.

Add Health is a program project designed by J. Richard Udry (PI) and Peter Bearman, and funded by grant P01-HD31921 from the National Institute of Child Health and Human Development to the Carolina Population Center, University of North Carolina at Chapel Hill, with cooperative funding participation by the National Cancer Institute; the National Institute of Alcohol Abuse and Alcoholism; the National Institute on Deafness and Other Communication Disorders; the National Institute of Drug Abuse; the National Institute of General Medical Sciences; the National Institute of Mental Health; the National Institute of Nursing Research; the Office of AIDS Research, National Institutes of Health (NIH); the Office of Behavior and Social Science Research, NIH; the Office of the Director, NIH; the Office of Research on Women's Health, NIH; the Office of Population Affairs, U.S. Department of Health and Human Services (DHHS); the National Center for Health Statistics, Centers for Disease Control and Prevention, DHHS; the Office of Minority Health, Centers for Disease Control and Prevention, DHHS; the Office of Minority Health, Office of Public Health and Science, DHHS; the Office of the Assistant Secretary for Planning and Evaluation, DHHS; and the National Science Foundation. Persons interested in obtaining data files from the National Longitudinal Study of Adolescent Health should contact Jo Jones, Carolina Population Center, 123 West Franklin Street, Chapel Hill, NC 27516-3997 (email: jo_jones@unc.edu).

REFERENCES

Angeles, G., Guilkey, D. K., & Mroz, T. A. (1998). Purposive program placement and the estimation of family planning program effects in Tanzania. *Journal of the American Statistical Association, 93* (443), 884–899.

Brooks-Gunn, J., Duncan, G. J., Klebanov, P. K., & Sealand, N. (1993). Do neighborhoods influence child and adolescent development? *American Journal of Sociology, 99* (2), 353–395.

Mason, W. M., & Entwisle, B. (1982). *A better way to do contextual analysis.* Presented at the Annual Meetings of the Population Association of America, San Francisco.

Mroz, T. A., & Guilkey, D. K. (1992). *Discrete factor approximations for use in simultaneous equation models with both continuous and discrete endogenous variables*. Mimeo. Carolina Population Center, University of North Carolina at Chapel Hill.

Solon, G., Page, M. E., & Duncan, G. J. (1997). *Correlations between neighboring children in their subsequent educational attainment*. Ann Arbor, MI: University of Michigan.

10

One Step Forward and Two Steps Back: Neighborhoods, Adolescent Development, and Unmeasured Variables

Linda M. Burton

The Pennsylvania State University

Seven days before this symposium began, I traveled to my birthplace, Los Angeles, California, for a brief visit with my parents. While there, I frequented the neighborhoods of my youth—South Central Slauson and Eastside Compton. As I journeyed through these neighborhoods, I was reminded of the day-to-day survival strategies, I, my siblings, and several of our friends adopted to navigate these challenging terrains. Over the course of my childhood, teen, and young adult years, these neighborhoods transitioned from village-like communities to public spaces characterized by social isolation, severe economic deprivation, and a precipitous rise in gang warfare. According to prevailing pedagogic perspectives on neighborhoods and human development, these spaces would have been designated a high-risk environment for children and teens (Crane, 1991; Jencks & Mayer, 1990; Sampson, 1992; Wilson, 1987).

After completing the tour of my old neighborhoods, I returned to my parents' home and talked with my mother about my childhood and adolescent neighborhood experiences. Ensconced in personal biography, academic neighborhood theories, and an emerging critique of Greg Duncan and Stephen Raudenbush's symposium paper, I posed the following questions to her—How do you think that growing up in South Central Slauson and Eastside Compton affected the behavior of neighborhood children and teens? What did parents and adult neighbors do to help their children survive, and in some cases, thrive in these neighborhoods?

My mother sat quietly for a moment, then abruptly left the room without answering either question. She returned ten minutes later with a tattered, faded-pink box in hand. It was my childhood idea box. She handed the box to me and suggested I consult its contents for answers to my queries. I was quite surprised that my mother proposed I find answers to these questions in notes I had written as an 8-year-old. Nonetheless, I delicately perused the contents of the box, carefully taking in the childhood musings it tendered.

Albeit fate or coincidence, I discovered a scribbled note in the box that helped my thinking about the questions I had posed to my mother—questions that, in fact, are of central concern to this symposium. The note read:

You only see what your fear tells you to look at. You see what is right in front
of your face. You have to look through that. You will take one step forward
and then many steps backwards before you understand. (Miss Estelle Washington, May 8, 1962)

These were the words of Miss Washington, an elderly African American
woman who was South Central Slauson's sage, "other mother" (Collins, 1991, p.
119), and protector of neighborhood children. Miss Washington shared these words
with me one afternoon when I returned home from school angry and perplexed
about why my sisters and I had to physically defend ourselves everyday against a
band of warring kids who lived two blocks over. As I recall, Miss Washington
was trying to explain to me that these kids constantly tyrannized others not because they didn't like them, but because their warring behavior was influenced by
factors that were not readily apparent to me. If I was to understand the menacing
behavior of these children, I would have to look beyond the surface of their actions, " take a step back" as it were, and determine the **unmeasured** influences that
were contributing to their conduct.

The timeless wisdom of Miss Washington's words are the inspiration for my
comments on Greg Duncan and Stephen Raudenbush's paper, "Neighborhoods
and Adolescent Development: How Can We Determine the Links?" Indeed, their
paper offers an eloquent assessment of conceptual and methodological issues concerning existing survey research on neighborhood effects and adolescent development. In the spirit of Miss Washington's philosophy, clearly delineating these
issues is " one step" forward in advancing neighborhood research. Implicitly,
however, Duncan and Raudenbush also suggest that neighborhood researchers
may need to "take several steps backwards" before this field of study can advance
further. The backward steps comprise identifying, conceptually defining, and measuring critical neighborhood-, family-, and individual-level variables that have yet
to be systematically assessed in neighborhood effects research (Burton, Price-
Spratlen, & Spencer, 1997; Tienda, 1991).

I contend, as Duncan and Raudenbush imply, that in extant survey research
on this topic, neighborhood context, family processes, and adolescent outcomes
are measured as omnibus variables comprising multiple undefined features of a
particular domain, or as variables that by the nature of their conceptual definitions
exclude subtle, yet critical processes related to the outcomes of interests. These
unmeasured features probably represent the mechanisms that produce true neighborhood and family effects in the lives of adolescents. Clearly identifying and
including them in analyses may tell us more precisely what aspects of neighborhoods and families influence adolescent outcomes of interests.

A growing number of social scientists have suggested that ethnographic research is particularly well suited for identifying unmeasured variables in neighborhood effects research (Burton, 1997; Jarrett, 1995, 1998; Korbin & Coulton,
1997). Ethnographic studies, given their focus on intense, continuous, and often

microscopic observations of individuals and families in specific environments or cultures, can provide valuable insights on *nuanced* neighborhood and family processes that are not captured in survey research but, in fact, may profoundly influence adolescent outcomes (Denzin & Lincoln, 1994; Spradley & McCurdy, 1972).

Drawing on existing ethnographic neighborhood research, my comments on the Duncan and Raudenbush paper takes " two steps back" and discusses several domains of unmeasured variables that may be important to consider in neighborhood effects research. Extensive reviews of the ethnographic literature on this topic indicate that there are clearly more unmeasured neighborhood, family, and adolescent outcome variables than can be outlined in this essay (Jarrett, 1998). Consequently, only three of the more prevalent domains of unmeasured variables are discussed here—linear development and the adultification of adolescents in high-risk environments (Burton, Brooks, & Clark, 1998; Jurkovic, 1997; Kotlowitz, 1991); the fluidity of family structure (Stack, 1996); and the multiple neighborhood memberships of teens (Burton & Graham, 1998; Noack & Silbereisen, 1988).

Linear Development: High-risk Neighborhoods and the Adultification of Children

One of the more prevalent domains of unmeasured variables in neighborhood effects research concerns the use of traditional developmental perspectives to frame adolescent outcomes for teens residing in high-risk environments. Although not explicitly discussed in the Duncan and Raudenbush paper, these approaches commonly undergird survey research on neighborhood effects and adolescent outcomes (Spencer, 1995; Spencer & Dornbush, 1990).

Traditional developmental approaches define adolescence as an age period marking the linear progression from childhood to adulthood. Occurring between the ages of 11 to 20, normative adolescent development is characterized by predictable qualitative biological, social, and cognitive changes for the individual (Feldman & Elliott, 1990). In mainstream contexts, social institutions and families provide specific guidelines concerning the role expectations and behaviors of adolescents. Schools, for example, plan developmentally appropriate curricula and activities for teens. Parents offer directives to adolescents concerning their place in families and society. Under these directives, adolescents are often reminded that they are no longer children but are not yet adults. While the activities adolescents engage in are designed to progressively prepare them for adulthood, in most cases adolescents are not allowed to fully assume adult roles, such as parenthood, until their post-teenage years.

These linear notions of development often determine what neighborhood researchers view as positive (e.g., high school completion) or negative (e.g., teen pregnancy) outcomes for adolescents and consequently drive how such variables are measured. The argument I extend here is a simple one. I contend that using traditional developmental approaches in the study of neighborhood effects research, by default, contributes to the prevalence of unmeasured variables, particularly in studies involving teens growing up in economically disadvantaged, high-risk neighborhoods. Teens growing up in these environments may attach different meanings to adolescent roles and behaviors than do their mainstream counterparts, thus calling in to question the relevance of individual-level variables derived from traditional developmental approaches and applied to these populations (Burton, Obeidallah, & Allison, 1996; Ogbu, 1985; Seidman, 1991; Spencer & Dornbusch, 1990). For example, some teens may move from childhood to adulthood without distinctly experiencing the intermediate stage of adolescence, in part because they have been exposed prematurely to extraordinary stresses in their environment that demand they develop hyper-advanced skills to survive (Burton, 1991; MacLeod, 1987; Williams, 1978). The experience of Lafayette escorting his younger sister home from school illustrates this point:

> Suddenly, gunfire erupted. The frightened children fell to the ground. 'Hold your head down!' Lafayette snapped, as he covered Dede's head with her pink nylon jacket. If he hadn't physically restrained her, she might have sprinted for home, a dangerous action when the gangs started warring. 'Stay down,' he ordered the trembling girl. The two lay pressed to the beaten grass for half a minute, until the shooting subsided. Lafayette held Dede's hand as they cautiously crawled through the dirt toward home (Kotlowitz, 1991, p. 9).

In addition, teens growing up in high-risk neighborhoods, and in families with severe economic and structural constraints, out of necessity, often assume adult responsibilities at remarkably early ages. In a recent review of the qualitative literature on this topic, Burton, Brooks, and Clark (1998) referred to this process as the "adultification of children and adolescents". Adultification is the downward extension of adult responsibilities to children and teens. These responsibilities may include a child or teen: (1) taking on a parental role vis-à-vis younger siblings and possibly the parent as well; (2) being a parent's confidant; and (3) supporting the family financially. The life situation of Joe provides further insight:

> My brother Joe had to quit school when he was sixteen years old. He had to go out and get a job...to support all the kids...He's our father. That's what he really is—he's our father. Every.... penny that my brother got he threw right into the family, right into the house...cuz my mother can't work (MacLeod, 1987, p. 51).

Burton, Brooks, and Clark (1998) noted that the adultification experiences of teens represent a non-linear form of development. What is most relevant about adultification in terms of the Duncan and Raudenbush paper is that survey researchers studying adolescents in high-risk environments may derive outcome variables that are not consistent with the realities of the adolescent's environment and may omit, by default, more salient developmental variables if adultification processes are not included in their conceptual framework. Moreover, when adultification is not considered, researchers also risk erroneously assigning aberrant attributions to teens when, in fact, their behavior appropriately fits the demands of the context. The comments of this 15-year-old underscores this contention:

> Sometimes I just don't believe how this school operates and thinks about us. Here I am a grown man. I take care of my mother and have raised my sisters. Then I come here and this know-nothing teacher treats me like I'm some dumb kid with no responsibilities. I am so frustrated. They are trying to make me something that I am not. Don't they understand I'm a man and have been a man longer than they have been a woman? (Burton, Obeidallah, & Allison, 1996, p. 404).

Fluid Families and Omitted Variables

A second domain of unmeasured variables in neighborhood effects research concerns the conceptualization and measurement of family structure as a mediating or moderating influence on adolescent outcomes. A common measure of family structure used in these studies is a dichotomized construct which contrasts the effects of intact and non-intact families relative to a specific adolescent outcome (e.g., school achievement). Intact families are often defined as those where both biological parents are present in the household. Non-intact families are principally characterized as single-parent households (Wu & Martinson, 1993).

The ethnographic literature clearly indicates that static, narrowly defined conceptualizations of family structure are poor substitutes for unmeasured family variables that are more likely to be directly related to teen outcomes. One of the more important unmeasured variables in survey research is the fluidity of family structure (Stack, 1996; Stack & Burton, 1993; Zollar, 1985). The fluidity of family structure concerns the frequency and pace of changes in family composition as a function of marriage, childbearing, conjugal dissolutions, death, economic hardship, familial excommunication, or personal choice. The flexibility inherent in some family structures permits change to occur constantly. Constant changes in family structures over time pose a noteworthy difficulty for survey researchers who study neighborhoods, families, and teens at one point in time. Cross-sectional surveys are not likely to identify the effects of structural fluidity on the relationship between neighborhoods and adolescent development.

Two patterns of fluidity have been identified in ethnographic studies— bundled chaos and stable maintenance (Burton & Jayakody, 1997; Jarrett & Burton, in press). The former represents a pattern in which changes in family structure are fast-paced, constant, and simultaneous. The latter reflects a pattern in which changes are often predictable and relatively infrequent and, in general, occur one at a time.

The pacing and sequencing of these changes differentially impact family processes and outcomes for teens. Using case-study profiles of the Samuels and Mack families reported in two ethnographic studies of urban African Americans, examples of the differential impact of bundled chaos and stable maintenance families on neighborhood effects and adolescent outcomes are provided below (Burton & Jayakody; Jarrett & Burton, in press).

The Samuels family represents the bundled chaos form of family structure. This family is headed by 35-year-old Jeannie Samuels who is the mother of three— two young adult daughters and an adolescent son. Her son, 15-year-old Terrance, who has been involved in fighting and vandalism in his neighborhood, described the constant changes that the family has experienced:

> So many things keep happening all at one time. My mother gets married. My real father gets a divorce for the fifth time. My youngest sister has her third baby. My oldest sister leaves to go live with boyfriend. One of my brothers [his father's child] dies. My grandpop is dying. Another woman says she is having a baby by my father. Hey, what's up with all this! Too many changes all the time. Who is my family anyway? (Burton & Jayakody, 1997)

Table 1 profiles Terrance's perception of who comprised his family during a six month period. As this table indicates, Terrance's definition of family changed constantly during this period. In terms of the unmeasured variable issues raised by Duncan and Raudenbush, two critical questions emerge regarding Terrance's family situation: How does a family that experiences constant structural changes mediate or moderate the impact of neighborhood context on an adolescent's behavior? What crucial information is lost or mis-specified when researchers do not include fluidity in family structure variables in neighborhood effects research?

Terrance's own analysis of the relationship among his neighborhood, family, and behavior addresses these questions. Terrance reported that in the context of his family's instability, he had difficulty resisting the security he found in neighborhood "posses". In Terrance's neighborhood, posses are groups of young males and/ or females who "hang out together" and occasionally get into trouble. The posse Terrance joined, however, was involved in some criminal activities (e.g., vandalism and fighting). Terrance believed, as other ethnographic studies report, that if he were part of a family network that experienced fewer changes, he might not have become involved in the posse (MacLeod, 1987; Sullivan, 1989). The stable maintenance pattern of fluidity exhibited by the Mack family affirms his thesis:

> Our family is pretty stable. We don't have lots of babies. We plan our marriages so that there is no surprise. We only had one death in the last 10 years...my father. I'm glad our family is this way. We have enough to deal with trying to survive in this neighborhood and keeping our kids out of trouble. We don't

Table 10.1

Terrance's Family Composition Profile

January 1991	March 1991	June 1991
Family Changes	**Family Changes**	**Family Changes**
• Biological Parents Divorce is Final	• Biological Mother Marries Boyfriend	• Biological Mother Files for Divorce
	• Maternal Grandfather Dies	• Stepfather Moves to Another State
	• Biological Father Changes Girlfriends	• Biological Father Marries Girlfriend
	• Sister 2 Leaves the State with Unknown Boyfriend	• Brother 1 is Killed
	• Cousin Moves in with Paternal Grandmothe	• Sister 1 Gives Birth to First Child
		• Sister 2 Returns Home, and is Married
		• Paternal Grandmother Dies
		• Aunt and Four Cousins Move into Paternal Grandmother's House
Family Composition	**Family Composition**	**Family Composition**
• Biological Mother (divorced)	• Biological Mother	• Biological Mother
• Mother's Boyfriend	• Stepfather	• Biological Father
• Biological Father (divorced)	• Biological Father	• Stepmother
• Biological Father's Girlfriend	• Biological Father's New Girlfriend	• Maternal Grandmother
• Maternal Grandmother	• Maternal Grandmother	• Sister 1
• Maternal Grandfather	• Paternal Grandmother	• Sister 2
• Paternal Grandmother	• Sister 1	• Brother
• Sister 1 (mother's child)	• Brother	• Brother
• Sister 2 (mother's child)	• Brother	• Sister 3
• Brother 1 (father's child)	• Brother	• Sister 4
• Brother 2 (father's child)	• Sister 3	• Brother
• Brother 3 (father's child)	• Sister 4 (father's girlfriend's child)	• Nephew
• Sister 3 (father's child)	• Brother 4 (father's girlfriend's child)	• Brother-in-Law
• Mother's Friend	• Cousin	• Aunt
	• Mother's Friend	• Cousins 1-5
		• Mother's Friend

need no crazy unpredictable stuff in our family to make things harder. We don't need to lose any of our family to the streets (Jarrett & Burton, in press).

From these examples we see that constant changes in family structure keep teens off balance while predictable changes allow families to satisfactorily manage neighborhood trapping, thereby enhancing the likelihood of their teens achieving desirable outcomes (Furstenberg, 1993). Relative to the issue of unmeasured variables, these examples also illustrate the potential conceptual and methodological problems that arise in the interpretation of neighborhood research that does not include more dynamic features of family structure as mediating or moderating influences on adolescent outcomes.

Multiple Neighborhood Memberships: An Unmeasured Effect

A third source of unmeasured variables in neighborhood effects research concerns the use of a teen's single residential address as the principal location of their neighborhood experiences. Ethnographic family research has consistently found that using a single residential address as an identifier of the primary neighborhood in which a teen develops may not provide an accurate view of the impact of neighborhoods on adolescent outcomes (Bell-Scott & Taylor, 1989; Burton & Graham, 1998; Williams & Kornblum, 1985; Zollar, 1985). In some situations, teens concurrently call a multiplicity of residences their homes—that is, they may be members of families who simultaneously coreside across multiple households located both within and across a variety of neighborhoods. The comments of Wylene, who resides across three households, underscore this point:

People be studying me and everything and they think they know about me and how I live. They don't know nothing cause they don't pay attention to what I say. I live in three places and I'm different in every one. Each place makes me different. Even I know that (Burton & Price-Spratlen, in press).

Dwight, an 11-year-old who resides two days a week with his mother in a poor, high-risk neighborhood and five days a week with his grandmother in a stable, working-class neighborhood, had this to say:

When I go to my momma's I have to be a bad ass or I will get beat up. So if you see me over there, I look like that. But when I'm with Nana (grandmother) I'm another way cause the kid's over there don't fight that much so I don't have to swell up (act like he's tough) (Burton & Price-Spratlen, in press).

Both Wylene's and Dwight's comments speak to the inappropriateness of using a single residence identifier in assessing the impact of neighborhoods on their lives. More importantly, their comments showcase their awareness of how each of the contexts they reside in demand different behaviors from them. Such developmental insights would not be captured in research that uses a teen's single reported address as the sole indicator of neighborhood membership.

In light of Duncan and Raudenbush's methodological charge to survey researchers to "get the context right", the multiple neighborhood membership variable appropriately suggests that researchers "get the *contexts* right".

Neighborhoods Effects Research and Unmeasured Variables: Summary Thoughts

Inspired by the wisdom of Miss Washington's words, and the discussion of unmeasured variables presented by Duncan and Raudenbush, the purpose of this commentary has been to briefly describe three domains of unmeasured variables in neighborhood research—linear development and the adultification of adolescents; the fluidity of family structure; and the multiple neighborhood memberships of teens. While drawing attention to these domains may enlighten survey researchers on a few unmeasured variables, the primary message of this commentary is a much simpler one. Essentially, the message is that ethnographic research has much to offer the field in terms of discovering, identifying, and defining critical neighborhood and family variables that influence adolescent development. If this field continues to move forward, as Duncan and Raudenbush are hopeful that it will, future studies of neighborhood effects will require the integration of ethnographic and survey methodology. This integration means that ethnographers and survey researchers will have to take "two steps back", as partners in the enterprise, to define and refine those unmeasured variables and processes that are truly responsible for neighborhood effects on families and their adolescent children.

REFERENCES

Bell-Scott, P., & Taylor, R. (1989). The multiple ecologies of black adolescent development. *Journal of Adolescent Research, 4,* 119–124.

Burton, L. M. (1991). Caring for children: Drug shifts and their impact on families. *American Enterprise, 2*(3), 34–37.

Burton, L. M. (1997). Ethnography and the meaning of adolescence in high-risk neighborhoods. *Ethos, 25*(2), 208–217.

Burton, L. M., Brooks, J., & Clark, J. (1998). Dancing in the moonlight: Ethnography, prevention/intervention research, and the adultification of children. Paper presented at Family Research Consortium II Summer Institute, Blaine, WA.

Burton, L. M., & Graham, J. (1998). Neighborhood rhythms and the social activities of adolescent mothers. In R. Larson & A. C. Crouter (Eds.), *Temporal rhythms in adolescence: Clocks, calendars, and the coordination of daily life.* San Francisco, CA: Jossey-Bass.

Burton, L. M., & Jayakody, R. (1997). Rethinking family structure and single parenthood: Implications for future studies of African-American families and children. Paper presented at the NICHD Family and Child Well-Being Network Conference, "Research Ideas and Data Needs for Studying the Well-Being of Children and Families," Warrenton, VA.

Burton, L. M., Obeidallah, D. O., & Allison, K. (1996). Ethnographic perspectives on social context and adolescent development among inner-city African American teens. In R. Jessor, A. Colby, & R. Shweder (Eds.), *Essays on ethnography and human development.* Chicago: University of Chicago Press.

Burton, L. M., Price-Spratlen, T., & Spencer, M. (1997). On ways of thinking about and measuring neighborhoods: Implications for studying context and developmental outcomes for children. In G. Duncan, J. Brooks-Gunn, & L. Aber (Eds.), *Neighborhood poverty: Context and consequences for children.* New York: Russell Sage Foundation.

Burton, L. M., & Price-Spratlen, T. (in press). Through the eyes of children: An ethnographic perspective on neighborhoods and child development. In A. Masten (Ed.), *Minnesota symposium on child psychology* (Vol. 29). Hillsdale, NJ: Lawrence Erlbaum.

Clark, R. M. (1983*). Family life and school achievement: Why poor black children succeed or fail.* Chicago, IL: University of Chicago Press.

Collins, P. H. (1991). *Black feminist thought.* New York: Routledge.

Crane, J. (1991). The epidemic theory of ghettos and neighborhood effects on dropping out and teenage child bearing. *American Journal of Sociology, 96,* 1126–1260.

Denzin, N. K., & Lincoln, Y. S. (Eds.), (1994). *Handbook of qualitative research.* Thousand Oaks: Sage Publications.

Feldman, S. S. & Elliott, G. R. (Eds. (1990). *At the threshold: The developing adolescent.* Cambridge, MA: Harvard University Press

Furstenberg, F. F., Jr. (1993). How families manage risk and opportunity in dangerous neighborhoods. In W. J. Wilson (Ed.), *Sociology and the public agenda.* Newbury Park, CA: Sage.

Jarrett, R. L. (1995) Growing up poor: The family experiences of socially mobile youth in low-income African American neighborhoods. *Journal of Adolescent Research, 10,* 11–135.

Jarrett, R. L. (1998). Indicators of family strengths and resilience that influence positive child-youth outcomes in urban neighborhoods: A review of qualitative and ethnographic studies. Report to the Annie Casey Foundation. Baltimore, MD.

Jarrett, R. L., & Burton, L. M. (in press). Dynamic dimensions of family structure in low-income African-American families: Emergent themes in qualitative research. *Journal of Comparative Family Studies.*

Jencks, C., & Mayer, S.E. (1990). The social consequences of growing up in a poor neighborhood. In L.E. Lynn, Jr., & M.G.H. McGeary (Eds.), *Inner-city poverty in the United States* (pp. 111–186). Washington, DC: National Academy Press.

Jurkovic, G. J. (1997). *Lost childhoods: The plight of the parentified child.* New York: Brunner/Mazel, Inc.

Kotlowitz, A. (1991). *There are no children here.* New York: Anchor.

Korbin, J. E., & Coulton, C. J. (1997). Understanding the neighborhood context for children and families: Combining epidemiological and ethnographic approaches. In J. Brooks-Gunn, G. J. Duncan, & J. L. Aber (Eds.), *Neighborhood poverty: Context and consequences for children.* New York: Russell Sage Foundation.

MacLeod, J. (1987). *Ain't no makin' it: Leveled aspirations in a low-income community.* Boulder, CO: Westview Press.

Noack, P., & Silbereisen, R.K. (1988). Adolescent development and the choice of leisure settings. *Children's Environments Quarterly, 5,* 25-33.

Ogbu, J. (1974). *The next generation: An ethnography of education in an urban neighborhood.* New York: Academic Press.

Sampson, R. J. (1992). Family management and child development: Insights from social disorganization theory. In J. McCord (Ed.), *Advances in criminological theory* (Vol. 3, pp. 63–93). New Brunswick: Transaction Books.

Seidman, E. (1991). Growing up the hard way: Pathways of urban adolescents. *American Journal of Community Psychology, 19*(2), 173–205.

Silverstein, B., & Krate, R. (1975). *Children of the dark ghetto: A developmental psychology.* New York, NY: Praeger.

Spencer, M. B. (1995). Old issues and new theorizing about African American youth: A phenomenological variant of ecological systems theory. In R.Taylor (Ed.), *Black youth: Perspectives in their status in the United States.* Westport, CT: Praeger.

Spencer, M. B., & Dornbusch, S. M. (1990). Challenges in studying minority youth. In S. S. Feldman & G. R. Elliott (Eds.), *At the threshold: The developing adolescent.* Cambridge, MA: Harvard University Press.

Stack, C.B. (1974). *All our kin: Strategies for survival in a black community*. New York: Harper and Row.

Stack, C. B. (1996). *Call to home*. New York: Basic Books.

Stack, C. B., & Burton, L. M. (1993). Kinscripts. *Journal of Comparative Family Studies, 24*(2), 157–170.

Sullivan, M. (1989). *Getting paid: Youth crime and work in the inner-city*. Ithaca, NY: Cornell University Press.

Tienda, M. (1991). Poor people and poor places: Deciphering neighborhood effects on poverty outcomes. In J. Huber (Ed.), *Macro-micro linkages in sociology*. Newbury Park, CA: Sage.

Williams, M. (1978). Childhood in an urban black ghetto: Two life histories. *Umoja, 2*, 169–182.

Williams, T., & Kornblum (1985). *Growing up poor*. Lexington, MA: Lexington Books.

Wilson, W. J. (1987). *The truly disadvantaged: The inner city, the underclass, and public policy*. Chicago, IL: University of Chicago Press.

Wu, L. L., & Martinson, B. (1993). Family structure and the risk of premarital birth. *American Sociological Review, 58*, 210–232.

Zollar, A. C. (1985). *A member of the family: Strategies for black family continuity*. Chicago, IL: Nelson-Hall.

11
Communities as Systems: Is a Community More Than the Sum of Its Parts?

Stephen Small
Andrew Supple
University of Wisconsin-Madison

Duncan and Raudenbush (chap. 8, this volume) provide an excellent summary of the most pressing methodological difficulties in assessing neighborhood effects. The authors rightly note that although there is a growing interest by social scientists in understanding the roles that neighborhood and community influences play in the lives of children, adolescents, and families, the research thus far has not been very successful at capturing these neighborhood effects or providing much insight into the processes that might account for them. Duncan and Raudenbush attribute much of this problem to deficiencies related to method, measures, and analytic techniques. Although they do an excellent job overviewing a number of these difficulties and suggesting some possible solutions, we believe the problem is more fundamental and resides earlier in the research process.

From our perspective, the problem results from a deficiency of current theory and conceptualizations of neighborhood and community. To the degree that our conceptualizations of neighborhood and community are deficient, so are the measures and methods that follow. Consequently, in this chapter, we focus our attention primarily on what we believe to be some fundamental issues regarding how community and neighborhood are defined and operationalized and we present a preliminary systemic framework for conceptualizing and organizing how communities might affect the development and well-being of children and adolescents.

The primary contribution of our framework to the field lies in the conceptualization of communities as systems comprised of interrelated parts. We also argue that the most theoretically meaningful and methodologically promising effects exist at higher order levels and are products of the transactional relationships existing between elements in the system. This framework calls attention to several factors not typically addressed in neighborhood effect studies or related theory, and answers in the affirmative the question posed in the title of this chapter, "Is a community more than the sum of its parts?"

DEFINING TERMS

Before we begin our explication of this framework, we consider how neighborhood and community have traditionally been defined and operationalized and offer some suggestions about how these terms might be distinguished from one another. A review of the literature on neighborhood and community effects (including the community psychology literature and the recent anthology, *Neighborhood Poverty, Vol. I,* Brooks-Gunn, Duncan, & Aber, 1997) indicates that the terms *neighborhood* and *community* are typically used interchangeably. Although it appears that historically the terms neighborhood and community were often used to describe the same concept, we believe that such usage can be confusing both conceptually and practically.

In this chapter we consider *neighborhood* to refer to a physical place, defined by socially shared boundaries, that include a population of people who usually share similar life chances, socioeconomic status, and physical proximity. *Community*, on the other hand, refers to social relationships that individuals have based on group consensus, shared norms and values, common goals, and feelings of identification, belonging, and trust. These conceptualizations are consistent with dictionary definitions, the root origins of each word, and previous conceptualizations from the community psychology (Heller, 1989; McMillan & Chavis, 1986) and developmental psychology literatures (Bronfenbrenner, Moen, & Garbarino, 1984). Moreover, this conceptualization recognizes that sociotechnological changes have created the possibility for people to become part of communities that are outside of their immediate physical environs.

The key element that differentiates neighborhoods from communities is that whereas a neighborhood can be the physical location where a community occurs, community is not necessarily tied to a physical place or locality, but rather is a more relational and psychological construct that goes beyond physical boundaries (Heller, 1989). That is, a community refers to a psychological place where an individual feels a sense of connection, identity, trust, mattering, and relationship. The critical question for conceptualization, theory, and research, however, is which entity (neighborhood or community) is more important when it comes to understanding the development and well-being of youth? It is our view that for both conceptual and methodological reasons, community is the more useful concept.

Neighborhood would seem to be an easier concept than community to measure because it is grounded in place and researchers can at least make an attempt to estimate its boundaries. In contrast, community is a psychosocial construct that, to some degree, resides in people's heads and derives its significance from the relationships people form and the meanings that are associated with them. Even though neighborhoods are physical entities, however, defining meaningful spatial boundaries is not a straightforward task. Such spacial boundaries and definitions of neighborhood are likely to vary from individual to individual and probably also are related to one's social class, developmental status, and race or ethnicity. For example, for very young children, the most important physical and social environments are likely to be the home and family, and the functional neighborhood is fairly small in size. For the adolescent, the physical boundaries of the neighborhood expand further and might include the school, the local YMCA, the community youth center, and blocks where close friends live. For many adolescents, the neighborhood has become somewhat obsolete as a meaningful physical location. Contemporary urban and suburban teens may spend time in many different neighborhoods. They may work in a fast food restaurant across town, attend a magnet or consolidated school miles from where they live, and "hang out" at a church-sponsored youth group located several neighborhoods away. A family's financial status is also likely to influence the size of their neighborhood. For example, wealthier families are more likely to have the means to participate in settings located in neighborhoods far from their home. They can afford to send their children to private schools or to cultural and recreational activities located elsewhere and to shop in malls that are many miles from their home. For these families, the composite of these settings constitutes their actual neighborhood.

The problem of looking at community effects by using spatial definitions of neighborhood was alluded to by Duncan and Raudenbush (chap. 8, this volume). They noted that defining neighborhood by even fairly limited geographic areas using measures derived from zip codes, census tracts, or block groups, has not been very productive. The failure of such spacial definitions of neighborhood should not really surprise us. There is no reason to believe that how the U.S. Postal Service or Census Bureau defines neighborhood is in any way consistent with how people actually do. All this suggests that in order to develop a functional and meaningful measure of neighborhood, we must first go inside people's heads and gain an understanding of how they define, perceive, and organize the physical settings in which they participate. In other words, before we can derive meaningful measures of an individual's neighborhood, we must first understand how they define their community.

TOWARD A NEW FRAMEWORK FOR CONCEPTUALIZING COMMUNITY EFFECTS

The framework we present should be considered preliminary and speculative. We offer it as a small attempt to reframe an important but not well conceptualized area of study. Its value depends not only on whether it can provide some guidance to future conceptualization for research on the effects of communities on children and adolescents, but also on whether it has practical utility to practitioners in the field.

Three principles guide this framework. First, the communities that children and their families belong to socially and psychologically are more important influences than the actual physical place or neighborhood where they reside. We recognize that there is an overlap between the two concepts and that physical place does impact individuals and their families. However, as we noted earlier, to meaningfully define the spatial boundaries of neighborhood, one must first have an understanding of how individuals define and perceive them. In other words, we must know about their *community*.

Second, we think it will be more fruitful and instructive to focus on the mechanisms or processes by which communities affect human development rather than spatial features, structural characteristics, or demographic markers. In the early stages of an area of study, it can be useful to identify structural characteristics and demographic factors because they are easy to locate and measure and because they can often provide useful initial insights. But sometimes, as seems to be the case with many of the current approaches to the study of neighborhood effects, these demographic and structural factors are such imprecise measures or so distal that the effects of interest are barely perceptible. Even more importantly, these marker variables usually tell us little about the actual processes or mechanisms that account for the developmental, behavioral, or health-related outcomes of interest. Focusing on underlying mechanisms is crucial for theoretical reasons as well because very little is currently known about the mechanisms that explain the ways by which neighborhoods and communities can influence the well-being and development of its children and youth. Perhaps even more importantly, efforts to furnish practitioners and policy makers with tangible strategies for using communities to support adolescent development must focus on underlying processes.

The final and key principle of our framework is that communities are complex systems. As such, they are comprised of smaller interacting subsystems that are organized in unique ways. This final assumption might seem obvious, but an examination of the literature indicates that such a concept is rarely incorporated into either theoretical models or research strategies. Most social science research on community effects on human development has tended to examine either demographic factors or processes in isolation, or at best, in small clusters. As Duncan and Raudenbush (chap. 8, this volume) noted, looking only at social addresses or isolated processes makes it appear that there are few or no community effects or that they are inconsequential. Conceptualizing communities as complex systems, rather than as the sum of isolated parts, calls attention to several important processes that occur at different levels within the community and that typically have been overlooked.

The remainder of this chapter is devoted to the presentation of an organizing framework for thinking about some of the ways that communities can affect children and adolescents. In contrast to other approaches to the study of community, we argue that communities are complex systems that are far more than and different from the sum of their parts and that an accurate assessment and understanding of community effects on human development must take this into account. Our framework proposes that communities influence children and youth on at least three levels: first order, second order, and third order community effects. A heuristic diagram of this framework is presented in Fig. 11.1.

Figure 11.1
Heuristic Diagram of First, Second, and Third Order Community Effects

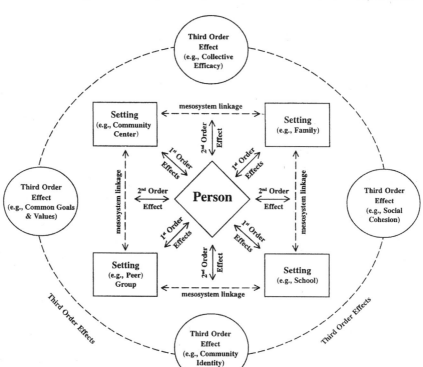

FIRST ORDER COMMUNITY EFFECTS

First order community effects are the direct aggregate influences of the universe of community settings and institutions in which adolescents participate. In the child development literature, these individual settings are referred to as microsystems (Bronfenbrenner, 1979); other social scholars refer to them as *social mediators* (Connell, Aber, & Walker, 1995). Some examples of significant community settings for children and youth include families, schools, peer groups, recreational youth programs, health care facilities, religious institutions, and child care settings. From a developmental perspective, what is most important about these settings is not the settings themselves, but the *processes* occurring within them that promote or undermine youth development and well-being. Examples of some of these processes include parental socialization, positive (or negative) peer influence, modeling by older youth and adults, and the development of self-efficacy and self-confidence. When taken together, in the aggregate, they constitute first order community effects. From a statistical standpoint, first order community effects are an additive function of all the significant community settings in which individuals participate and that influence their development and well being.

Both the quantity and quality of these settings vary from place to place as a function of a range of economic, political, and social factors. For example, poorer families are less likely to have access to a wide range of settings, and the settings that they do participate in are more likely to be of inferior quality. It is also worth noting that children grow older, the number of significant settings in which they participate typically expands. This is usually viewed as a positive developmental sign and an important force in promoting development (Bronfenbrenner, 1979). For example, very young children may only participate in (and be influenced by) a few settings such as the immediate family and child care, whereas adolescents typically participate in and are directly influenced by a much broader range of settings, including peer group, school, workplace, family, nonformal educational and recreational programs, and religious settings.

Suffice it to say that first level community effects are the aggregation of those primary influences that occur within the individual settings that comprise one's community. Within these settings, important and influential processes occur; any effort to understand human development or behavior or to strengthen a community must take them into account.

SECOND ORDER COMMUNITY EFFECTS

Even if it were possible to know about the influence of every single community setting on adolescent development (i.e., if we could overcome what Duncan and Raudenbush [chap. 8, this volume] refer to as omitted variable bias), we still would not have a complete picture of community effects. This is because community effects are greater than the sum of the effects from individual settings. Community effects also consist of effects of the second order, which are determined by relationships and linkages between settings in a community, or, in the words of Bronfenbrenner (1979), "a set of interrelations between two or more settings in which the developing person becomes an active participant" (p. 209). These linkages include the social networks that children and their families are a part of and that often serve as the "social glue" that bridges different settings. We view second order community effects as including many of the *mesosystem effects* described by Bronfenbrenner in his Ecological Systems theory (1979, 1992); however, we believe there are additional, critical elements as well.

Building on Bronfenbrenner's conception of mesosystem, we propose several ways that second order community effects—the linkages and relationships between community settings—may serve to enhance the development and well-being of children and adolescents who participate in them. We do not view this list as exhaustive or definitive, but rather as an initial effort to suggest some possible interconnections and relationships characteristic of healthy, vital communities that could affect youth.

Cross-Setting Consistency

To the degree that community settings in which children and youth participate share common goals and values, the potential positive effects in each setting are reinforced and enhanced. Particular settings may have different immediate purposes, but when common values and general goals are consistent across settings, young people are likely to be exposed to the same normative messages, be held to similar standards of behavior, and be exposed to adults and others who consistently model behavior that embodies these norms and expectations. Such cross-setting consistency also helps to legitimize and consequently strengthen the effect of a particular practice or value. Conversely, where such cross-setting consistency occurs, but where the values and behavior being modeled and encouraged are deviant or delinquent, the effects are still likely to be reinforced, but in a direction consistent with the deviant behavior and values.

Cross-Setting Presence of Adults and Older Youth

The developmental potential of individual settings is likely to be further enhanced if there are individuals, especially adults and older, mature youth, who are present in more than one setting where the young person participates (Bronfenbrenner, 1979) and who uphold and model positive community standards and values. Not only will this contribute to greater consistency across settings in norms, values, and expectations (as mentioned previously), but it will increase the likelihood that positive relationships will develop between the young person and the adult or older youth, further enhancing the settings' potential to positively contribute to the young person's development.

Quality of Communication and Exchange Across Settings

The quality of individual settings can be enhanced by high levels of cross-setting communication, especially when adults in one setting are knowledgeable about the people, activities, norms, and expectations present in other settings in which children participate. In the words of Bronfenbrenner (1979), "The developmental potential of participation in multiple settings will vary directly with the ease and extent of two-way communication between those settings" (p. 216). For example, there is substantial evidence that children do better in school when parents and teachers communicate with one another about the child's needs (Epstein, 1990; Stevenson & Baker, 1987). Similarly, parents of adolescents who are acquainted with and communicate regularly with the parents of their children's friends are better able to establish common rules and expectations as well as more effectively monitor the peer groups' whereabouts and activities (Small & Eastman, 1991). In addition, being knowledgeable about what occurs in other settings can help youth and their parents better prepare for the child's transition into new settings and inform parents about the appropriateness of specific settings for the child.

Availability of Structurally Different, Appropriate, and Supportive Settings

Bronfenbrenner (1979) proposed that "Development is enhanced as a direct function of the number of structurally different settings in which the developing person participates in a variety of joint activities and primary dyads with others, particularly when these others are more mature and experienced" (p. 212). This suggests that healthy communities not only provide appropriate, high quality settings, but that they possess a variety of settings offering a range of different activities, opportunities, and experiences and that they involve cross-age participants. The need for structurally different and challenging settings and exposure to a variety of non-familial adults may be especially important for adolescents who need increasingly challenging experiences, and opportunities where they can explore new roles and identities, and who could benefit from the development of relationships with nonparental adults in whom they can confide. Communities that do not provide positive challenges and opportunities risk having youth who rely primarily on peer culture for a sense of identity and who engage in deviant behaviors as a way to create personal challenges and test out emerging abilities.

Complementarity and Fit of Community Settings

This refers to how well available community settings complement one another. In contrast to the other second order community effects discussed thus far, this concept is not primarily concerned with linkages between settings but with the "fit" of existing settings. Well functioning, supportive communities are characterized by complementarity in the settings and institutions available to children and their families. This suggests that there is an ideal balance in the types of settings and institutions that exist within an individual's community. Although the fit between settings partly depends on the quality and quantity of existing settings within an individual's community, the concept of complementarity assumes that not all communities must have the same number and types of settings. The ideal balance and mix of settings most likely depend on the characteristics and needs of the people living there. For example, in communities where there is a high degree of seasonal summer employment, it is probably very important to have day-long recreational activities and child care available for children and youth during the summer months.

Another way to look at the concept of setting complementarity and fit is to consider the developmental needs of a particular child and the ways that these needs are being met. If a child's needs are not being met in one setting, such as the family, then whether or not the child thrives or suffers will depend on whether these needs are being met in other available settings. Research on resilient children suggests that such children are better able to locate and draw out what they need from other settings and people when they are not receiving what they need in the settings where those needs are typically met. Their resiliency is not only a result of their personal characteristics, but also depends on the availability of settings and people that can provide the support, structure, or opportunities that they need.

Physical and Social Accessibility

Finally, the ability of community members to both physically and socially navigate between settings and institutions has important implications for young people. The degree of accessibility in a community determines how often youth can take advantage of the benefits of various settings and also affects the quality of linkages between settings.

Barriers to accessibility can be both physical and social. Physical barriers include a lack of convenient transportation, environments in which people feel unsafe, and programs or settings that are not available at convenient times or places. They might also include barriers that result from natural or man-made geographical features that inhibit movement from one setting to another. Social barriers might include such factors as language, social class, or cultural differences between a program's providers and those it serves, as well as social or cultural boundaries. For example, an individual may perceive a particular setting as being located in an area "owned" by a rival gang or ethnic group and refuse to utilize facilities, programs, or businesses that are located within that territory.

The concept of second order community effects has rarely been discussed or examined in the research literature. However, recent approaches to community building on behalf of youth emphasize the need for building cross-setting, community collaborations. The reasons and benefits for such cross-setting approaches, although rarely stated, seem to be, in part, related to the perceived value of creating stronger intersetting linkages and improving the level of complementarity between them.

We suggest that the theoretical concept of social capital might best be conceptualized as the aggregation of second order effects that exist within a community. This appears consistent with Putnam's (1993) definition of social capital as "features of social organization, such as networks, norms, and trust, that facilitate coordination and cooperation for mutual benefits" (p. 36), as well Coleman's (1990) claim that "social capital is lodged not in individuals but in the structure of social organization" (p. 302).

THIRD ORDER COMMUNITY EFFECTS

The core tenet of our conceptual framework posits that among the most important influences that communities exert on youth are those of a higher order, what we refer to as *third order community effects*. We hypothesize that when second order effects or the level of social capital in a community reaches a critical mass, then the potential of a community system to operate at a new, higher level of complexity may emerge.

Third order community effects are the product of interactions of various elements in a community system. They are a manifestation of processes taking place at higher order levels of community organization. Third order effects are not simply the aggregation of settings, processes, or intersetting relationships that occur at lower levels of social structure or organization, but rather are effects that are unique to the system as a whole. Higher order effects cannot be explained by reducing them to their smaller, constituent parts because they are more than the sum of their parts. Higher order effects include and incorporate lower level effects, but also possess properties that are unique to the higher level system of which they are a part. The relationship between the parts and the whole is characterized by *emergence* (Colarelli, 1998). The concept of emergence is based on the idea that higher levels of a system are more complex and encompassing than are lower levels in that they include the capacities, processes, and settings of lower levels but then add their own unique, system-level capacities. The combination of parts produces a whole that is greater than and different from the sum of the parts (Colarelli, 1998).

Higher level systems properties can also influence and determine the meaning and function of a lower order part of the system. The whole, in other words, is not only more than the sum of its parts, but it can, in some cases, influence the function of its parts. Another way to think about third order community effects is that they are located in the collective rather than in the individual parts and that they derive both their meaning and their influence as properties of the whole.

At first glance, third order community effects may sound nebulous, difficult to identify, and elusive to measure. However, we believe that much of the most recent and productive research on community influences focuses third order effects, even though it is not identified as such. Other authors in this volume have also begun to argue that collective properties of communities are important to identify as processes that influence youth development (Sampson, chap. 1, this volume). Drawing on this emerging literature, we discuss several examples.

Social Cohesion

Social cohesion is a term used by community psychologists to refer to a sense of emotional closeness among community members as a result of shared real-world-lived experiences, common life changes, and similar personal histories (Heller,

1989). *Emotional cohesion* is likely to be characterized by a sense of trust and solidarity among individuals and a feeling that others in a community can be counted on to look out for one another and the good of the community. What makes social cohesion a third order, community level property, rather than a second order effect or dimension of social capital, is that the emotional closeness that is experienced is not just to a few key people or institutions but is more a generalized emotional connection to a critical mass of others in the community.

Community Identity and Membership

Closely related is the concept of *community identity and membership* (McMillan & Chavis, 1986). When it emerges in a community, citizens feel a sense of belonging, ownership, and community spirit. They also feel that they are a part of an entity that is larger than oneself. One's personal identity becomes defined in part by the community in which one is a member. Community identity and membership is neither an individual characteristic nor a dyadic one, but emerges out of a collective sense of being part of something larger than oneself.

Superordinate Values, Goals, and Norms

When members of a community feel an emotional connection to one another and some form of shared identity and group membership, they are likely to recognize that part of what unites them with others are common norms, values, and goals. They share a collective sense about what is expected, valued, and desirable. Unlike the mesosystem linkages between two or more settings, the norms, values, and goals that are shared are not just common to a small group of individuals or settings but are perceived as being shared by most people in the community. Part of their justification and importance comes from the fact that they are viewed as agreed on and accepted by members of the community. They are seen as values or norms that are at the core of what the community represents and what it desires for its members.

Collective Efficacy

Finally, we view the concept of *collective efficacy* (Sampson, Raudenbush, & Earls, 1997) as another example of a third order community effect. Sampson, Raudenbush, and Earls define collective efficacy as "the linkage of mutual trust and the willingness to intervene for the common good." Or as Sampson (chap. 1, this volume) stated, "Collective efficacy is meant to signify an emphasis on shared beliefs in a neighborhood's conjoint capability for action, coupled with an active sense of engagement on the parts of residents." It seems clear from this definition that collective efficacy is a system-level property that is located in the collective and directed to regulating and benefitting the community as a system.

Because third order effects are properties of the community system, they are likely to be highly interdependent and interrelated. It seems reasonable to posit that some third order community effects are dependent not only on the existence of lower order effects, but on the prior emergence of other third order effects. For example, collective efficacy appears to be a fairly advanced higher order community system property because it is contingent on other third order community effects. Before collective efficacy within a community can occur, there must first be a sense of shared values and goals around which the community will unite, a belief in and commitment to a common good, a sense of cohesion and mutual trust among citizens so that they are willing to work together, and finally, the human and material resources to draw on to bring about community action.

To implicate a third order community effect, it would be necessary to demonstrate that the observed effect is a function of forces lying outside the direct effects of the universe of community settings (first order effects) and the linkages between such settings (second order effects). Consequently, the influence of the community on families and the individuals who reside within it cannot be validly measured solely by assessing and aggregating the contributions of each of its constituent subsystems. Third order community effects are probably interactive and multiplicative rather than additive. The effects derive from the coexistence and joint impact of particular subsystems, the nature of the linkages between them, and unique properties that characterize the system as a whole.

IMPLICATIONS FOR POLICY AND PRACTICE

Like most systems, it seems reasonable to assume that community systems are hierarchically organized and that lower level effects precede higher level ones. Before a second order effect like mesosystem linkages can be formed, you must first have individual community settings to be linked. Before you can have a third order effect like collective efficacy or community identity, you must have both a critical mass of quality settings in a community and a sufficient number of intersetting linkages.

There are important practical and policy implications for such a hierarchical sequencing of levels of community effects. It means that, because third order effects build on and incorporate second order effects, it is probably unrealistic to try to promote third order effects like collective efficacy, social cohesion, or community spirit before creating sufficient second order linkages. Similarly, it makes little sense to put energy into creating second order linkages if there are not first a sufficient number of quality, primary community settings. What this implies for practice and policy is that we need to begin by creating and enhancing settings, then work at optimizing their fit and creating meaningful linkages between them. Finally, not until these first two levels of community effects have been achieved can we expect conditions to be present where third order system effects can emerge or be promoted. In other words, it is folly to think that we can promote community efficacy, cohesion, or identity if fundamental settings do not exist or where important setting linkages have not yet been established.

Given our inability to simply infuse communities with constructs like cohesion, efficacy, or social capital or to make people feel more connected to their community, we argue that interventions should focus on first and second order level effects. We hypothesize that the interactions between various community subsystems such as families, schools, churches, and businesses contribute to higher order community effects. The extent to which youth belong to a community with strong, healthy, and positive frequent interactions among subsystems leads to the promotion of a sense of community, social cohesion, and collective efficacy that enhances the environmental context in which youth develop.

Programmers and policy makers should endeavor to identify interventions that strengthen the bonds and links between subsystem settings to create second order effects. Improving the quality of communication across settings, encouraging adults to participate in a range of different settings in which children spend time, working towards common community values, goals, and norms across settings, and inculcating a sense of trust among community members should be emphasized as potential points for intervention. Based on our model, we hypothesize that community collaborations that enhance second order effects contribute to the emergence of desirable third order effects.

CONCLUSION

We believe that the communities in which children and adolescents live can have important influences on their well-being and development. Unfortunately, current efforts to understand community influences have thus far not been very successful at either finding community effects or identifying underlying mechanisms. In our view, the primary reason for this lack of success is conceptual: Researchers have failed to conceptualize communities as the complex systems that they are and have instead looked for community effects where it is most convenient. Although a conceptualization of communities as multilevel, complex systems will not be easy to operationalize or study, we believe it provides a more accurate and honest description of the complexity inherent in community effects and will result in more useful theoretical and practical insights than current conceptualizations have thus far provided.

REFERENCES

Bronfenbrenner, U. (1979). *The ecology of human development: Experiments by nature and design.* Cambridge, MA: Harvard University Press.

Bronfenbrenner, U. (1992). Ecological systems theory. In R. Vasta (Ed.), *Six theories of child development: Revised formulations and current issues* (pp. 187–249). London: Jessica Kingsley.

Bronfenbrenner, U., Moen, P., & Garbarino, J. (1984). Child, family, and community. In R. D. Parke (Ed.), *Review of child development research* (Vol. 7, pp. 283–328). Chicago: University of Chicago Press.

Brooks-Gunn, J., Duncan, G., & Aber, L. (Eds.). (1997). *Neighborhood poverty, Vol. 1.* New York: Russell Sage Foundation.

Colarelli, S. M. (1998). Psychological intervention in organizations. *American Psychologist, 53,* 1044–1056.

Coleman, J. S. (1990). *Foundations of social theory.* Cambridge, MA: Harvard University Press.

Epstein, J. L. (1990). School and family connections: Theory, research and implications for integrating sociologies of education and family. In D. G. Unger & M. B. Sussman (Eds.), *Families in community settings: Interdisciplinary perspectives* (pp. 99–126). New York: Hayworth Press.

Heller, K. (1989). The return to community. *American Journal of Community Psychology, 17,* 1–15.

McMillan, D. W., & Chavis, D. M. (1986). Sense of community: A definition and theory. *Journal of Community Psychology, 14,* 6–23.

Putnam, R. (1993, Spring).The prosperous community: Social capital and community life. *The American Prospect,* 35–42.

Sampson, R. J., Raudenbush, S., & Earls, F. (1997). Neighborhoods and violent crime: A multilevel study of collective efficacy. *Science, 277,* 918–924.

Small, S. A., & Eastman, G. E. (1991). Rearing adolescents in contemporary society: A conceptual framework for understanding the responsibilities and needs of parents. *Family Relations, 40,* 455–462.

Stevenson, D. L., & Baker, D. P. (1987). The family-school relation and the child's school performance. *Child Development, 58,* 1348–1357.

IV

What Policies can Strengthen Neighborhoods as Contexts for Child and Adolescent Well-being?

12

Community Approaches to Improving Outcomes for Urban Children, Youth, and Families: Current Trends and Future Directions

James P. Connell
Institute for Research and Reform in Education

Anne C. Kubisch
Roundtable on Comprehensive Community Initiatives
for Children and Families
The Aspen Institute

INVESTING IN COMMUNITIES TO IMPROVE RESIDENTS' WELL-BEING: A BRIEF HISTORY

In the United States, the history of community-based initiatives to improve poor urban neighborhoods and the lives of their residents dates to settlement houses of the late 19th century. In the 20th century, neighborhood-based efforts include the fight against juvenile delinquency in the 1950s, the War on Poverty in the 1960s, and the community development corporation movement of the last 30 years.[1] Over this period, several themes have cycled in and out of the antipoverty field in policy discussions, programmatic trends, and related research. The themes are, perhaps, best expressed as efforts to find the right balance between perspectives that are in tension for ideological, political, technical, or financial reasons. They include the tensions between:

- People versus place: interventions designed to benefit particular groups of individuals who live in distressed neighborhoods versus interventions aimed at improving neighborhood conditions for all present and future residents.
- Public versus private: relying on resources from the public sector versus resources from the private sector (corporate, church, voluntary, philanthropic, etc.).
- Top down versus bottom up: leadership from those in established positions of power versus leadership from the affected community or intended beneficiaries.

---

[1] For further discussion of the evolution of CCIs and the state of the field today, see Halpern, 1994; Jackson & Marris, 1996; Kingsley, McNeely, & Gibson, 1997; Kubisch, Brown, et al., 1997; Kubisch, Weiss, et al., 1995; Leiterman & Stillman, 1993; O'Connor, 1995, forthcoming; Pitcoff, 1997; Stone, 1996; Walsh, 1996.

- Deficit oriented versus asset oriented: interventions that are designed to fix specific problems versus interventions designed to reinforce the strengths and assets of an individual or community.
- Categorical versus comprehensive: interventions that focus on specific problems or outcomes versus interventions that address multiple problems and the interactions among them.
- Technology application versus capacity building: interventions that apply a particular model program or technology versus interventions that focus on building the capacity of individuals or neighborhoods to develop solutions to their own problems.

The antipoverty field has come to a moment in history when the key actors are trying to bridge the divides and bring the best elements of these themes together in a new approach to poverty alleviation that addresses both individual well-being and community development. This chapter describes how comprehensive, community-building initiatives based on these themes are unfolding, and then focuses on the youth development field as an in-depth case illustration. The chapter also points out the areas needing additional work to implement and learn from these initiatives and to assess the progress and potential of them.

RECENT RESEARCH TRENDS HIGHLIGHTING THE IMPORTANCE OF NEIGHBORHOOD IN INFLUENCING OUTCOMES FOR INDIVIDUALS AND THEIR POLICY IMPLICATIONS

Since the 1970s, researchers have increased their efforts to understand the causes of urban community distress and its effects on the children and families who live in poor neighborhoods. As developmental psychologists, community psychologists, economists, sociologists, anthropologists, and political scientists addressed these problems, we learned a great deal about the inter-relationships among poverty, poor physical and mental health, crime, crumbling infrastructure, low business activity, racism, and weak social and cultural institutions in American cities. The growing understanding of these inter-relationships also has increased awareness of the interaction between individual outcomes and the conditions of the surrounding environment, and more recent research has attempted to describe and analyze this phenomenon.

With regard to early child development, for example, many scholars followed Bronfenbrenner's (1977, 1979) early lead and worked to define the importance of *context* on a child's well-being, including family, child care and educational circumstances, neighborhood attributes, and sociocultural practices. Research has begun to demonstrate how children are influenced by the resources and risks in their neighborhoods, including institutional supports, presence or absence of affluent residents, neighborhood stability, and density of social networks. (See Aber, Brooks-Gunn, & Duncan, 1997, for an excellent review of literature in this domain.) These factors intersect with individual attributes to produce healthy or unhealthy outcomes for children as they develop.

In the last decade, research on youth development also has begun to demonstrate the critical relationship between contextual and individual factors. To become economically self-sufficient adults with healthy relationships and good citizenship practices, youth must accomplish certain things (Connell, Aber, & Walker, 1995). But the developmental processes involved in reaching those accomplishments are influenced by the physical and demographic characteristics of neighborhoods (Briggs, 1996; Brooks-Gunn, Duncan, Klebanov, & Sealand, 1993; Crane, 1991; Sampson, 1996), by the structure of economic opportunities (Freedman, 1982; Wilson, 1996), by social and cultural contexts (Burton, Allison, & Obeidallah, 1995; Spencer, 1986), and by institutional capacities and resources in the neighborhood (Case & Katz, 1991; Wynn, Costello, Halpern, & Richman, 1994).

The newest line of research into the community-individual relationship highlights the importance of *social capital*—dense social networks, a sense of community, strong informal associations, and similar types of qualities—in maintaining the overall well-being of a community and residents. That research was spurred by Coleman (1990) and then Putnam (1993), but has been helped along by social network analysis experts (Castells, 1996; Wellman & Leighton, 1979) and community psychologists (Wandersman, Roth, & Prestby, 1985). This perspective attempts to analyze the attributes of healthy communities from a social perspective and to link them to healthy individual behavior and outcomes. Sampson (chap. 1, this volume) reviews this literature in a thorough and clear way.

From a range of different starting points, social scientists are beginning to focus on the importance of the relationship between individual-level and community-level variables. Whereas the developmental psychologists find that healthy communities can enhance child and youth development, sociologists and anthropologists find the converse—that healthy individuals help create healthy communities.

This multidisciplinary and integrative social science approach to understanding the causes and consequences of urban poverty in the United States has challenged the traditional ideological divide between behavioralists and structuralists in U.S. social policy-making circles. Behavioralists tend to ascribe poor outcomes such as unintended teen pregnancy, unemployment, or criminal behavior to individual-level characteristics, including intelligence, values, attitudes, and motivation. Their policy prescriptions have tended to focus on changing individual people through skills development, attitude change, reduction of their dependency on public assistance, and incentives to change their behavior. Structuralists, on the other hand, have focused on how changes in the macro-economy have produced deleterious effects on low-skilled workers, racist practices in housing and employment, and lack of investment in the public school system. Their policy prescriptions focus more on contextual factors, either at the macro level, such as working toward more equitable regulatory or tax policies, or at the local level, seeking to revitalize communities (economically, politically, and socially) that are most hurt by these macroeconomic forces.

Recent Programmatic Trends

These research findings have been reinforced by program-level experience that increasingly shows that singular and highly focused strategies, no matter how effective they might be, have inherent limitations and cannot be expected to achieve sustained improvements in individual and community well-being in poor urban neighborhoods in the United States. This lesson emerges from many programmatic directions.

We can learn a great deal from one of the most successful and best studied programs for children living in poor communities in the United States: Head Start, an enriched development program for children aged 3 to 5 years old. Children living in extremely disadvantaged, high-risk families and neighborhoods who participate in Head Start often make major developmental gains and enter school better equipped than children who do not participate in the program. According to the longitudinal study of the pilot program in the 1960s, those children go on to exhibit fewer problem outcomes such as teen pregnancy, dropping out of high school, and criminal behavior than do their peers at age 19 (Berrueta-Clement, Schweinhart, Barnett, Epstein, & Weikart, 1984). However, they still have higher teen pregnancy rates, drop-out rates, and arrest rates than the national average. We have found that 2 years of enriched education at ages 3 and 4, however powerful, do not eliminate the long-term disadvantage children face when they've grown up in economically distressed families and communities. The effects of early intervention wear off when the children go on to underfunded elementary schools, in low-income neighborhoods, where crime rates are high and employment rates are low. The effects are more robust when the enriched educational environment is sustained.

A similar lesson comes from those who have been engaged in the physical revitalization of low-income urban neighborhoods. During the 1970s and 1980s, a strong and well-funded movement dedicated to building or rehabilitating housing in the inner city blossomed. These community development corporations (CDCs) became the largest producers of low-income housing in the country, but most of the neighborhoods in which they are active are still poor and their residents continue to experience a range of social and economic problems. The CDCs, as a result, are seeking ways to complement their infrastructure work with human development work.

The lesson that we can draw from the Head Start program and from the CDC example—that neither a one-shot experience, no matter how positive, nor a single narrow intervention, no matter how good, can do it all—is being learned in a whole range of social and economic programs. Across the United States, agencies and their funders have begun to recognize the limitations of operating solely in specialized niches and have begun to reorient their ways of doing business to reach beyond traditional boundaries. Many types of experiments are attempting to link program components that have been proven to work. The strategies that result have been more comprehensive and, one hopes, more effective.

At the same time, over the course of the last decade or so, program planners, managers, and funders have grown increasingly concerned about the rigidity of institutions dedicated to improving the well-being of individuals and families in distressed neighborhoods. The main types of institutions are best categorized according to their principal programmatic emphasis:

- Human development, notably social service agencies and schools;
- Physical and economic development, notably community development corporations (CDCs) and other housing, economic, and business development groups; and
- Social and political development, focusing on strengthening of what is variously called civic life, the social fabric, and sense of community. Groups that work with this approach tend to be local religious, cultural, civic, and recreational organizations and community organizers.

The concern centers on whether there are too few institutional vehicles with the flexibility and capacity to incorporate the lessons of this recent research and program experience into new initiatives. In response, a number of experiments have been launched to develop the capacity in distressed neighborhoods to integrate resources and knowledge to revitalize neighborhoods for a sustained period of time. The programs are known in the field as *comprehensive community initiatives*, or CCIs, and they represent an attempt to put into practice the findings that have emerged from both social science research and programmatic experience. They are neighborhood-based efforts to improve the lives of individuals and families as well as their neighborhoods, by working comprehensively across social, economic, and physical sectors. They are also built on evidence from the social capital and social network theorists: They are structured to promote *community building*, meaning individual and community empowerment and social capital.

At the individual and family levels, CCIs seek to improve the quality of life of children and their families. Much of what CCIs actually do is targeted at individuals through, for example, education, employment training, service provision, social supports, and leadership development. CCIs generally aim to expand the quantity and to improve the quality of services and activities in those domains and to add a developmental, human capital-building orientation to them. These strategies are intended to increase an individual's skills, identify and enhance existing capacities, change attitudes and values, and build motivation.

At the neighborhood level, CCIs are concerned with the accessibility and quality of social support, economic opportunity, and physical infrastructure. This generally encompasses efforts to improve or increase housing, neighborhood infrastructure, the business sector, education and training institutions, the social and civic support network, cultural vitality, and other quality-of-life factors. CCIs also are concerned with the qualities of collective life provided through strong personal networks, social capital, and a "sense of community," as well as the neighborhood's capacity to handle conflict, solve problems, and express its voice and represent its interests in the larger economic and political arena.

Most of the 50 to 100 CCIs were created by and receive support from private foundations, although there is a growing number of federal, state, and locally sponsored initiatives. At the same time, many institutions have undertaken activities to provide technical assistance to CCIs, to evaluate and carry out research to increase understanding of their work, to share knowledge among CCIs, and to disseminate information about them to a broader audience. Perhaps more important, however, is the way the principles that underlie CCIs are increasingly guiding a wide range of publicly and privately sponsored social welfare and economic development efforts. A growing number of sector-specific or outcome-specific initiatives in education, health, youth development, crime prevention, substance abuse, child development, and child welfare are being guided by principles of comprehensiveness and community building. CCIs may represent the "purest" application of comprehensiveness and community building, but they are by no means the sole expressions of those principles.

Recent trends in research are making their way into policy design primarily in the form of more comprehensive approaches to urban development and innercity revitalization. The best-informed interventions today are no longer based on the premise that a single programmatic activity will lead to impressive outcomes for all individuals in a distressed neighborhood. Moreover, the research that has described and analyzed the interaction between individual outcomes and the conditions of the surrounding environment has helped bridge the divide between "people-oriented" strategies and more "place-oriented" strategies.

KEY ISSUES RAISED BY EARLY EXPERIENCE WITH CCIs: AN AGENDA FOR POLICY, RESEARCH, AND PRACTICE

One of the great strengths of the CCI field is that it was born out of the common knowledge base and experience of the policy, research, and practitioner constituencies. The collective wisdom and skills of these three constituencies must now be directed toward the next generation of issues, ones that are raised in the process of implementing, managing, and evaluating CCIs. These emerging issues are as

complex as the ambitious community change initiatives themselves and will require deliberate and sustained attention. Three priority issues are discussed here.
They certainly do not represent all of the topics needing attention, but they do give
a sense of where new efforts need to be directed.

The Need for Better "Theories of Change"

Those in the community revitalization field have grown impatient about achieving
outcomes that will affect residents' lives in meaningful ways. Does the program
reduce poverty rates, reduce un- and underemployment, decrease the incidence of
low birthweight babies, decrease drop-out and crime rates, and improve the stock
of affordable housing? These types of outcomes are difficult to achieve, especially quickly. Yet program directors, agency heads, and others, because they
must compete for program funding, commit themselves to achieving significant
changes in these broad social indicators, even if they know their modest program
is unlikely in and of itself to transform their neighborhood.

The challenge to the social science community is to lay out, in a much more
sophisticated and detailed manner, the paths leading to those outcomes. Social
scientists, policy makers, and program staff need to work together to define the
paths that individuals, communities, institutions, and programs should be encouraged to follow toward improved well-being. This means developing more nuanced theories of change at the individual, institutional, and community levels that
are based on both scientific evidence and program experience. (See Connell &
Kubisch, 1998, for a discussion of theories of change and their importance to
policy and program evaluation.)

The focus needs to be on developing three distinct but interrelated pathways.
One is relatively straightforward—linking longer term outcomes back to well-
known precursors of those outcomes. For example: elementary school completion predicts secondary school completion, which predicts university attendance,
which predicts employability, which predicts employment, which predicts income.
The second is linking sets of intentional activities to these outcomes over the course
of the initiative—integrated and responsive human services, reformed schools,
safer streets, and more and better jobs in the community lead to better educational
outcomes and employment levels for the community's residents. The third set of
pathways is more complicated—it includes building the conditions and capacities
at the individual or neighborhood level to get these activities implemented and
sustained. These paths include creating political empowerment, building social
capital, strengthening institutional capacity for reform, and developing effective
local leadership. These latter paths need to be better understood, both theoretically and empirically.

By not investing enough in defining these pathways, policy makers and funders
will be able to judge an initiative only by whether it results in the ultimate outcomes at which point political, human and economic resources can no longer be

reallocated. New tools are desperately needed to permit promising initiatives to demonstrate short-term achievements over time periods that are meaningful to politicians, to funders who do not easily take a long-range view, and to community residents who are eager for documented evidence of progress.

The Need to Develop Evaluation Approaches That Elucidate How and Why Change Occurs

The second area needing attention from practitioners and researchers is improving understanding of *how* initiatives work. The emphasis placed on detecting and measuring ultimate outcomes has robbed the second and third paths of the attention they deserve and that policy makers and program managers need. As a result, much of what is currently called *process evaluation* is unhelpful, often offering only anecdotal evidence with no analysis. Alternatively, process evaluations fall back on documenting the inputs—how many units of service were provided, how many loans were made, or how many participants enrolled in the program—without linking them to results. These process measures may even act as a substitute for outcome measures because they provide comforting evidence of activity even if the logic linking these activities to intended outcomes is not apparent or compelling.

Documenting whether and how a policy or program was implemented and how it produced outcomes can be done with rigor, but it requires some work. Meta-analyses seeking to distill "best practices" from multiple studies on the part of the evaluation industry represent one step in the right direction. But policy makers and program directors need a broad range of tools to find out *how* and *why* a policy or program produces (or does not produce) outcomes. For example, pathways including contextual influences on implementation, changes in institutional capacities, and CCIs sorting out competing priorities, must be important foci of evaluators' work. This information will help ensure that the policies and activities are more intelligently implemented in the future.

The Need to Understand the Role of Social Capital and Community Building in Neighborhood Revitalization

The notion of *community building* is front and center in current community revitalization strategies. It is generally defined as strengthening the capacity of residents, neighborhood associations, and neighborhood organizations to work toward sustained change in conditions. Early outcomes could include a widely shared vision for the community and a strategic plan for achieving the vision (a broadly accepted, compelling and specific theory of change); strengthened informal associations among neighborhood residents; more well-functioning community institutions; racial equity and healthy interracial dynamics; and "early wins" through productive collaboration among neighborhood organizations.

The emphasis on community building was a reaction to the "top down" and technocratic nature of the social policy and community development field during the 1970s and 1980s. The trend was toward a more community-driven agenda that respected community strengths, culture, wisdom, and capacity. It recognized that for a neighborhood effort to be sustained over time, the community needed to "own" it. It also grew out of a concern that anomie had replaced a sense of community in distressed inner cities. This perception on the part of practitioners and policy makers mirrored the research community's new efforts to define and understand the role of *social capital*.

The cutting-edge questions that need answering under the new comprehensive community-building initiative are:

- Does enhanced social capital (or community building) lead to improved outcomes in priority policy areas such as health, income, and crime?
- If the answer to the first question is yes, then can social capital or community building be promoted? How?
- Are the investments that we make in social capital and community building working? How do we define and measure whether social capital is being increased? How much is required to move community initiatives toward their goals?

These questions become extremely important in the context of efforts to improve conditions in poor communities. Policy makers must always consider the value of investing in one strategy over another when resources are scarce and the stakes high.

The growing number of studies correlating social capital with desirable outcomes is helping to motivate the community-building emphasis of many of the current policies and programs, but we have only a preliminary understanding of the "texture" of that correlation. Sampson and his colleagues have done excellent work as it relates to crime. (Sampson, chap. 1, in this volume.) Others have focused on dimensions such as good government (Putnam, 1993), civic engagement of youth and young adults (Youniss, McLellan, and Yates, 1997), and even health (Kawachi, 1998). However, as the scientific community would be quick to note, correlation does not equal causation. We need to gain clarity on issues surrounding the links between investment in social capital or community-building activities and more programmatic activities. We need to understand, for example, whether sequencing of activities makes a difference, whether levels of investment in one kind of activity "tips" other outcomes, and the conditions under which investing in one strand of activity has higher or lower returns.

As to whether social capital can be promoted through intervention, there is much less evidence. A 1996 report by the Community Development Research Center at The New School found that relationships within communities can be strengthened by the activities of CDCs, but only when the CDCs deliberately put into place activities designed to build and strengthen these relationships. In this case, an increase in "acquaintanceships" led to greater feelings of connection, greater sense of community, and more faith in the ability of residents to work together to solve neighborhood problems (Briggs & Mueller, with Sullivan, 1996). These results are quite clearly relevant to the goals of community-building initiatives, but we need much more evidence of whether and how this can be accomplished.

Finally, evaluation of CCIs probably will allow researchers to make progress on developing measures of social capital and related community-building concepts. Funders of several CCIs have invested significantly in evaluation, and developing surveys and other instruments to measure the social capital and community-building dimensions of the work. The field will benefit from this methodological and measurement development work.

A CASE IN POINT: COMMUNITY APPROACHES TO YOUTH DEVELOPMENT

We now turn to an example of a comprehensive, community-based approach to improving outcomes for youth. We chose youth development as our focus because of its relevance to the theme of this volume and because the youth development field has made considerable progress on the three issues described that are challenging the overall CCI field: the need for better theories of change, the need for better evaluation, and the need for a better understanding of the role of community building. We have drawn this example from the work of the Community Action for Youth Project (CAYP) (e.g., Connell & Gambone, 1998; Connell, Gambone, & Smith, 1998; Connell, 1998; Gambone, in press).

The Youth Development Field

The history and emergence of the youth development field parallels that of CCIs. Youth policy in the United States historically has been a fragmented set of programs without a center. No single entity addresses youth issues holistically at the national level. As the social science research community began to highlight the importance of community level influences on youth outcomes, practitioners also began experimenting with new, more comprehensive, and community-based approaches to improving outcomes for youth. At its inception 10 years ago, *youth development* was neither a field nor an approach. It was a movement that united around two central axioms.

Axiom 1: Program thinking fails as a basis for policy thinking. This point was painfully supported in the late 1980s and early 1990s by substantial research findings that past approaches to specific youth problems produced weak, transient, or no results (Walker & Villella-Velez, 1992). These publicly funded approaches centered on *interventions* that assumed the problem lay with a deficit in the young person. The intervention sought to provide youth with the skills or knowledge that would correct the deficiency. Such approaches failed to take into account the complexity of young people's lives or the environment in which they still had to function. The pattern of disappointing results seemed to suggest that policy expectations needed to be rethought (and lowered), and that *social engineering* had its limits.

Axiom 2: Youth policy and youth interventions should be guided by a "developmental" framework. Converging evidence and findings from the adolescent development field, youth resiliency studies, and applied social research provided a credible platform for the movement. The work of the Center for Youth Development (e.g., Pittman & Cahill, 1992) in articulating the issues and advocating a new approach to youth issues helped create wider policy awareness. Applied research findings, particularly the work of Public/Private Ventures and The Search Institute, brought new substance and credibility to a set of ideas that already were intuitively appealing.

At the center of this thinking was the idea that young people are assets in the making, whose development depends on a range of supports and opportunities that come from family, community, and the other institutions that touch them. When the supports and opportunities are plentiful, young people can and do thrive; when their environments are deficient or depleted, youth fail to grow and progress.

Like CCIs, the compelling nature of this logic has led to great expectations for interventions based on it. Also like CCIs, the need to develop compelling theories of change to guide these interventions is pressing. Fortunately, the youth development field has made considerable progress in defining some of the elements of these theories—specifically, the linkages between the experiences of youth as they grow up, the effects of these experiences on their accomplishments as young people, and the probable impacts of these accomplishments in adulthood. As a field, we are ready to articulate a compelling and unifying statement of what the basic supports and opportunities all youth need to grow up healthy are—the nonnegotiables of youth development—and what these nonnegotiables can realistically be expected to yield when in place within and across settings where youth spend time.

However, to advance the field of comprehensive community initiatives focused on youth development, a theory of change guiding these interventions will have to include at least two other elements. Both elements will extend the framework beyond the individual level of analysis and intervention to the organizational and community levels where most CCIs operate. We must formulate a set of community strategies that, when implemented, will close the gap from existing levels of the supports and opportunities youth are experiencing to thresholds that meaningfully increase the chances of achieving our goals for youth, and we must offer ways to mobilize and build the capacities of stakeholders at all levels to embrace and then implement these community strategies.

The balance of this chapter presents one such framework.

A COMMUNITY ACTION FRAMEWORK FOR YOUTH DEVELOPMENT

The framework presented in Fig. 12.1 was developed by Connell and Gambone. It is a hybrid: elements A, B, and C reflect many well documented linkages between the experiences and accomplishments of youth and their long-term prospects as adults, whereas the linkages among elements E, D, and C are grounded much more in practical experience and common sense than in research studies or rigorous program evaluations.

The framework builds on three main sources of work: other youth development frameworks that have been influential in shaping the field; reviews of academic theory and research on adolescent development (Connell, Aber, & Walker, 1995; Gambone, 1998); and lessons learned either directly or indirectly from intermediary organizations working on the following initiatives:

Figure 12.1
Community Action Framework for Youth Development

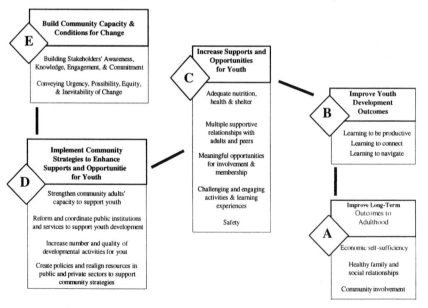

- P/PV's *Community Change for Youth Development*;
- The Center for Youth Development and Policy Research's *Youth Development Mobilization*;
- Search Institute's *Developmental Assets for Children*;
- National Urban League's *Community Youth Development Mobilization Initiative*;
- Development Research and Programs Inc.'s *Communities That Care;* and
- The Institute for Research and Reform in Education's *First Things First.*

A more complete explication of the evidence—from research, practical experience, and common sense—for the framework's validity is forthcoming (Connell & Gambone, 1998).[2] As it stands, the framework is meant to be a practical guide for investors, planners, practitioners, and evaluators involved in community-based youth development initiatives.

Although the logical flow of the framework in Fig. 12.1 moves from left to right, the framework was derived from right to left (for example, from Box A to Box C), from what it is that we want and expect youth to achieve as young adults (A) back to developmental outcomes we seek for youth to lead to these achievements (B) and then further back to the supports and opportunities that youth need to reach these developmental outcomes (C).

What Outcomes Should a Community Realistically Expect?

According to the framework, the long-term goals of community-based youth development initiatives are to improve the long-term life chances of young people to become economically self-sufficient, to be healthy and have good family and social relationships, and to contribute to their community.

For economic self-sufficiency, all youth should expect as adults to be able support themselves and their families and have some discretionary resources beyond those required to put food on the table and a roof over their heads. They should have a decent job and the education or access to enough education to improve or change jobs.

For healthy family and social relationships, young people should grow up to be physically and mentally healthy, be good caregivers for their children, and have positive and dependable family and friendship networks.

Contributions to community could come in many forms, but we hope that our young people will look to do more than be taxpayers and law abiders—to contribute at a threshold level where they give something back to their community, however they define that community.

By highlighting these positive indicators, we do not mean to exclude negative markers of outcomes in these three areas. Meaningful decreases in welfare rolls,

---

[2] The following sections are abstracted from Connell and Gambone (1998).

behavior-based physical and mental health problems, child abuse and neglect, and incidences of violent crimes are important, but less ambitious, markers of these same three long-term outcomes.

What Developmental Outcomes are Most Likely to Lead to Early Adult Success?

Our review of the relevant literature suggests that the likelihood of these three goals being achieved increases dramatically if youth accomplish certain things as they move from childhood through adolescence. They must learn to be productive—to do well in school, develop outside interests, and acquire basic life-skills. They must learn to connect—to adults in their families and community, to their peers in positive and supportive ways, and to something larger than themselves. They must learn to navigate—on three fronts:

- Among changing conditions in their multiple worlds—their peer groups, families, schools, social groups, and neighborhoods, each of which may require different ways of behaving and, in some cases, even different languages.
- Along the developmental transitions from being taken care of to taking care of others, from mastering the physical challenges of being a child to the sexual challenges of being an adult, and from just learning about their world to developing their own identity and role in it.
- Around the lures of unhealthy and dangerous behaviors (drugs, alcohol, and unsafe sexual activity) and experiences of unfair treatment, rejections, and failures—challenges that all youth face but that are much more prevalent for children living in economically disadvantaged circumstances.

Research and common sense tell us that if young people can achieve these outcomes, their prospects as adults improve dramatically; if they don't, success as defined by the three long-term outcomes in this framework will be difficult to achieve.

What Supports and Opportunities Must Communities Provide to Youth?

The framework asserts that for youth to learn to be productive, connected, and able to navigate, they must experience a set of supports and opportunities that are the critical building blocks of development across all of the settings in which they spend their time. Research points to a short list of key experiences that are associated with the capacities we expect young people to have in order to achieve our goals for them:

- Adequate nutrition, health, and shelter. This first set of supports are the foundation on which youth can benefit from the others. If a young person is hungry, ill, or inadequately sheltered, it is much more difficult for him or her to benefit from even the most developmentally enriched social environment. Although every setting or organization may not be responsible for providing these supports, they must be addressed if we expect young people to grow.

• Multiple supportive relationships with adults and peers. Perhaps the most consistent and robust finding on human development is that experience of support from the people in one's environment, from infancy on, has broad impacts on later functioning across multiple domains. Relationships with both adults and peers are the source of the emotional support, guidance, and instrumental help that are critical to young people's capacity to feel connected to others, navigate day-to-day life, and engage in productive activities. Key experiences in supportive relationships include high, clear, and fair expectations and a sense of boundaries, respect, and dedication of key resources.

• Challenging and engaging activities and learning experiences. Youth, especially adolescents, need to experience a sense of growth and progress in developing skills and abilities. Whether in school, sports, arts, or a job, young people are engaged by—and benefit from—activities where they experience an increasing sense of competence and productivity. Conversely, they are bored by activities that do not challenge them in some way. Often in adolescence this boredom can lead to young people participating in high-risk activities because the healthier options in their lives do not offer the appropriate blend of challenge and sense of accomplishment.

• Meaningful opportunities for involvement and membership. As young people move into adolescence and need to begin the critical transition from being taken care of to taking care of themselves and others, they need ample opportunities to try on the adult roles they are preparing for. This means they need to participate in making age-appropriate decisions for themselves and others, ranging from deciding what activities to participate in to choosing responsible alternatives to negative behaviors and taking part in setting group rules for classrooms, teams, organizations, and the like. They also need to practice taking on leadership roles, such as peer leader, team captain, council member, or organizational representative. In order to develop a sense of connectedness and productivity, and to begin making decisions from a perspective that is less egocentric, young people also need to experience a sense of belonging. Specifically, they need to participate in groups of interconnected members, such as their families, clubs, teams, churches, theater groups, and other organizations that afford opportunities for youth to take on responsibilities. They also need to experience themselves as individuals who have something of value to contribute to their different communities. When healthy opportunities to belong are not found in their environments, young people will create less healthy versions, such as cliques and gangs.

- Physical and emotional safety. Finally, young people need to experience physical and emotional safety in their daily lives. With these supports, young people are able to confidently explore their full range of options for becoming productive and connected, and, when they experience challenges to navigate, they can focus their full attention on meeting these challenges. The absence of these supports has profound effects on their options and decisions: they become distracted from opportunities to be productive in school and other settings; some join gangs or carry weapons to protect themselves; and if youth feel consistently rejected, discriminated against, or under physical threat, adults' arguments for avoiding high risk behaviors become less compelling.

In sum, this framework suggests that the presence of these five supports and opportunities across settings at the community level will result in dramatic and immediate improvements in young people's productivity, connectedness, ability to navigate, and, in the longer term, their success as adults. Conversely, if these investments in youth are *not* made, we will continue to see a growing proportion of our young people move into adulthood ill-equipped, at best, to achieve the goals we have for them and, at worst, dangerous to themselves and others.

The presence of these supports and opportunities, then, becomes the non-negotiable of the youth development approach. They are the lens through which a community should first examine its ecology to identify what resources are available in the lives of its young people. They are the guideposts that communities can use to plan and assess these supports and their efforts to enrich and realign resources, with confidence that when these supports and opportunities are available for all youth, across settings, from ages 10 to 18, their developmental outcomes will improve dramatically. These are also the standards of practice to which individual organizations and programs working with youth should commit themselves and against which they should document their accomplishments.

COMMUNITY ACTION STRATEGIES

Figure 12.1 presents additional elements of the framework (Box D). These include three strategies that communities can implement to increase supports and opportunities for youth across the major settings in which they spend time: family and neighborhood, schools and other public institutions, and activities during gap periods. A fourth community strategy calls for policy and resource realignments to support the first three strategies. These strategies extend beyond the current focus in the youth development field on "gap" activities. Applying a youth development approach to this wider range of settings is essential if we are to achieve meaningful change in a broad and diverse population of youth at the community level.

We briefly describe and present a rationale for including these strategies in a youth development framework.

Strengthen the capacities of adults who live and work with young people in our communities to provide these supports and opportunities. History, research, and common sense tell us we cannot "program" or "service" young people into healthy development. Specific programs and high-quality youth services are key strategies for optimizing youth development outcomes, but, without caregivers, neighbors, and employers of young people providing the supports and opportunities at home, in their neighborhoods, and where they work, the impact of these strategies on youth will be minimal.

Any honest community effort to increase the supports and opportunities in the everyday lives of youth will and should inevitably bump up against the sensitive question of how to deal with families and family issues. In one sense, the case is clear-cut to include families in youth development approaches: the family is the single most critical source of support, encouragement, moral development, love, and sustenance for a young person. However, governments have limited their interventions in the families of youth on the principle that because children are under the jurisdiction of their parents, the state should not interfere, but rather play a protective or supportive role. Until recently, the state would intervene in family life only in instances of demonstrable and egregious failure to meet the basic needs of youth, resulting in foster care, child protection, and juvenile justice activities, or in the case of certifiable need, through the welfare system. However, in recent years there has been an increasing recognition that public policy and institutions have a role to play in supporting parents as they work to raise their children. This is evidenced in the creation of community-based, family support centers, a growing investment in developmental child care programs like Early Start and Head Start, and an increase in child rearing programs and interventions for parents in high risk categories (such as teen parents).

Nevertheless, most of the supportive interventions and policies have, to date, focused on the parents of young children in the hopes that early intervention would prevent problems and make it unnecessary to "interfere" later. However, parents of adolescents are in as great a need of support as are the parents of young children, especially in disadvantaged communities where the networks and resources for children from ages 10 to 18 are particularly thin. The youth development field has not directly involved families of youth, for the most part, and has not yet found a rationale or mode to do so comfortably and coherently. The reluctance to address the issue head-on is understandable, but that reluctance also circumscribes the impact our field and our approach can have and the issues we can give voice to.

Optimizing adult support of youth will also have to involve neighbors (many of whom are themselves parents) and employers of youth. Communities will need to understand and then build on youths' often casual but sometimes crucial contacts with neighbors and on their early work experiences to increase the supports and opportunities available to youth.

Specific interventions and broad, community-wide strategies to clarify and support what caregivers, neighbors, and employers can and should provide to youth must be brought into our field's purview. Otherwise, community initiatives are not going to achieve adequate thresholds of supports and opportunities to produce meaningful change in many young people's life chances.

Integrate and reform the large institutions and systems that affect young people. Reforming and coordinating public institutions have proven formidable challenges—that the field has usually sidestepped. The most glaring example is public education. Outside the home, schools are the main environment for young people. Long before youth development became a widely accepted concept, there were clamors for those institutions to change, to become more responsive and effective. *School reform* is still a central topic in most large cities, yet public education is an immense and densely packed sector—at times defensive and at times quite justified in being so. It also has a thicket of peripheral organizations working to serve, improve, and reform it, and its core activities have remained outside the scope of youth development efforts. Because public education has seemed too tough a nut to crack, youth development has avoided taking it on.

Reluctance to take on institutional issues extends beyond schools. Juvenile justice systems bear directly on the lives of many young people—young people whose development is most seriously devoid of support and opportunities and who are least likely to gain access to traditional, youth-serving organizations. Other public institutions and policies touch youth through separate funding streams that originate at federal and state levels—welfare, housing, drug and alcohol treatment, child care—and the programs often end up unorganized, unstrategic, and underfunded in poor communities. Seldom do these services build from a coherent recognition of what needs to be done to support youth. They respond most of all to the dictates of funders and must constantly order their work and priorities to keep their funding, even when inadequate. The past efforts to achieve "service integration," whether at national, state, or local levels, have generally had discouraging results. The few incentives to work together are heavily outweighed by funding dependency, inflexible rules, and institutional habits and culture long in the making.

The supports and opportunities described in the framework extend the idea of appropriate standards to all these institutions that serve youth. Once these non-negotiables for youth are embraced, these institutions can grapple with developing strategies and concrete processes for providing the supports and opportunities for their "shared" clients.

It is encouraging to note that some major educational reform efforts are using the supports and opportunities included in this framework—or conditions closely aligned with them—as guideposts. Comer's work is a prominent example. First Things First, the school reform framework of the Institute for Research and Reform in Education (IRRE; Connell, 1996), makes explicit links from changes in school structures and classroom practices to these supports and opportunities and, ultimately, to youth development outcomes.

Increase the number and quality of developmental activities available for young people before and after school, on weekends and holidays, and over the summer. Here is where our traditional definition of the youth development field fits into this unifying framework. Stronger and more widespread supports for youth outside their homes, schools, social service, and work experiences are essential to optimize youth development outcomes.

Key to this third strategy will be a full assessment of the supports and opportunities available in gap periods to all youth and particularly to youth that are hard to reach. Another key will be the capacity of the organizations currently providing these activities to absorb expanded responsibilities for different youth from those currently served.

Given what we already know from research on these gap periods, areas of programming and community-based activities that need to be strengthened and made more accessible are social-recreational, athletic, cultural, educational, and spiritual. We also must realize that adding new programming and activities is not enough. We need to set standards for the quality of these activities to provide designers, operators, and consumers of these programs and activities with ways of knowing that what is going on there, at minimum, does no harm and, at best, maximizes the supports and opportunities young people get.

Realign policies and resources in the public and private sector in ways that support the implementation of these strategies. The youth development field, even as it is currently defined, has recognized that without policy supports from municipal, state, and federal government, it will remain marginalized in its efforts to affect youth development outcomes. This framework broadens the field's purview to incorporate family supports, neighborhood revitalization, and institutional reform, as well as expanded youth development programming and activities. Common sense, if not scientific research, makes it clear that public policies will have to be realigned if this expanded set of strategies is to have any chance of being implemented. Policy should support thoughtful, innovative, and rigorous proposals by community stakeholders for providing supports and opportunities to youth across the settings in which they grow up. These proposals can include recommendations for policy realignments at the state and federal levels to support the proposed community strategies.

New resources will also be necessary, but from a political and practical standpoint, policy-makers will need evidence early on that existing resources are being realigned to begin implementing these three sets of community strategies. Without this step, result-free resource allocations of the past will haunt and ultimately undo any efforts to marshall new resources.

Our own strong belief is that all four of these strategies must be in place if we are to ever see the change that we are seeking for our youth. In some communities, some of these strategies are already in place and only need to be augmented by those that are not. For other communities—particularly those where youth experience very few supports and opportunities and have little chance to prepare for successful adulthood—the price of piecemeal interventions for them and our country is severe and disturbing. First, if we continue to tinker around the edges of these young people's lives, community-level outcomes for youth will not improve in any meaningful way. This failure will only deepen the cynicism of investors in youth development, including participants themselves, and make future investments more difficult to obtain. Second, the final fall-out of a "big goals, little intervention" approach will be further entrenchment of "blame the victim" scenarios in some professional, community, and policy quarters.

Building Community Capacity and Conditions for Change

By definition, realignment of political, economic, and human resources toward new and better youth development practices means some old practices and policies will have to go. For adults living and working with youth, for public institutions, and for community-based organizations that serve youth and their families, making these choices and living with their personal and political consequences will not be an easy task. Therefore, these choices and their associated risks cannot be delegated or assigned to any single community stakeholder group.

Communities will need mobilization efforts to create conditions that encourage *all* stakeholders to put their oars in the water and pull together. In this framework (Fig. 12.1, Box E), we have identified four conditions that mobilization efforts should seek to achieve to launch and sustain implementation of the community strategies (Fig. 12.1, Box D).

First, there must be a sense of urgency among all stakeholders—a sense that "Something that I care about is very wrong and must be made right."

Second, stakeholders must believe that these changes are possible to achieve. Success stories have to be told and believed and credible evidence of the efficacy of these strategies must be made available in compelling ways.

Third, people asked to risk their comfort with the status quo have to see others doing the same; they have to sense equity in the pain and gain of change. For instance, when school reform means teachers change what they do but no one else does, it doesn't work.

Finally, before individual and institutional stakeholders put themselves on the line, they will have to believe that business as usual is going to give way to innovation. The decline in supports and opportunities available to youth in many economically threatened communities over the past 50 years has been clear and dramatic. At times it appears inexorable. Conversely, intentional programmatic investments to enrich these supports and opportunities over this same period have been intermittent, erratic in approach, and ephemeral in impact. With this back-drop, this new generation of community initiatives needs a collective sense by all stakeholders that "this is the big one," that this, too, will not pass, or the energy necessary to implement these bold and high-stakes strategies will not be there.

Creating these conditions is a tall order but we believe that activities focused on building stakeholders' awareness, knowledge, engagement, and commitment to the story this framework tells can work. For example, stakeholders who see the gap between where youth are and where they need to be can create a sense of urgency. Stakeholders who interact with youth and adults in other communities like theirs, where their concerted efforts are closing this gap, gain a sense of pos-sibility that this can happen in their community too. Achieving a sense of equity will require that stakeholders across existing power relationships engage in honest discussions about what they can do individually and collectively to implement these community strategies, the risks involved in doing so, and the supports needed from each other to pull it off. Finally, change of this kind only becomes inevitable when key stakeholders—those who control political and financial resources in the community and those who have immediate and persistent impact on the lives of youth—jointly agree that the risk-reward ratio makes business as usual the more painful option.

CONCLUSIONS AND RECOMMENDATIONS

Public and private investments in improving individual and collective quality of life have returned to more place-based, locally driven strategies. These compre-hensive community initiatives (CCIs) are being implemented primarily in urban areas—in neighborhoods and cities unaffected or even adversely affected by the same macro-economic forces that have brought increased prosperity to other geo-graphic areas and economic segments of our society. Fortunately, the planning and implementation strategies for revitalizing these communities are now being enriched by unprecedented levels of research on how individuals and their con-texts interact in these communities.

In our example, we presented a research-based theory of change for commu-nity action, where community action is focused on improving youth development outcomes (Connell & Gambone, 1998). Some of this theory's hypotheses are not yet grounded in research, particularly those specifying links between community mobilization (Box E) and the successful implementation of the four community action strategies (Box D). As with broader based CCIs, these mobilization issues of how to create community conditions and build capacity for change are the most pressing. In our view, formulating and testing these hypotheses about what it will take to implement a broad but targeted set of community action strategies should provide vital information to the dozens of CCIs now underway. Community initiatives focusing on youth development offer a unique opportunity to contribute to this broader CCI movement. Why? Because the targets of these capacity-building activities are clearer and more easily understood by community and external stakeholders than are those in other community-based initiatives with broader human, social, and economic agendas. Yet, the community action strategies proposed in the youth development framework engage a broad array of community stakeholders and issues.

Given the potential these community-based youth development initiatives have to inform the broader CCI agenda, we concur with Connell and Gambone (1998), who have made ten recommendations for how investors, intermediaries, and researchers can strengthen these initiatives and maximize learning from them.

For Public and Private Investors:

1. Adopt a community focus to financing youth activities that recognizes the fundamental need for young people to receive supports and opportunities (Box C) across all of the settings where they spend time (Box D) in order to have a reasonable chance of achieving the youth development outcomes (Box B).
2. Provide funding and technical assistance to communities to develop new or strengthen existing local intermediaries to act as managers/conveners, capacity-building agents, mobilization centers, and accountability coordinators (Box E) for these initiatives.
3. Work with community stakeholders to define benchmarks for each stage of investment: creating conditions for change, planning change, implementing change, learning from change.
4. Have achievement of these outcomes trigger new investments in the next stage of work.
5. Support technical assistance providers (local and national) to anticipate and be responsive to mobilization, planning, implementation, and evaluation challenges faced in these initiatives.

For National Intermediaries
(Research and Technical Assistance Organizations):

1. Assess your organizations' capacities to support these initiatives as they mobilize around, plan, implement, and evaluate the community action strategies in the framework.
2. Disseminate this information immediately to communities, investors, and other intermediaries involved in community-based youth development initiatives.
3. Use these organizational assessments to create intermediary partnerships that can respond to a given community initiative's full range of external support needs.

4.   Conduct formative research on early work with communities using this and similar frameworks and meet to discuss implications for future support   activities.

For Researchers and Scholars:

Develop research and scholarly agendas that test and enrich key hypotheses guiding current initiatives. For example:

- Examine how different dimensions of social capital affect parenting practices.
- Delineate dimensions of work-related experience most beneficial to youth development outcomes.
- Identify gap period activities yielding highest levels of engagement and participation for youth within and across diverse groups.
- Isolate key elements of collaborative activities among community stakeholders that yield sustained and effective implementation of community action strategies.
- Provide description and analysis of institutional reform processes leading to effective practices with youth and their families.
- Document variation in development of community leaders—youth and adults.

REFERENCES

Aber, J. L., Brooks-Gunn, J., & Duncan, G. (Eds.) (1997). *Neighborhood poverty: Context and consequences for children,* Vol. 1. New York: Russell Sage Foundation.

Berrueta-Clement, J., Schweinhart, L. J., Barnett, W. S., Epstein, A. S., & Weikart, D. P. (1984). *Changed lives: The affects of the Perry Preschool Program on studies through age 19.* Ypsilanti, MI: High School Educational Research Foundation.

Briggs, X. N. (1996). *Brown kids in White suburbs: Housing mobility, neighborhood effects and the social capital of poor youth.* Ph.D. dissertation. Teachers College, NY.

Briggs, X., & Mueller, E. J. with Sullivan, M. (1997). *From neighborhood to community: Evidence on the social effects of community development.* New York: Community Development Research Center, New School for Social Research.

Bronfenbrenner, U. (1977). Toward an experimental ecology of human development. American Psychologist, *32,* 513–31.

Bronfenbrenner, U. (1979). *The ecology of human development: Experiments by nature and design.* Cambridge, MA: Harvard University Press.

Brooks-Gunn, J., Duncan, G. J., Klebanov, P. K., & Sealand, N. (1993). Do neighborhoods influence child and adolescent development? *American Journal of Sociology, 99*(2), 353–395.

Burton, L. M., Allison, K., & Obeidallah, D. A. (1995). Social context and adolescents perspectives on development among inner-city African-American teens. In L. Crockett & A. C. Crouter (Eds.), *Pathways through adolescence: Individual development in relation to context.* Hillsdale, NJ: Lawrence Erlbaum.

Case, A. C., & Katz, L. F. (1991). *The company you keep: The effects of family and neighborhood on disadvantaged youths.* Working Paper 3705. Cambridge, MA: National Bureau of Economic Research.

Castells, M. (1996). *The rise of the network society* (Vol. 1). Oxford: Blackwell.

Coleman, J. S. (1990). *Foundations of social theory.* Cambridge, MA: Harvard University Press.

Comer, J. P., Hayes, N. M., Joyner, E. T., & Ben-Avic, M. (Eds.) (1996). *Rallying the whole village: The Comer process for reforming education.* New York: Teachers College Press.

Connell, J. P. (1996). *First things first: A framework for successful school-site reform.* Philadelphia, PA: Institute for Research and Reform in Education.

Connell, J. P. (1998). Comment on: What community supplies, by Robert Sampson. In W. T. Dickens & R. F. Ferguson (Eds.), *Urban problems and community development* (pp. 279–286). Washington, DC: Brookings Institution.

Connell, J. P., Aber, J. L., & Walker, G. (1995). How do urban communities affect youth? Using social science research to inform the design and evaluation of comprehensive community initiatives. In J. P. Connell, A. C. Kubisch, L. Schorr, & C. Weiss (Eds.), *New approaches to evaluating community initiatives: Concepts, methods, and contexts* (pp. 93–125). Washington, DC: Aspen Institute.

Connell, J. P., & Gambone, M. A. (1998). A community action framework for youth development: Rationale and early applications. In G. Walker, K. Pittman, & D. Watson (Eds.), *Directions for youth development.* Lawrence, KS: Conestoga Press.

Connell, J. P., Gambone, M. A., & Smith, T. (1998). *Youth development in community settings: Challenges for our field and our approach.* Philadelphia, PA: Institute for Research and Reform in Education.

Connell, J. P., & Kubisch, A. C. (1998). Applying a theory of change approach to the evaluation of comprehensive community initiatives: Progress, prospects, and problems. In K. Fulbright-Anderson, A. C. Kubisch, & J. P. Connell (Eds.), *New approaches to evaluating community initiatives: Theory, measurement, and analysis* (pp. 1–44). Washington, DC: Aspen Institute.

Crane, J. (1991). *Effects of neighborhoods on dropping out of school and teenage childbearing.* In C. Jencks & P. Peterson (Eds.), *The urban underclass.* Washington, DC: Brookings Institution.

Freedman, R. (1982). Economic determinants of geographic and individual variation in the labor market position of young persons. In R. Freedman & D. Wise (Eds.), *The youth labor market problem: Its nature, causes, and consequences.* Chicago: University of Chicago Press.

Gambone, M. A. (1998). Challenges measurement in community change initiative. In K. Fulbright-Anderson, A. C. Kubisch, & J. P. Connell (Eds.), *New approaches to evaluating community initiative: Theory measurement and analysis* (pp. 149–164). Washington, DC: Aspen Institute.

Gambone, M. A. (1999). *Community action and youth development.* Maryland: Aspen Institute Roundtable for Comprehensive Community Initiatives.

Halpern, R. (1995). *Rebuilding the inner city: A history of neighborhoods initiatives to address poverty in the United States.* New York: Columbia University Press.

Hawkins, D. J., Catalano, R. F. Jr., & Associates. (1992). *Communities That Care: Action for Drug Abuse Prevention.* San Francisco: Jossey-Bass.

Jackson, M., & Marris, P. (1996). *Collaborative comprehensive community initiatives: Overview of an emerging community improvement orientation.* Washington, DC: The Urban Institute.

Kawachi, I. (1998). *Social cohesion and health.* Boston, MA: Harvard School of Public Health.

Kingsley, T. G., McNeely, J., & Gibson, J. O. (1997). *Community building: Coming of age.* Washington, DC: The Urban Institute.

Kubisch, A. C., Brown, P., Chaskin, R., Hirota, J., Joseph, M., Richman, H., & Roberts, M. (1997). *Voices from the field: Learning from comprehensive community initiatives.* Washington, DC: Aspen Institute.

Kubisch, A. C., Weiss, C. H., Schorr, L. B., & Connell, J. P. (1995). Introduction. In J. P. Connell et al. (Eds.), *New approaches to evaluating community initiatives: Concepts, methods, and contexts.* Washington, DC: The Aspen Institute.

Leiterman, M., & Stillman, J. (1993). *Building community.* New York: Local Initiatives Support Corporation.

O'Connor, A. (1995). Evaluating comprehensive community initiatives: A view from history. In J. P. Connell, A. C. Kubisch, L. Schorr, & C. Weiss (Eds.), *New approaches to evaluating community initiatives: Concepts, methods, and contexts* (pp. 23–63). Washington, DC: The Aspen Institute.

O'Connor, A. (1999). Swimming against the tide: A brief history of federal policy in poor communities. In W. T. Dickens & R. F. Ferguson (Eds.), *Urban problems and community development* (pp. 76–137). Washington, DC: The Brookings Institution.

Pitcoff, W. (1997). Redefining community development. *Shelterforce, 19*(6), 2–14.

Pitcoff, W. (1998). Redefining community development, Part II: Collaborating for change. *Shelterforce, 19*(1), 2–17.

Pittman, K., & Cahill, M. (1992). *Pushing the boundaries of education: The implications of a youth development approach to education policies, structures, and collaborations.* Commissioned paper for Council of Chief State School Offices, Washington, DC: Center for Youth Development and Policy Research.

Putnam, R. (1993a). The prosperous community: Social capital and public life. *American Prospect, 25,* 26–28.

Putnam, R. (1993b). *Making democracy work: Civic traditions in modern Italy.* Princeton, NJ: Princeton University Press.

Sampson, R. J. (1999, November). *What community supply.* In W. T. Dickens & R. F. Ferguson (Eds.), *Urban problems and community development* (pp. 241–279). Washington, DC: Brookings Institution.

Schorr, L. B. (1997). Synergy: Putting it all together to transform neighborhoods. In *Common purpose: Strengthening families and neighborhoods to rebuild America* (pp. 301–379). New York: Doubleday.

Spencer, M. B. (1986). Risk and resilience: How black children cope with stress. *Journal of Social Science, 71*(1), 22–36.

Stone, R. (1996). *Core issues in comprehensive community-building initiatives.* Chicago: Chapin Hall Center for Children.

Unger, D., & Wandersman, A. (1982). Neighboring in an urban environment. *American Journal of Community Psychology, 4,* 185–193.

Walsh, J. (1996). *Stories of renewal: Community building and the future of urban america.* New York: The Rockefeller Foundation.

Walker, G., & Villela-Velez, F. (1992). *Anatomy of a demonstration: The Summer Training and Education Program (STEP) from pilot through replication and postprogram impact.* Philadelphia, PA: Public/Private Ventures.

Wanderman, A., Roth, R., & Prestby, J. (1985). Keeping community organizations alive. *Citizen Participation, 6*(4), 16–19.

Wandersman, A., Heller, K., Price, R., Riger, S., & Reinbarz, S. (1984).*Psychology and community change* (2nd ed.). Homewood, IL: Dorsey. (Citizen participation, chap. 10.)

Wellman, B., & Leighton, B. (1979). Networks, neighborhoods, and communities: Approaches to the study of the community question. *Urban Affairs Quarterly, 14,* 363–390.

Wilson, W. J. (1996). *When work disappears: The world of the new urban poor.* New York: Alfred A. Knopf.

Wynn, J. R., Costello, J., Halpern, R., & Richman, H. (1994). *Children, families, and communities: A new approach to social services.* Chicago: University of Chicago, Chapin Hall Center for Children.

Youniss, J., McLellan, J. A., & Vates, M. (1997). What we know about engendering civic identity. *The American Behavioral Scientist, 40*(5), 620–631.

13

On Mount and Fayette: Implications for Comprehensive Youth Development Approaches

Ralph B. Taylor

Temple University and National Consortium on Violence Research

RECENT URBAN ETHNOGRAPHIES

Let me start my comments on Connell's and Kubisch's paper by pointing our attention in a seemingly unrelated direction: recent urban, inner-city ethnographies. To mention just a few—and I apologize if I am leaving out your favorite: Philippe Bourgois's *In Search of Respect* done in Spanish Harlem, Terry Williams' *The Cocaine Kids* done on the upper west side of New York City, Mercer Sullivan's multi-neighborhood *Getting Paid*, and Eli Anderson's *Streetwise*, done in some neighborhoods near the University of Pennsylvania (Anderson 1991; Bourgois 1996; Sullivan 1989; Williams 1989).

But let me turn to one you may not have heard of: David Simon's and Ed Burns' *The Corner: A Year in the Life of an Inner-City Neighborhood* (New York: Broadway Books, 1997). Simon is a former *Baltimore Sun* reporter and author of *Homicide;* Burns is a former Baltimore City detective.

They spent a year—1993—"hanging out" with people on a drug corner—Mount and Fayette—in the Franklin Square neighborhood on the west side of Baltimore. Their purpose was to learn about the lives these people led, and understand things from their point of view. The corner was one of about 120 open air drug markets active at the time in the city. In about a 10 block radius there were about 15 open air drug markets.

The neighborhood in 1990 was extremely impoverished. If we look at the census tract information for the two block groups nearest the main location, we see poverty numbers that are high, and extremely high for very young children under five.

Census Tract 1901 2 Block Groups Closest to 1625 W. Fayette		
1990 % in Poverty	Block Group 4	Block Group 5
All	46	82
17 and under	49	64
5 and under	80	100

I mention this ethnography for three reasons. It centers much of its attention on a teenager, DeAndre McCullough, making his transition to adulthood. He is fifteen when the story starts. During the course of the year in which he is followed he gives up on school, serves time in a juvenile lockup, gets sentenced to juvenile probation, increases his profile in the local drug dealing trade, becomes a father, participates in a city-wide oratory contest, joins and leaves a rec center basketball team, and more. Second, the ethnography, following DeAndre and his relatives, friends, and acquaintances, provides detail on the kinds of settings inhabited by teens and children in extremely disadvantaged neighborhoods. We can gain a sense of where the resources and threats are for children of different ages as they navigate their neighborhood. It is possible through the ethnography to gain a sense of the lifespace of these individuals. Third, although I am not intimately familiar with the neighborhoods described I was conducting research in adjoining neighborhoods, Southwest Civic and Union Square, in 1994, the year after the ethnography was completed. The context resonated for me.

The drug corner, not surprisingly, dominated the lives of preteen and teen males. It was the dominant arena for economic activity. But the lure was not just economic even though "the money is its own argument - not punch-the-clock, sweep-the-floor, and wait-for-next-Friday money, but cash money, paid out instantly to the vacant-eyed kids serving the stuff" (p. 59). The lure that Simon and Burns describe and that Williams and Bourgois detail similarly, is self respect.

> They are working the package with the hidden knowledge that they will fall, that with rare exception, the money won't last and the ride will be over in six months, or four, or three. They do it not so much for the cash ... but for the brief sense of self. All of them are cloaked in the same gangster dream, all of them cursed by the lie that says they finally have a stake in something. By such standards, the corner proves itself every day. That it destroys whatever it touches hardly matters; for an instant in time, at least, those who serve the corners have standing and purpose (p. 59).

The intrusion of the drug corners even into the lives of those years from being teenagers is apparent as well. The rec center leader, Ella Franklin, negotiated with corner dealers to suspend their activities for a short time one day each week while summer campers walk past. Her negotiations had some impact.

> 'Time out' yells one of the lookouts, seeing the six-year olds leading the way out of St. Martins and down the sidewalk past Echo House, on their way to the Francis Woods Pool. The bird-call hawking of the touts dies away; the slingers take a step or two down Mount.
>
> It's not a complete concession by any means – the corner world is too far gone to get everything right on the first day. As the children saunter hand-in-hand across Mount, Buster is still at the pay phone, arguing with one of his runners. Down the block, Alfred keeps working that ground stash, unwilling to give a white boy chance enough to talk past him and cop from some-one else ... By the second Monday, with camp in full swing, she can watch as the children file out the church doors and tramp down the sidewalk, knowing that what awaits them down at the corner is nothing worse than an awkward pause in the action. Every now and then, she hears someone trying to keep it in check (p. 297).

In a later scene at the rec playground, the authors describe third, fourth, and fifth graders arguing about whether two people in a car, sitting on a house across the street, are shooters or not.

Four points are clear from this ethnography. Drug buying and selling activities loom extremely large in the lives of male children and male teens in extremely disadvantaged neighborhoods. Second, the draw here is not just economic but, when seen from the participants' perspective, psychological as well. They can be somebody, even though they know the run is short. Third, much of the funds pumped into these markets come from welfare payments. Those payments are slated to end in March of next year. The impacts on local drug markets are not clear. Finally, given the scale and immediacy of the drug-based economy, other entry level jobs are simply not competitive, even if they were easy to get to, which they are not.

Comprehensive Approach to Initiatives

Let me now turn to the paper just presented, and point toward some key features of that, and then use those comments to ground one small suggestion.

James Connell's and Anne Kubisch's paper on community approaches to improving outcomes for urban children, youths, and values proves valuable for many reasons. Most importantly, the authors detail the limitations of previous community-based initiatives, contrasting those with the more comprehensive approaches currently being applied. They highlight the limited conceptual thinking that has guided the narrower approaches up to now. They underscore the challenges to the more comprehensive approaches coming from policy makers placing themselves either among the behavioralists or the structuralists. These divisions in the worldviews of policy makers exist as well among academic researchers and program evaluators.

I agree with these authors when they point toward a perhaps brighter future where "people oriented" and "place oriented" strategies are being replaced by research examining interactions between individual outcomes and the surrounding social, institutional, physical, economic, and cultural contexts.

The authors point out areas where program impacts, even if they are comprehensive, are likely to be limited: schools, juvenile justice, and families, among others. In a masterful understatement the authors tell us "reforming and coordinating public institutions [such as schools] have proven formidable challenges." The family is out of bounds, the authors point out, in many circumstances because on principle the state should not be interfering when the parents have jurisdiction. As one who many years ago worked with pre-delinquents in a residential treatment center, and wanted to strangle parents on more than one occasion, I am pleased to see the slow changes described by the authors where outside supports for parents of children and teens seem to be increasing.

The more comprehensive approach detailed by the authors recognizes two fundamental points about the lives of children and teens. First, what happens in different formal and informal institutional settings—family, school, and rec center for example—weave together. What happens in one setting carries over to the other. Second, children spend substantial amounts of time in "gap" activities when they are transiting their neighborhood or occupying locations without direct adult supervision, walking to school, or hanging out front after school waiting for their mothers or fathers to come home and let them in, or on the playground without supervision. What is happening in these gap periods, the comprehensive programs recognize, is important.

The authors advocate, after identifying which particular supports and opportunities are required— they term these the "non-negotiables of the youth-development approach"—programs that systematically increase available resources. In order to learn more about these resources they suggest "a community should first examine its ecology to identify what resources are available in the lives of its young people."

I want to take this suggestion seriously, and amend it slightly. A community should first examine its ecology to identify *both* what resources are available and what threats exist to the lives of its young people. In the same way that if we focus solely on deficits we have half the picture, if we focus solely on opportunities and ignore threats, we still have half the picture. Such a directive points us towards a comprehensive community assessment. How are we to do this?

Before I get to the how let me also underscore the importance of such a venture from an evaluation perspective. Connell and Kubisch point out two problems with evaluations. Either they concentrate on "hard" outcomes that are too far removed from the program efforts themselves—they term them broad social indicators that are relatively easy to measure—or evaluators complete process analyses that are little more than stories. If we are to learn more about what programs are achieving, we need well-grounded indicators for intermediate outcomes.

In short, what I am suggesting is that if we take the criticisms being leveled here against both limited program initiatives and limited assessment ventures, and if we take the "comprehensive" idea seriously, we need to gauge on an ongoing basis the shifts taking place in resources and threats present in the lives of the children and teens whose lives we hope to affect.

The same comprehensive assessment is suggested, albeit along different lines, by Sampson in his reference to ecometrics in his work with Raudenbush, and by Spencer, again along some very different lines too, with her focus on the Phenomenological Variant of Ecological Systems Theory. But the suggestions in the current paper being discussed, and in these other two papers, point us toward a more comprehensive understanding of the spaces the children and teens move through.

What is needed, I would suggest, to get toward this more comprehensive understanding, is a theoretically grounded assessment **that can tell us how the conditions around children and pre-teens are changing as a result of comprehensive initiatives.** In short, we need to build the research infrastructure to obtain comprehensive measurements of changes in the threat and opportunity structures.

To get at these structures I suggest we use ecological psychology, originally developed by the late Roger Barker and his many colleagues, including Herbert Wright, Phil Schoggen, Paul Gump, and many others (Barker, 1968; Wicker, 1979, 1987; Willems & Raush, 1969).

One of the key findings emerging from ecological psychology was the behavior setting (Wicker, 1987). Behavior settings are freestanding 'natural' units of the everyday environment with recurring patterns of behavior—standing patterns of behaviors—surrounded and supported by a physical environment. These units, behavior settings, organize and **are** community life. From the Simon and Burns ethnography examples would include the corner store; classes at the rec center; church services; funerals; basketball practices at the rec center; various corner drug markets; the drug rehab center; the scrap iron yard where you could trade metal for cash; and so on.

Barker and his colleagues carried out years of field research in a small Kansas town, and later in a small town in England, documenting and describing the extant behavior settings through which children and adults moved. In a related vein of research they focused on the individual stream of behavior, seeking to understand how a child's stream of ongoing behavior was conditioned by various behavior settings.

Barker's rules for identifying behavior settings are clear and straightforward. The work is not easy, and is labor intensive, but the result can be an agreed-upon, externally valid description of the comprehensive community through with a child or a pre-teen moves.

Simon and Burns' book provides numerous examples detailing how different youth's participation in resource-laden and threat-laden settings varied across individuals, and across time for specific individuals, **and** how those variations linked to prosocial or antisocial outcomes.

In a couple of papers, one recent, one not so recent, I have tried to apply behavior setting theories to our understanding of order and disorder in urban residential environments (Taylor, 1987, 1997). Other researchers likewise are attempting that connection (Mazzerolle, Kadleck, & Roehl, 1998).

I would suggest that one of the most important intermediate outcomes to be measured in a comprehensive community initiative is shifts in types and strengths of behavior settings in the target community that draw in children, preteens, and teens. Behavior settings, such as drug markets, that represent threats to the goals described by Connell and Kubish, should decline in spatial extent, hours of operation, the number of people involved in maintaining those settings, or how actively people are involved in those settings. Particularly important from a youth development perspective will be the rates at which youth aged 11–17 participate in these settings.

Behavior settings through which targeted youth can reach some of the positive goals described should increase in spatial extent, number that can be accommodated, density of adult supervision networks, intensity of youth involvement, and hours of operation. These settings would include after-school programs, mentoring programs, supervised sports or recreation activities, and the like.

If a comprehensive community initiative is having an impact, across the community targeted we should see shifts in teen and pre-teen participation rates in threatening vs. supportive behavior settings, or at the least decreasing involvement in the first type and increasing involvement in the second type.

What is needed are a series of urban field stations documenting shifts in community behavior settings over time, staffed by researchers in combination with local residents. We need an assessment approach that taps the intermediate shifts as a program alters events and opportunities in a locale, and that has a scope broad enough to match with the initiative itself.

Such an approach goes beyond the relatively innovative ecometrics suggested by Sampson and Raudenbush because it will unearth the free-standing units in the public social environment, and it will document how those shift over time. If we are changing the lives of youth in communities, we need to be able to document the ways that that is happening.

Setting up and maintaining urban field stations to document shifts in community public life presents numerous challenges. I mention just a few here.

(1) The researcher needs to know beforehand which communities are in future likely to be sites for comprehensive communities. This requires local knowledge of community dynamics. The researcher needs to know who the actors are and when an initiative is likely. An alternative, and perhaps easier approach, how-

ever, would be for the researcher in collaboration with local community leaders to commit to a particular locale, and then seek subsequent funding for a comprehensive initiative. It the community has strong, documented needs, and an operating field station generating data to assist in evaluating initiatives, a stronger case can be made for attracting funding.

(2) It will take considerable time and effort for the researchers to develop working relationships with local leaders and residents. The difficulties in establishing trust are not to be over-estimated. But if local leaders can be treated as partners in the setup phase, and if researchers convincingly demonstrate their commitment to training and employing local residents in observing, data recording, and data processing, these barriers can be overcome.

(3) The continuous funding of such a field station is expensive; researchers will devote significant fractions of their efforts to seeking additional funding sources. This enterprise is not a quick-return venture, but rather one for committed researchers.

To focus for a moment on children and violence in inner-city neighborhoods, consider the advantage of developing comprehensive profiles of the behavior settings through which children move. Surveys tell us that children are exposed to a high level of violence in inner-city locations, and that high levels of exposure link to social deficits and feelings of vulnerability (Cooley-Quille et al., 1995; Schwab-Stone et al., 1995). But these studies can only provide a general indication of the amounts and types of violence experienced by children and pre-teens in these settings. Detailed descriptions of the behavior settings through which they move may help us better understand how violence emerges from everyday routine activities, and, therefore, how best to prevent it in these contexts.

I recognize that the clarion call being issued here is a simple one to sound and an extremely difficult one to act on. But the important points would seem to be first, that we do have models of how to do this successfully and, second, that if we want to promote evaluations that do justice to the truly comprehensive initiatives to which neighborhood leaders are turning, we need such an approach.

ACKNOWLEDGMENTS

The author appreciated helpful comments on an earlier draft from Ron Davis. Address correspondence to the author at Department of Criminal Justice, Gladfelter Hall, Temple University, Philadelphia, PA 19122 (ralph@blue.temple.edu).

REFERENCES

Anderson, E. (1991). *Streetwise: Race, class and change in an urban community.* Chicago: University of Chicago Press.

Barker, R. G. (1968). *Ecological psychology.* Stanford: Stanford University Press.

Bourgois, P. (1996). *In search of respect.* Cambridge: Cambridge University Press.

Cooley-Quille, M. R., Turner, S. M., & Beidel, D. C. (1995). Emotional impact of children's exposure to community violence: A Preliminary study. *Journal of the American Academy of Child and Adolescent Psychiatry, 34,* 1362–1368.

Mazzerolle, L. G., Kadleck, C., & Roehl, J. (1998). Controlling drug and disorder problems: The role of place managers. *Criminology, 36,* 371–404.

Schwab-Stone, M., Ayers, T. S., & Kasprow, W. (1995). No safe haven: A Study of violence exposure in an urban community. *Journal of the American Academy of Child and Adolescent Psychiatry, 34,* 1343–1352.

Simon, D., & Burns, E. (1997). *The corner: A year in the life of an inner-city neighborhood.* New York: Broadway Books.

Sullivan, M. (1989). *Getting paid: Youth crime and work in the inner city.* Ithaca, NY: Cornell University Press.

Taylor, R. B. (1987). Toward an environmental psychology of disorder. In D. Stokols & I. Altman (Eds.), *Handbook of environmental psychology.* New York: Wiley.

Taylor, R. B. (1997). Social order and disorder of streetblocks and neighborhoods: Ecology, microecology and the systemic model of social disorganization. *Journal of Research in Crime and Delinquency, 33,* 113–155.

Wicker, A. W. (1979). *Introduction to ecological psychology.* Monterey: Brooks/Cole.

Wicker, A. W. (1987). Behavior settings reconsidered: Temporal stages, resources, internal dynamics, context. In D. Stokols & I. Altman (Eds.), *Handbook of environmental psychology.* New York: Wiley.

Willems, E. P., & Raush, H. L. (1969). *Naturalistic viewpoints in psychological research.* New York: Holt, Rinehart, and Winston.

Williams, T. (1989) *The cocaine kids.* Reading, MA: Addison-Wesley.

14

Developmental and Ecological Considerations in Implementing Community Action Strategies for Children and Youth

Mark Greenberg
The Pennsylvania State University

"The test of the morality of a society is what is does for its children."
—Dietrich Bonhoffer

THE CURRENT STATE OF AFFAIRS

As we approach the 21st century, many young people face greater risks to their health and social development than ever before (Hamburg, 1992; Takanishi, 1993). Damaging adolescent problems such as drug abuse, teenage pregnancy, delinquency, suicide attempts, and school failure are strongly related to lack of parental monitoring, inconsistent discipline, poor communication, and family discord (Dryfoos, 1990).

In certain domains, today's young people engage in substantially more health-risk behavior than did their counterparts from the 1960s (National Commission on the Role of the School and the Community in Improving Adolescent Health, 1990). Dryfoos (1997) recently estimated that 30% of 14- to 17-year olds regularly engage in multiple high-risk behaviors, and an additional 35% experiment with various high-risk behaviors.

Zill and Nord (1994) pointed out that structural changes in families are not as critical for successful child development as how a family carries out three core responsibilities that society expects from it. First, families are expected to provide for the basic physical needs of young people, including food, clothing, and shelter. Second, families have the primary responsibility to educate children to respect the rights of others, to differentiate right from wrong, and to value other societal institutions. Third, it is important for families to monitor and supervise children's daily activities to protect them from harm and to make sure that they conform to society's rules. But of course families don't do this alone; they do it in concert with friends, relatives, churches, and other social institutions.

Changes in the American economy have made it increasingly difficult for many parents to provide for the basic needs of their children (Zill & Nord, 1994).

It is also difficult for families to combat negative peer influences that may be contrary to the priorities of parents. Such influences are often extended and reinforced by the media. At the same time, adult authority has become weaker and more fragmented in recent years. It is a challenge for parents to maintain control as their children grow older. Parents face the task of helping their children become more independent as they mature, while concurrently monitoring the influences of peers and other forces in their children's lives.

In her assessment regarding the functioning of children and families, Dryfoos (1994) pointed out the following: (a) A significant proportion of children will fail to grow into contributing adults unless there are major changes in the way they are taught and nurtured; (b) Although families and schools traditionally carried out the responsibilities for raising and educating children, they require transformation to fulfill these obligations more effectively; and (c) New kinds of community resources and arrangements are needed to support the development of children into responsible, productive, fully contributing members of society.

It is within this social-historical context that Connell and Kubisch (chap. 12, this volume) present their comprehensive model, which attempts to unite and integrate effective models of youth development and the community action framework. By utilizing an ecological-developmental framework, they advance both domains towards a new level of integration. In doing so, they elaborate on a number of tensions in the field, on which I comment.

THE DIALECTIC OF PEOPLE VERSUS PLACES

As Connell (chap. 12, this volume) points out, the balance of people versus places is an important one. This is because developing a community's infrastructure, both from an economic and a services perspective, is likely to lead to changes that might also improve the skills or tools of individuals in those neighborhoods. For example, creating jobs, attracting better quality service-oriented businesses and shops to a neighborhood, and improving the quality of community services (for example, policing) make that neighborhood more attractive to others. As a result, there is likely to be less out-migration and greater stability in the neighborhood. This stability itself provides instrumental and emotional support and a sense of belonging to residents. As a result of this economic and structural stability, there is also likely to be greater investment in school, agencies, and youth development.

An opposite causal effect is also likely. That is, providing individuals with new skills or abilities may lead to improvements for the neighborhood itself. For example, having children and youth remain in school and involving them in healthy activities is likely to reduce crime and thus attract investment in the neighborhood; as a result, the neighborhood is apt to stabilize. However, if there is little investment in the neighborhood, it is likely that there will be more out-migration by the persons who benefit most from the "people-oriented" interventions. For example, my own experience with preventive intervention in high-crime neighborhoods showed that as parents become more aware of the developmental and social issues that they and their children face, one of the most beneficial moves parents believe they can make is to decide to leave a particularly "dangerous" neighborhood and find housing in one that is less threatening. Findings described by Duncan and Raudenbush (chap. 8, this volume) indicate that parent beliefs can indeed be true; families who move their children from more dangerous and unsafe housing situations to other neighborhoods with less disadvantage have children who show improvements in competence. Thus, an individual-skills level intervention alone may benefit a particular child or family, but not the neighborhood as a community.

This dialectic between people and places has slowly moved to a more synthetic model that attempts to incorporate both person and places models in new-look community initiatives. The newer models attempt to utilize both citizen-shaped decision-making and expert advice in order to both make structural changes at the level of institutions and their policies and provide more integrated skills and services to individuals at most need in the community. These Comprehensive Community Initiatives (CCIs) attempt to combine efforts to work across the social, economic, and physical spheres of action. New terms such as *comprehensive* and *community-building* are "in."

The great value in Connell and Kubisch's contribution (chap. 12, this volume) is integrating developmental models of youth development with a broad community action framework that is now increasingly being adopted by communities across the county. By doing so, he and his colleagues have crafted a clear model of the multiple steps of both process and outcome. This model can serve as an organizing principle, a guide for integration of process and program changes, a device to assess gaps in community-wide program development and delivery, and an assessment for mediation or short-term theoretically based change.

DEVELOPING A THEORY OF CHANGE: THE CONTRIBUTION OF DEVELOPMENTAL-ECOLOGICAL THEORY

As Connell and others recognize, the evaluation of these large-scale initiatives provide numerous challenges to which there are no clear solutions (Connell, Kubisch, Schorr, & Weiss, 1995). Thus, there has been widespread adoption of Weiss's notion of developing a "theory of change" that assesses the effects of interventions and initiatives by linking them to short-term theory-based mediators (Weiss, 1995). Following from Weiss's conceptualization, as it is unlikely that long-term outcomes (rates of youth delinquency, teen pregnancy, school-dropout) will be rapidly changed, there is an urgent need for developing measures of near and midterm mediation of longer term changes. In chapter 12, Connell and Kubisch provided examples of mediated processes that can be used as markers on the way to successful youth initiatives.

A central question here is, at what levels in the system is change to be expected? The use of Bronfenbrenner's (1979) ecological model is instructive here because it provides a conceptual mapping of differentiated levels of systemic influences. That is, change might be assessed at the level of the individual, their closest relationships (e.g., parent, peer, teachers, or other adults), the relationship between ecological settings that impact children and youth (school-home, school-community, home-community), and policies that affect these institutions; finally, one would examine change in the systems themselves.

Connell provides the example of elementary school completion as a predictor (or short-term mediator) of eventual secondary school completion. That is, if a systemic change leads to greater elementary school or middle school completion, this could be considered an important signpost of later improved rates of high school graduation. Although such a variable may be of some use, other variables that are more skills-oriented and psychological in nature are likely to be stronger predictors and closer to developmental theories of change. Examples would be changes in early reading achievement in the elementary years, as well as children's attachment to school during the late elementary and early adolescent periods. Similarly, although statistics on the rate of foster-care or maltreatment might be used to characterize change in the quality of family life, variables closer to developmental theory such as parents' ability to monitor their child's whereabouts and parents' sense of connection and frequency of communication with their child's school may be more instructive of change. Furthermore, they are more likely to yield changes in a shorter period of time. Most important here is the child or youth developing healthy relationships with others (Greenberg, 1999). It is important here to recognize that these short-term criteria for evidence of success are quite similar to those used in medicine; short-term, theory-based mediators, often seen as indicators of risk reduction, are conventionally used as the primary indicator for the efficacy of a treatment. For example, new drugs or therapies to reduce heart disease do not need to reduce morbidity, they need to reduce a risk factor such as level of cholesterol/LDL (low density lipid) levels in the bloodstream.

COMMUNITY READINESS AND COMMUNITY-BUILDING

Connell and Kubisch (chap. 12, this volume) also call for improved research that provides a fuller understanding of the process of implementation of community initiatives. That is, how is community change best implemented, by whom, with what goals? This would include examining the readiness of communities to engage in the change process (Arthur et al., 1998; Butterfoss, Goodman, & Wandersman, 1996; Goodman, Wandersman, Chinman, & Imm, 1996; Orting et al., 1995). Although concepts of readiness have been borrowed from treatment research (Prochaska, DeiClemente, & Norcross, 1992), there is a need for a more refined assessment of the construct of community readiness (Glisson & Hemmelgarn, 1998). As Connell discusses, Sampson's model of collective efficacy (chap. 1, this volume) may be an important aspect of this larger construct of readiness.

As I have served on community boards attempting service systems reform, the issue of resource reallocation is one of the greatest obstacles to such reform. As a colleague of mine says, "Collaboration is when you put your money on the table and then remove your hand!" It is not only money that is at issue, however; it is the psychological turf and identity that community and social service agencies have developed that is very difficult to change. Although it is easier if a community can implement something that builds new resources instead of redistributing them, I have reservations about this strategy. There is unlikely to be sustainability of change over time if there is not reallocation of existing dollars; as the new dollars disappear, so do the systems changes that had been successfully implemented.

In the area of child services and resources, one of the great problems is that of categorical funding streams. As Connell and Kubisch have discussed, systems that serve children and families overlap in some areas and there are great gaps in others, I have gone to meetings to discuss the disposition of a child having social and behavioral difficulties at which as many as 15 professionals from eight different agencies are working in a piecemeal, uncoordinated fashion on the same child and family; this is the real world of turf. Relatedly, categorical streams of dollars that create separate programs for child abuse, drug and alcohol abuse, foster care, violence prevention, AIDS prevention, abstinence promotion, mental health, juvenile justice diversion, and so forth belie a lack of developmental thinking, and this does little to promote protective factors that decrease risk and danger (Coie et al., 1993). The issue of service integration in the social services end is critical— agencies are dependent on not changing the funding streams; the culture is one of division, not integration. As Connell reiterates, systems integration will only occur when key stakeholders, who control political and financial resources, and those who work directly with youth jointly agree that the risk-reward ratio of current systems must change. The great problem of categorical funding streams—the failure to create systems change—leads to many people serving the same children in families in an uncoordinated, nondevelopmental, cost-ineffective manner. Second, there is lack of developmental thinking that can lead to promoting protective factors that decrease risk and danger. The issue of service integration in the social services end is critical. Agencies are dependent on not changing the funding streams; the culture is one of division, not integration. Thus, in order to capture "real-world" conditions, the assessment of community readiness must include assessment of the issues of flexibility and openness to change and to create service integration.

This broad construct of community readiness can also be viewed as a predictor of potential outcomes. More importantly from a practical standpoint, it may be that a certain level of community readiness (in terms of readiness to change institutional structures as well as neighborhood leadership) is necessary for the initiation of a CCI. As Kozol said, "Pick battles big enough to matter, and small enough to win."

MEASURING THE EFFECT OF NEIGHBORHOOD ON CHILDREN'S OUTCOME

The importance of the relationship between individual level and community level varies. Childhood development occurs within the multiple contexts of the home, the school, and the neighborhood (Bronfenbrenner, 1979). Thus, to adequately study it, the growth and adjustment must be embedded in analyses of the contextual risks to which children are exposed (Sameroff & Seifer, 1990).

In the Fast Track project, we (Greenberg et al., 1999) examined how the combined effects of demographic, family psychosocial, and neighborhood risk factors on children's development will be examined in families from four American communities. The study involved 382 children who were representatively drawn from 25 elementary schools in four U.S. locations; three urban neighborhoods (Durham, Nashville, Seattle) and a fourth location including three communities in rural Pennsylvania. The urban schools were chosen from those neighborhoods showing the highest rates of youth delinquency in their cities. The study involved a test of the hierarchical and unique contributions of three major dimensions of social context on the behavioral, academic, and psychological outcomes of a culturally and geographically diverse combination of child populations. Most literature on the effects of neighborhoods has hypothesized impact primarily in the preadolescent and adolescent periods. In this study, we examined the potential role of neighborhood effects when children first enter formal schooling.

Levels of neighborhood poverty, crime, residential instability, and concentrations of lower income families have been related to higher levels of stress, exposure to violence, child maltreatment, parents' mental health, and child psychological adjustment (Aber, 1994; Attar, Guerra, & Tolan, 1994; Duncan et al., 1994; Lindgren, Harper, & Blackman, 1986; Melton, 1992; White, Kasl, Zahner, & Will, 1987). However, as noted by Duncan and Raudenbush (chap. 8, this volume) and Sampson (chap. 1, this volume) many studies measure only one aspect of the neighborhood construct. Burton, Price-Spratlen, and Spencer (1997) emphasized the importance of understanding the different meanings of neighborhood context and their relation to developmental outcomes. *Neighborhood*, as measured by social address (Bronfenbrenner, 1986), reflects physical or demographic properties, whereas *perceptions of neighborhood* capture residents' personal evaluations of their social milieu. Neighborhood can also be conceived of as social networks, as well as subcultures with shared social practices and beliefs. As Burton et al. (1997) noted, each construct has its strengths and its limitations. In the present study, the

quality and social aspects of the neighborhood were measured using both participant perceptions and staff ratings of the neighborhood.

During home visits to each of our study families, the interviewers made objective ratings of the quality of the neighborhood using a scale developed for this
project. The primary caregivers' perception of the neighborhood was also assessed
by their reports of the neighborhood's safety, violence, drug traffic, satisfaction,
and stability. Of interest here is the factor termed *neighborhood safety* (e.g., How
often are there problems with muggings, burglaries, assaults, etc.? How much of
a problem is the selling and using of drugs around here?). Our overall neighborhood risk variable consisted of a single factor that was a composite of the interviewers' assessment inventory and the Neighborhood Safety subscale of the par-
ent-report Neighborhood Questionnaire.

The first question we addressed was whether the neighborhood-level variable
predicted child outcomes in first grade after demographic and family psychosocial
variables were taken into account; these measures include ethnicity, SES, single-
parenting, number of children, family communication, maternal social support,
family life stress, and maternal depression. Thus, this study met Duncan and
Raudenbush's criteria (chap. 8, this volume)—to use geographically diverse
samples, examine contextually based mediators, attempt to include often omitted
contextual variables, and have independent measures of outcome.

After demographic and family context variables had been entered, neighborhood added significantly to the prediction of both parent-reported and teacher-
reported externalizing behavior, as well as teacher report of social competence.
However, the absolute increment in prediction by neighborhood context was small.
This suggests that neighborhood, as a distal factor, accounted for a small but unique
portion of the variance in young children's externalizing problems. Further, we
found an interaction between neighborhood risk times child gender for both parent and teacher reports of externalizing difficulties. In both cases, the relation
between neighborhood risk and the outcomes was stronger for boys than for girls,
indicating that neighborhood context may influence the functioning of boys and
girls differently. The reasons for this are unclear. It may be that boys who are
difficult and troublesome are more affected by extrafamilial influences in the surrounding ecology, whereas girls are less likely to venture out and be exposed to
other neighborhood influences at this young age. Alternatively, it may be that
boys are more responsive to the negative influences of the neighborhood, such as
older males who get in trouble. This may be another example of the fact that boys
appear to be more vulnerable to the effects of their environment (Bolger, Patterson,
Thompson, & Kupersmidt, 1995; Joffe, Offord, & Boyle, 1988; Simcha-Fagan,
Gersten, & Langner, 1986; Vaden-Kiernan, Ialongo, Pearson, & Kellam, 1995).

Finally, using path analyses, we found that the effects of neighborhood risk
were only partially mediated by psychosocial (home environment and social support) or demographic (single parent status) variables. These findings corroborate
other recent findings on the effects of neighborhood. In the present study, it should

be noted that other, unmeasured variables such as parenting style or school level contextual variables may further mediate the relationship between neighborhood and child outcome.

WHAT IS THE MEANING AND LEVEL FOR DEFINING NEIGHBORHOOD?

The finding of a significant effect for neighborhood level influences on children's behavioral development led me to further consider the meaning of the term *neighborhood*. We found a strong relationship between how residents subjectively defined their neighborhood and our staff ratings of the appraisal of the immediate area surrounding their residence. As Sampson (chap. 1, this volume) and Lee (chap. 2, this volume) discuss, residents' subjective appraisal is important. There are obviously different levels of local social organization, and there is a clear differentiation for most people between the meaning of their neighbors versus their neighborhood (Lee, chap. 2, this volume). One might visualize concentric circles that would first include your actual spatial neighbors on all sides, then your own street or building, next, the areas you walk to, and then the larger neighborhood; in many cases, these differing levels will have differing influences on child and family life. For example, close bonds or isolation from one's immediate neighbors, or those persons who are either part of your street or the building you live in, are likely to have quite different effects on child and family development than will other, more distal characteristics of your neighborhood. Having lived in three neighborhoods as a parent with young children, I know that children open doors and create links to neighbors as well as other parents, and these links change the nature of neighborhood for families. However, as children become teens and are more mobile, neighbors may have less impact (Gonzales, Cauce, Freidman, & Mason, 1996).

Returning to Connell's chapter, this raises the issue of what size or scope do or should community initiatives take? Is there a "right" level? When organizing for systemic change, is the "right" level a neighborhood that is a well-known spatial and social subdivision of a city? Is it the catchment area of an elementary school that ties its citizens together? Is it smaller units of social organization? This is of great interest as we are now involved in the evaluation of "community"-based prevention programs in 21 communities in Pennsylvania in which the Communities That Care (CTC) model has been introduced.

CTC is a comprehensive, community-wide, risk- and protective-factor prevention strategy that mobilizes community members to plan, implement, and evaluate coordinated positive youth development programs (Hawkins, Catalano, & Associates, 1992; Hirachi, Ayers, Hawkins, Catalano, & Cushing, 1996; Peterson, Hawkins, & Catalano, 1992). The CTC process has three phases. First, key community leaders (e.g., the mayor, chief law enforcement officer, superintendent of schools, business and religious leaders, etc.) are oriented to the project. If they commit to the project, they agree to serve as an oversight board and appoint a prevention board of diverse community members. Second, the community board is trained to conduct a risk and resource assessment that provides an empirical foundation to identify priorities for preventive action. Third, during a planning and implementation phase, the board selects programs from a menu of interventions that have been evaluated for efficacy in addressing their priority risk areas and develops detailed action plans for program implementation. Baseline assessment data serve as the benchmark against which to measure community progress in targeted areas. In Pennsylvania, we found that the spatial size of CTC areas of focus ranged from entire counties that are primarily rural, to the catchment area of one elementary school, to one census track, or to a few political wards. It is obvious that choice of size, population density, and spatial externalities all affect the nature and scope of activities that can be accomplished in such an initiative. I believe that one of the major issues that systems change agents such as Connell will help us answer in the next decade is how we can begin to better characterize how such variables as size, density, and community readiness play important roles in the processes and outcome of the new look of community action research with children, youth, and families.

ACKNOWLEDGMENTS

This work was supported by National Institute of Mental Health (NIMH) Grants R18 MH48403, R18 MH50951, R18 MH50952, and R18 MH50953. The Center for Substance Abuse Prevention also provided support for Fast Track through a memorandum of agreement with the NIMH. This work was also supported in part by Department of Education Grant S184U30002.

REFERENCES

Aber, J. L. (1994). Poverty, violence, and child development: Untangling family and community level. In C. A. Nelson (Ed.), *Threat to optimal development: The Minnesota symposia on child psychology* (Vol. 27, pp. 229–272). Hillsdale, NJ: Lawrence Erlbaum Associates.

Arthur, M. W., Brewer, D. D., Hawkins, J. D., Graham, K. S., Tremper, M., Shavel, D. A., & Hansen, C. (1998). *Assessing state and community readiness for prevention.* Unpublished manuscript. Social Development Research Group, University of Washington, Seattle, WA.

Attar, B. K., Guerra, N. G., & Tolan, P. H. (1994). Neighborhood disadvantage, stressful life events, and adjustment in urban elementary school children. *Journal of Clinical Child Psychology, 23,* 391–400.

Bolger, K. E., Patterson, C. J., Thompson, W. W., & Kupersmidt, J. B. (1995). Psychological adjustment among children experiencing persistent and intermittent family economic hardship. *Child Development, 66,* 1107–1129.

Bronfenbrenner, U. (1979). *The ecology of human development: Experiments by nature and design.* Cambridge, MA: Harvard University Press.

Bronfenbrenner, U. (1986). Ecology of the family as a context for human development: Research perspectives. *Developmental Psychology, 22,* 723–254.

Burton, L. M., Price-Spratlen, T., & Spencer, M. (1997). On ways of thinking about measuring neighborhoods: Implications for studying context and development among minority children. In J. Brooks-Gunn & G. Duncan (Eds.), *Neighborhood poverty: Context and consequences for children* (pp. 147–192). New York: Russell Sage Foundation.

Butterfoss, F. D., Goodman, R. M, & Wandersman, A. (1996). Community coalitions for prevention and health promotion: Factors predicting satisfaction, participation, and planning. *Health Education Quarterly, 23,* 65–79.

Coie, J. D., Watt, N. F., West, S. G., Hawkins, J. D., Asarnow, J. R., Markman, H. J., Ramey, S. L., Shure, M. B., & Long, B. (1993). The science of prevention: A conceptual framework and some directions for a national research program. *American Psychologist, 48,* 1013-1022.

Connell, J. P., Kubisch, A. C., Schorr, L. B., & Weiss, C. H. (Eds.). (1995). *New approaches to evaluating community initiatives: Concepts, methods, and contexts.* Washington, DC: The Aspen Institute.

Dryfoos, J. G. (1990). *Adolescents at risk: Prevalence and prevention.* New York: Oxford University Press.

Dryfoos, J. G. (1997). The prevalence of problem behaviors: Implications for programs. In R. P. Weissberg, T. P. Gullotta, R. L. Hampton, & G. R. Adams (Eds.), *Healthy children 2010: Enhancing children's wellness* (pp. 17–46). Newbury Park, CA: Sage.

Duncan, G. J., Brooks-Gunn, J., & Klebanov, P. K. (1994). Economic deprivation and early childhood development. *Child Development, 65,* 296–318.

Glisson, C., & Hemmelgarn, A. (1998). The effects of organizational climate and the interorganizational coordination on the qualities and outcomes of children's service systems. *Child Abuse and Neglect, 22,* 401–421.

Goodman, R. M, Wandersman, A., Chinman, M., & Imm, P. (1996). An ecological assessment of community-based interventions for prevention and health promotion: Approaches to measuring community coalitions. *American Journal of Community Psychology, 24,* 33–61.

Gonzales, N. A., Cauce, A. M., Freidman, R. J., & Mason, C. A. (1996). Family, peer, and neighborhood influences on academic achievement among African-American adolescents: One-year prospective effects. *American Journal of Community Psychology, 24,* 365–387.

Greenberg, M. T. (in press). Attachment and psychopathology in childhood. In J. Cassidy & P. R. Shaver (Eds.), *Handbook of attachment theory and research* (pp. 469–496). New York: Guilford.

Greenberg, M. T., Lengua, L. J., Coie, J., Pinderhughes, E. E., & The Conduct Problems Prevention Research Group. (1999). Predicting developmental outcomes at school entry using a multiple-risk model: Four American communities. *Developmental Psychology, 35,* 403–413.

Hamburg, D. A. (1992). *Today's children: Creating a future for a generation in crisis.* New York: Times Books.

Hawkins, J. D., Catalano, R. F., & Associates (1992). *Communities that care: Action for drug abuse prevention.* San Francisco: Jossey-Bass.

Hirachi, T. W., Ayers, C. D., Hawkins, J. D., Catalano, R. F., & Cushing, J. (1996). Empowering communities to prevent adolescent substance abuse: Process evaluation results from a risk- and protection-focused community mobilization effort. *The Journal of Primary Prevention, 16,* 233–254.

Joffe, R. T., Offord, D. R., & Boyle, M. H. (1988). Ontario Child Health Study: Suicidal behavior in youth age 12–16 years. *American Journal of Psychiatry, 145,* 1420–1423.

Lindgren, S. D., Harper, D. C., & Blackman, J. A. (1986). Environmental influences and perinatal risk factors in high-risk children. *Journal of Pediatric Psychology, 11,* 531–547.

Melton, G. B. (1992). It's time for neighborhood research and action. *Child Abuse and Neglect, 16,* 909–913.

National Commission on the Role of the School and the Community in Improving Adolescent Health. (1990). *Code Blue: Uniting for healthier youth.* Alexandria, VA: National Association of State Boards of Education.

Orting, E. R., Donnemeyer, J. F., Plested, R. A., Edwards, R. W., Kelly, K., & Beauvais, F. (1995). Assessing community readiness for prevention. *The International Journal of Addictions, 30,* 659–683.

Peterson, P. L., Hawkins, J. D., & Catalano, R. F., (1992). Evaluating comprehensive community drug risk reduction interventions. *Evaluation Review, 16,* 579–602.

Prochaska, J. O., DiClemente, C. C., & Norcross, J. C. (1992). In search of how people change: Applications to addictive behaviors. *American Psychologist, 47,* 1102–1114.

Sameroff, A. J., & Seifer, R. (1990). Early contributors to developmental risk. In J. Rolf, A. S. Masten, D. Cicchetti, K. H. Nuechterlein, & S. Weintraub (Eds.), *Risk and protective factors in the development of psychopathology* (pp. 52–66). New York: Cambridge University Press.

Simcha-Fagan, O., Gersten, J. C., & Langner, T. S. (1986). Early precursors and concurrent correlates of patterns of illicit drug use in adolescents. *Journal of Drug Issues, 16*, 7–28.

Takanishi, R. (1993). The opportunities of adolescence—Research, interventions, and policy. *American Psychologist, 48*, 85–87.

Vaden-Kiernan, N., Ialongo, N. S., Pearson, J., & Kellam, S. (1995). Household family structure and children's aggressive behavior: A longitudinal study of urban elementary school children. *Journal of Abnormal Child Psychology, 23*, 553–568.

Weiss, C. H. (1995). Nothing as practical as a good theory: Exploring theory-based evaluation for comprehensive community initiatives for children and families. In J. P. Connell, A. C. Kubisch, L. B. Schorr, & C. H. Weiss (Eds.), *New approaches to evaluating community initiatives: Concepts, methods, and contexts*. Washington, DC: The Aspen Institute.

White, M., Kasl, S. V., Zahner, G. E., & Will, J. C. (1987). Perceived crime in the neighborhood and mental health of women and children. *Environment and Behavior, 19*, 588–613.

Zill, N., & Nord, C. W. (1994). *Running in place: How American families are faring in a changing economy and an individualistic society*. Washington, DC: Child Trends.

15

Community Approaches to Improving Outcomes for Urban Children, Youth, and Families

Dale A. Blyth
University of Minnesota

Before commenting on the strong chapter by Connell and Kubisch, as well as the larger issues they and others raised, I wish to make explicit up front that my comments come out of three recent experiences. First, efforts to help communities understand how they impact their youth's development: How do we, as professionals who study youth development, help communities become more intentional about their support of children and youth? Second, efforts to systematically evaluate such efforts: If we are to learn from what communities are trying, we must be able to establish evaluation systems that not only capture the impact of neighborhoods but also the impact of initiatives designed to improve the development of all children and youth within those "villages." And finally, direct observations of how the Community Action Framework for Youth Development is being applied to the 20-year initiative noted in their chapter. These experiences, often done in the framework of Search Institute's 40 assets youth need to succeed, have shaped my thinking and informed my perspectives.

DOES IT TAKE A VILLAGE?
AND OTHER RELEVANT QUESTIONS

Let me begin by saying I believe the "village" has an enormous influence on how children and especially adolescents develop. This belief comes from both an empirical and a theoretical understanding of how context and people's understanding of context affects their development in a host of direct and indirect ways. Although these effects are difficult to measure, and although we have only begun to have the sophisticated methodological approaches talked about by Sampson and his colleagues, the effects are real and important. This realization is especially true in an era where changes in families, macroeconomic factors, and policies have caused an erosion in how communities operate and in their ability to impact children and adolescents. The question in my mind, and the one that I believe the Connell and Kubisch chapter addresses most directly, is not whether it takes a village, or to what extent it takes a village, or even how we accurately capture the ways and extents to which it takes a village. Rather, the key question is: How can we utilize social science research and program experience to help communities maximize their positive influences on their own youth's development? The answer to this question, although greatly enhanced by the work of the other authors, must build on and go beyond what we know if it is to help frame how a community can become more intentional about how it supports youth development.

BALANCE AS OPPOSED TO CHOICE: AN APT ANALOGY

At the beginning of their chapter (chap. 12, this volume), Connell and Kubisch note five themes that operate and suggest that they are best thought of as finding the right balance between two perspectives. I could not agree more. The issue is not one of choosing a people-over-place approach to investing in communities—it must be both. It is not an issue of whether we rely on public versus private resources but rather finding the right balance. In short, finding the balance between what have often been dichotomous choices is a much more fruitful approach when working with communities than having someone, either the funder or the community, choose one option or the other. In working with communities as they try to increase the number of developmental assets their youth experience, using the Search Institute model of 40 developmental assets all youth need to succeed, it was often critical to help them take a balanced approach rather then make an arbitrary choice. To Connell and Kubisch's list of five tensions I would add two more—funder driven versus community driven, and formal programs versus informal relationship-based approaches.

By funder versus community driven, I refer to where the pressure for change originates and how it is used to move a comprehensive community initiative forward. One could argue that we are now on the third generation of efforts to help communities, especially poor ones, become better developmental contexts for children and youth. In the first generation, funders acted as though they had the answers and communities just needed to implement them for real change to occur. This proved ineffective for a variety of reasons, not the least of which was lack of community ownership, so we moved on to a second generation of efforts that were driven by the belief that the community has all the answers and just needs help in making the changes it believes are necessary. Such strategies tend to throw out what we know from previous efforts, and they consume an enormous amount of community energy and resources to get to what they believe is needed. This too often left few resources to actually make the changes. The third generation seeks to balance these two forces by utilizing what we know children and youth need for development, and how communities impact development. They seek to establish what youth need in order to develop and then to engage the community in a process that helps them drive how they reach these goals or outcomes. Balancing where different forces come from helps to take advantage of the strengths of both perspectives in an ongoing process of change. I am convinced that more often than not some external force or knowledge must play a key part in most community change efforts if they are to do business differently.

By formal programs versus broader, more informal relationship-based approaches, I am referring to the realization that we cannot simply program our youth's development. Youth development occurs, as Pittman (1991) would say, as the result of the accumulation of the everyday people, places, and possibilities they experience. It is the daily diet of these experiences that makes the difference, and these experiences are heavily influenced by family, peer, neighborhood, and community contexts. Thinking of development as occurring as the result of the daily diet of the people, places, and possibilities youth experience helps communities realize it is the balance of formal programs available and the types of informal social cohesion and social control that make up what Sampson's chapter refers to as *collective efficacy*. Neither formal program nor effective informal collective efficacy is likely to be enough alone in most current communities. This tension captures, in brief ways, some of the differences between Hawkins and Catalano's Communities That Care approach and the Search Institute's Healthy Communities, Healthy Youth emphasis. The Communities That Care model, based on social development theory, emphasizes using data profiles to help a community determine which of a range of proven programs or promising approaches it should use to change key risk and protective factors. The emphasis is on placing effective programs in place. In contrast, the Search Institute approach focuses more on broadening public awareness and a sense of responsibility for children and youth and the power of informal, relationship-based acts of asset building. Neither model excludes the other emphasis, but they each select very different balance points between programs and informal relationships as the place they encourage communities to seek.

COMBINING COMPREHENSIVE COMMUNITY INITIATIVE THINKING WITH A YOUTH DEVELOPMENT EMPHASIS: A SIGNIFICANT STEP FORWARD

Connell and Kubisch (chap. 12, this volume) do a nice job of summarizing and critiquing current trends in investment strategies and how they have led to more comprehensive community initiatives that seek to combine individual, family, and neighborhood level efforts to intentionally change how the community operates and impacts on children and youth. Their real contribution, however, is the Connell and Gambone (1998) work they cite (chap. 12, this volume) as responsible for the Community Action Framework for Youth Development (see Fig. 12.1). This framework is an explicit hybrid of what we know from research about the linkages between youth's experiences and positive outcomes and what we know from practical experience about what communities can do to increase those types of supports and opportunities in their communities. In short, unlike many other youth development frameworks, it builds a theory of how communities can change the necessary or nonnegotiable elements of youth development rather than just listing the elements themselves, as is done in many other frameworks. This theoretically driven linkage between what are reasonable and appropriate outcomes for youth—both as adults (Box A) and youth (Box B)—and what communities need to do to build the capacity and conditions for change (Box E) and implement key community strategies (Box D) in order to enhance the necessary supports and opportunities youth need to experience (Box C) is a major contribution to community mobilization work. As the authors themselves note, it is not a proven theory but a logical next step worthy of implementation and evaluation.

Based on my own experiences with the framework's application and my reading of the examples noted in the chapter, I believe that this framework proves useful because of its balance of breadth and depth. It not only helps a variety of people, both community people and the consultants and evaluators who work with them, see a larger picture, but it also adds specific details about what each of the elements means and how it can be assessed in greater depth. When Connell and Kubisch describe the use of the framework as an investment tool, I can attest to its utility. The framework allows a broad but cohesive set of goals, strategies, and more specific desired outcomes to be organized systematically and sequentially. It affirms the logic underlying the work and integrates it into a more natural flow. Furthermore, the cumulative efforts of the initiative over several years can be mapped against the framework to provide a sense of where investments have been made. Finally, by assessing the status of the community sites, in a very broad but appropriate way, it is helping staff identify gaps and plan new strategies for closing the gaps. In short, the framework appears as though it will be useful for planning, managing, evaluating, and investing as this major 20-year initiative moves forward.

I particularly want to comment on the extent to which the framework has done a good job of capturing both broad concepts and specific indicators through the use of some new language—such as the phrase "learning to navigate." It is not one of the normal outcomes that we think of for youth, but it is explicit and encompasses a variety of key concepts from the research literature while keeping it simple enough for use in such a complex, linked framework. Similarly, although the four community strategies for enhancing supports and opportunities for youth are broad, they neatly capture informal, people-based approaches, institutional reform approaches, program-centered approaches, and the need for policy work. In part, the likely success of the framework is based on this ability to see how it is all linked together while still focusing people's attention in detail on what is meant in each component of each box. In short, it mixes what needs to be done with a broad enough sense of how to stimulate people to want to fill in the details—a major accomplishment for what initially appears to be a too linear and static framework.

Another aspect of the framework I found particularly helpful was the way the authors suggest using it for everything from planning to evaluation and investment. Because of the breadth-depth issue noted earlier and the commitment to establish standards on which to judge success, the framework is indeed useful across all four aspects of a community mobilization initiative. This is important because it keeps various pieces working together rather than on separate levels with separate languages. Particularly helpful is the move to more intermediate and explicit outcomes of multiple types rather than relying on inputs and outputs or only long term outcomes for evaluation.

CONCLUSION

Although the initial recommendations in the chapter are all appropriate and sensible, they unfortunately do not go very far in advancing the nature of the work called for by the framework described. There is a real need to develop tools and training around the framework to help communities use it effectively in the variety of ways noted. Such tools might include incorporating what is known about specific linkages in the model, organizing the research literature in a way that is compatible with the framework, highlighting best practices that are consistent with the framework, and developing assessment tools to determine where the community stands in key areas. It will also be critical to assess whether or not it can actually change either the community's intentionality around youth development or the desired supports, opportunities, and short-range outcomes. Such work is undoubtedly underway by the authors and others, and the field will be enriched as this work comes to fruition. Finally, there is a need for the model to more adequately capture cultural differences and specific factors both within its boxes and across different populations. Some of the lessons coming out of the chapter by Spencer (chap. 4, this volume) may be useful in this arena. In summary, although no single framework or diagram can single-handedly help communities revitalize their efforts on behalf of children and youth, the issues discussed and the model put forth by Connell and Kubisch take a giant step forward in what I believe is the right direction. When combined with the research on how communities impact development and an understanding of ethnic and cultural differences, it can become a powerful tool for a reasoned, researchable approach to changes in the "villages" where our children and youth live.

REFERENCES

Connell, J. P., & Gambone, M. A. (1999). A community action framework for youth development: Rationale and early application. Philadelphia, PA: Institute for Research & Reform Education.
Pittman, K. J., & Cahill, M. (1991). A new vision: Promoting your development. Washington, DC: Center for Youth Development and Policy Research.

16

Neighborhood Effects on Child and Adolescent Development: Assessing Today's Knowledge for Tomorrow's Villages

Frank Avenilla
Susan Singley
The Pennsylvania State University

The title of this volume springs from an African proverb suggesting that the roles, responsibilities, and requirements of properly raising a child to adulthood extend beyond the reaches of the immediate family to include those in the community or neighborhood within which the child and the family are embedded. But, does it take a village to raise a child? Although it may have been true for peoples of the past, *is the same true for families and communities of today? And if so, exactly how does a village effectively help raise a child?* These questions lie at the heart of the current volume. They are particularly timely in light of the recent reformation of welfare and other social programs, the continual flow of international immigration and the growth of ethnic enclaves, and an economic boom that has largely bypassed many of the poor in America. Indeed, as we move into the 21st century, the villages and neighborhoods that house the poor and disenfranchised will be tested and called on to do even more for their residents.

Despite the potential importance of neighborhoods as contexts for childrearing and child and adolescent development, the contemporary research on community effects has been less than clear. Although a number of "standard" indicators of neighborhood characteristics have been associated with both positive and negative child and adolescent outcomes, a detailed picture of the precise processes through which neighborhoods exert their effects remains unidentified. More importantly, neighborhood-effects research is faced with a number of methodological challenges, not the least of which is the task of uncovering "unknown" aspects of neighborhoods that may have profound social and developmental impacts. The current volume represents a collection of ideas and empirical findings from researchers, policy makers, and interventionists who are at the forefront of neighborhood research. Together they have addressed several key questions: Does it "take a village" to raise a child? And if so, precisely *how* do communities foster healthy child and adolescent development? What aspects of communities and neighborhoods are particularly pertinent to the well-being and development of children and families? What are the methods by which we can best measure and understand the processes of neighborhood effects?

In this chapter, the four main chapters are reviewed and discussed in detail, with an eye toward synthesizing the state of our knowledge in this area. We begin with an overview of the underlying theories and concepts that provide the basis for our understanding of neighborhoods and neighborhood effects. In addition, this discussion includes examples from recent empirical research that document neighborhood effects at work. From there, our attention turns to the specific issue of precisely how neighborhoods help or hinder families in their efforts to raise children. In the following section, the focus shifts toward methodological issues and how we can better capture and measure neighborhood effects in action. We conclude with a discussion of how policy and intervention strategies directed at helping communities and neighborhoods can improve the lives of their inhabitants and the life chances of their youth.

SPECIFYING NEIGHBORHOOD EFFECTS

Sampson (chap. 1, this volume) argues that we already know that neighborhoods matter for human development: Robust empirical findings have demonstrated a neighborhood-level comorbidity of negative individual outcomes, such as adolescent delinquency, infant mortality, child abuse, and crime, which together are correlated with neighborhood socioeconomic disadvantage. Further, this concentration of social and economic disadvantage, which is associated with race, intensified during the 1980s and 1990s. What we know less about is *why* neighborhoods matter and exactly *for what*.

To this end, Sampson outlines a general theoretical framework centering on community social organization, that is, "the ability of a community structure to realize the common values of its residents and maintain effective social controls." Three mechanisms embedded within community social organization link neighborhood level structural characteristics with associated individual level outcomes: *social capital*, *collective efficacy*, and *routine activities*. In terms of the social organizational context of child rearing, Sampson identifies two important characteristics of neighborhood social capital: interlocking social networks that link adults in the community and facilitate informal social control and support of children, and *reciprocated transaction*, which might involve parents exchanging advice or goods related to child rearing. In order to activate social networks inherent in the community structure, communities also need *collective efficacy*, which refers to the cultural expectations for the informal social control and mutual support of children and involves shared values and mutual trust among adults in the neighborhood. Sampson also stresses the importance of a community's ability to create or take advantage of links outside the community, such as police and fire services, that promote a community's ability to maintain social control. Finally, Sampson suggests that we borrow the concept of *routine activities* from the criminology literature as a potential explanatory neighborhood-level mechanism. Threats to community well-being exist in the temporal and spatial structure of the neighborhood, particularly in land use patterns, such as the placement of bars or strip-malls. The ecological distribution of "daily routines" have an impact on how and when children come in contact with peers and adults, and in part determine opportunities for unsupervised activity on a daily basis.

These three social mechanisms are linked to structural differentiation through structural continuity, unequal resource distribution, racial segregation, and the broader ecological context. Residential stability, as indicated by levels of residential tenure and home ownership, allows for the development of social capital and social control via the formation of dense social networks. Meanwhile, the concentration and isolation of families and households characterized by multiple forms of disadvantage—for example, of lower-income, minority, single-parent families—diminish expectations for collective action and may lead to less diverse social networks (that, in turn, decrease the likelihood of a neighborhood being connected to more advantaged networks). Similarly, the concentration of socioeconomic *advantage* may lead to enhanced social capital and collective efficacy. Finally, Sampson stresses the importance of looking at the ecological context within which communities operate, including the citywide political economy and the social organization of adjoining neighborhoods.

Sampson uses data from the Project on Human Development in Chicago Neighborhoods to provide two empirical examples of how neighborhood-level constructs defined as important social mechanisms in the framework can be operationalized, and how their mediating effects on the link between community structure and individual outcomes can be measured and assessed. His first analysis measures the effect of structural characteristics on two independently measured outcomes—homicide and low birthweight. He also measures the mediating effect of both collective efficacy, measured using a summary two-component scale that taps "informal social control" and "social cohesion," and spatial dependence. Sampson finds strong evidence for spatial dependence, as well as a significant negative effect of collective efficacy on rates of homicide and low birthweight, after controlling for structural characteristics. The mediating effects of both spatial dependence and collective efficacy are net of prior rates of homicide and low birthweight, strengthening the conclusion that collective efficacy and spatial externalities are important neighborhood-level social mechanisms.

Sampson's second analysis examines more closely the connection between macrostructural characteristics of neighborhoods and neighborhood social mechanisms, specifically the "spatial context of social capital and collective efficacy specific to childrearing." He examines the effect of structural characteristics of neighborhoods on both "adult-child exchange" (which measures the extent to which adults know each other, look out for each other's children, and rely on each other for advice and help) and "child-centered social control" (which measures levels of neighborhood efficacy in areas specific to childrearing, such as the extent of tru-

ancy and graffiti). Results reveal that concentrated disadvantage has no significant effect on neighborhood levels of adult-child social exchange, whereas concentrated affluence significantly increases such levels. Residential stability emerges
as an important predictor: Net of concentrated disadvantage, racial or ethnic composition, and individual-level variables, stable neighborhoods exhibit higher levels of adult-child social exchange: "Although concentrated poverty seems to be
the privileged construct in mainstream urban research, these results call for a renewed look at residential stability and the perquisites of concentrated affluence."
Results for child-centered social control show similar patterns, with the important
exception of concentrated disadvantage: Poor neighborhoods exhibit significantly
lower levels of expectations for collective action regarding children. Importantly,
Sampson's analysis reveals that a neighborhood's ecological position within the
larger city is a significant predictor of its internal social organization. Neighborhoods appear to be influenced by the levels of adult-child exchange and child-
centered social control found in proximate neighborhoods, net of the other demographic and ecological controls.

Sampson's research indicates that the neighborhood mechanisms he identifies are important, and his work helps establish a crucial link between macrostructural characteristics of communities and individual-level developmental outcomes. In short, his research pushes us toward an understanding of why neighborhoods matter and for what. Left unanswered, though, is another set of "why"
and "how" questions: How do the structural characteristics of neighborhoods
influence the development and maintenance of social capital, collective efficacy,
and intergenerational closure? Why is there variation in the effect of structural
characteristics on neighborhood social organization? Expressing a theme that
emerges throughout this volume, Lee (chap. 2, this volume) stresses that residents' views of the structural characteristics of their neighborhood may differ
both from each other and from assumptions about objective qualities more commonly measured in neighborhood research. Subjectivity impinges on the effects
of structure, suggesting that researchers should not lose sight of the qualitative
aspects of the neighborhood measures they employ. For example, Sampson's
work implies that local institutions—neighborhood associations, churches—are
indicators of community cohesion and are assumed to have a positive effect on
social organization. Lee suggests that the role local institutions play in shaping
social organization should be treated as an empirical question rather than a fact.
To what extent and in what manner do these institutions engage residents? Only
by exploring such qualitative aspects of the neighborhood measures employed
can researchers advance our understanding of why neighborhoods matter. Such
an exploration may require going outside traditional disciplinary boundaries, in
order to effectively integrate both neighborhood-level quantitative measures—
the purview of quantitative sociologists and demographers—and qualitative and/
or individual level measures more commonly explored by ethnographers and psychologists.

Finally, as currently described, Sampson's framework does not specify what role the family plays in affecting individual developmental outcomes. Do all the effects of community social organization work through the family to affect child and adolescent development, or are some effects direct? Do various aspects of community social organization impinge on families of different structures differently? An important advancement for Sampson's model will be the specification of how family variables mediate the influence of or interact with neighborhood characteristics (Lee, chap. 2, this volume). Further, part of this specification may require attention to the more phenomenological aspects of neighborhood effects on parents and their chosen parenting strategies, as suggested by the work of Spencer (chap. 4, this volume), Korbin (chap. 5, this volume), and Burton (chap. 10, this volume), discussed in more detail later. Also in need of further attention are the interactive effects of the various levels—individual, family, and community (Massey, chap. 3, this volume). Are the disadvantages of living in a poor neighborhood and a poor family greater than the simple sum of their effects? Just as importantly (although, Massey argues, not enough researchers recognize it as such), are the *advantages* of living in an affluent neighborhood and an affluent family greater than the simple sum of their effects?

Many of the issues raised in reference to Sampson's work—incorporating meaning and perceptions of neighborhoods; defining the role of parents in mediating neighborhood effects on youth—are explored in more detail by Spencer in her contribution to this volume, to which we now turn.

THE CHILDREARING CAPACITY OF NEIGHBORHOODS

Spencer (chap. 4, this volume) focuses our attention directly on the observation that the ways in which residents are affected by and react to their neighborhoods vary greatly, and this fact has critical implications for how we conceptualize the ways in which different neighborhood mechanisms affect families. Unlike the other authors in this volume, who focus on neighborhoods and communities from sociological and demographic perspectives, Spencer takes a decidedly developmental and phenomenological approach. For her, the link between person and context is psychological and developmental in nature, and our conceptualizations of neighborhood effects must consider individuals' perceptions of their environments. It is these perceptions or psychological cues that help influence or determine the types of behavioral outcomes we see in response to contextual influences.

To illustrate her point, Spencer focuses on the experiences of African American adolescent males in low income urban neighborhoods and their responses to the dangers and risks inherent in their communities. Spencer highlights one response in particular—that of *hypermasculinity*, a reactive coping style characterized by a degree of heightened male bravado, a disdain for authority, social withdrawal, and a greater tendency toward delinquency. The picture painted by Spencer shows how the stresses and challenges of urban neighborhoods may cause some young males to react in seemingly negative, yet adaptive ways in an effort to survive the streets. Her model also considers the potential role of mothers as mediators or buffers of neighborhood stressors.

Spencer asserts that the lack of a clear understanding of and appreciation for the cultural context of minority families in poor communities, and the variation in individuals' and families' responses to negative contexts, has led to several critical misunderstandings and misinterpretations of the development and behavior of minority youth. To Spencer, these misunderstandings reinforce the need to develop a *phenomenologically* rooted conceptual model that centers on an identity-focused cultural ecological model of behavior, which she terms a *Phenomenological Variant of Ecological System Theory* or PVEST (for details see Spencer, chapter 4, this volume). This model emphasizes the importance of understanding how individual experiences and interpretations of neighborhoods contribute to our understanding of contextual effects on behavioral outcomes. A further advantage of this approach is its ability to examine how explicit parental strategies are used to mediate (or moderate) contextual influences.

Korbin's work (chap. 5, this volume) exemplifies the advantages of the phenomenological approach by demonstrating how variability in perceptions of neighborhoods may account for differences in the strategies that parents employ to monitor their children in the community. Korbin found that whereas a park or playground might be viewed objectively as a more suitable place for children to play, the parents in her study favored a less attractive but more easily observable alleyway because the park was further from view and more likely to be frequented by strange adults or gang members. As Sampson (chap. 1, this volume) stresses, land-use patterns and other ecological attributes that shape *routine activities* can have a large impact on children and adolescents and on the strategies parents employ to monitor them. Korbin's work is a good example of how routine activities, collective efficacy, and the phenomenological aspects of the neighborhood context interact. Her results reiterate the need to keep in mind how our hypotheses about neighborhood effects on outcomes coincide with the ways in which different individuals experience and interpret neighborhoods, which may also account for the variance found in individual outcomes. Similarly, Burton (chap. 10, this volume) provides critical insight into how the same "objective" environmental conditions can result in dramatically different social and developmental outcomes for innercity children, depending on the meaning and interpretation they attach to their experiences. Burton's argument is that the dangers and hardships exerted by impoverished and high-risk communities on children and adolescents can push them toward "nonlinear" developmental outcomes (e.g., adultification). As such, traditional developmental markers commonly used by researchers may not reveal a clear picture of the relationship between neighborhood effects and individual-level outcomes. Thus, a phenomenological approach focusing on the perception, meaning, and interpretation of these effects can be effective in helping us understand how and why nonnormative outcomes emerge.

Sullivan (chap. 7, this volume) stresses that it is not only the meanings and interpretations that vary among inner city youths but also external circumstances and situations, such that hypermasculinity may represent just one of many types of roles, behaviors, or personae that African American males may have to assume. Sullivan strongly urges caution in using the term when applied to minorities for fear that it may only reflect stereotypes or perceptions that minorities (African American males in this case) are perhaps more masculine in their behavior than men of other races would be in similar situations.

Research by Spencer and the other authors mentioned clearly demonstrates the importance of the phenomenological approach and the value of the PVEST model. However, a valuable addition to the model would be the specific contextual forces or factors that may influence individual outcomes. For example, empirically, Spencer concentrates on "the role of risks, stressors, and coping strategies" as they relate to hypermasculinity, grade point average, and school completion. The PVEST model implies that certain risks and stressors are in part due to more structural, contextual factors such as poverty, low socioeconomic status, crime, and the like. A potentially useful step for future research would be to actually include more objective indicators of neighborhood characteristics. The potential benefits are twofold, wherein both subjective self-report assessments of neighborhoods as well as objective assessments of neighborhoods are incorporated and examined in the same model. Indeed, such a procedure would help complete a test of the PVEST model because, as Spencer argues, the stresses and risks associated with living in dangerous neighborhoods are closely linked with or may in large part be due to the structural barriers and obstacles found in most poor communities of color. For example, South (chap. 6, this volume), reiterating the importance of identifying *objective* neighborhood effects, suggests that one way to establish whether and how neighborhoods have a significant effect on the behavior of African American males as hypothesized is to measure the degree of *contact* or *exposure* that young nondelinquent boys have with other boys, particularly those more involved in acts of delinquency.

Collectively, these authors recognize and underscore the importance of understanding the phenomenological meaning that individuals ascribe to their neighborhood experiences. At the same time, more objective indicators, like those described by Sampson (chap. 1, this volume) and South (chap. 6, this volume), have the potential to improve the explanatory power of the model presented. Obtaining and integrating both subjective and objective assessments of potential neighborhood effects represent a challenging research task. Our discussion turns now to addressing these methodological and measurement challenges.

MEASURING NEIGHBORHOODS EFFECTS:
PROBLEMS AND PROSPECTS

The current volume addresses the issue of whether neighborhoods matter at all; an equally important question deals with the issue of accurately detecting and measuring neighborhood effects and the primary mechanisms through which neighborhood effects operate. Identifying and measuring robust neighborhood effects has been such a difficult, and at times elusive, undertaking that it has prompted some social scientists to conclude that neighborhood effects matter very little, if at all, in terms of human development and behavior. However, Duncan and Raudenbush (chap. 8, this volume) have yet to come to a similar conclusion—indeed, their chapter is extremely useful.

In general, Duncan and Raudenbush point to what they, and previous researchers (see Manski, 1993; Moffitt, 1998), believe are the most critical methodological issues that neighborhood researchers must address: (a) the simultaneity problem; (b) the omitted-context variables problem; (c) the endogenous membership problem; (d) families as mediators and moderators of neighborhood effects; and (e) obtaining sufficient size and variability in neighborhood sample selection. Rather than discuss each of these issues separately, this review focuses on synthesizing these issues into critically distinct but related methodological themes that have broad implications for future neighborhood research and the prospects for identifying more robust neighborhood effects.

Each of the methodological issues just delineated is intrinsically related to specific points that Duncan and Raudenbush (chap. 8, this volume) argue have been the major obstacles to accurately determining neighborhood effects and understanding their true impact. The first critical point, for example, concerns the sufficient size and variability in neighborhood and resident samples. The authors argue that both large and small communities are vastly multidimensional in scope and function. Therefore, studies that rely only on a select number of neighborhoods reduce the likelihood of accurately assessing the variety of ways in which context can influence the individual and family. Moreover, greater neighborhood sampling variability increases the chances of accounting for the different sources of variability in child and family outcomes. Duncan and Raudenbush propose a solution in the form of *quasi* and *random assignment* experimental designs over a wide range of neighborhoods and samples. Sampson's assertion (chap. 1, this volume) that neighborhood effects are overlapping in nature, such that neighborhoods adjacent to each other impact one another, reinforces Duncan and Raudenbush's call to obtain a wider sampling of neighborhoods in order to obtain a true picture of neighborhood effects.

A second important point pertains to what Duncan and Raudenbush term *measuring the unmeasured.* Keeping in mind the complex and multidimensional nature of neighborhoods, researchers continually need to be aware of potential neighborhood effects that go unmeasured and omitted from theoretical models on contextual effects. Not only is thoughtful methodological planning required, but rigorous theoretical and conceptual thinking is necessary as well. For their part, the authors advocate the use of sibling and neighbor correlations based on the idea that a "correlation for children growing up in the same neighborhood but *not* in the same family indicates how much of what is important in the shared environments of siblings lies outside the immediate family." The authors note that sibling-based correlation estimates have the advantage of providing an upper bound estimate of "both measurable *and unmeasurable* aspects of the environments shared by siblings and neighbors." However, they are also quick to note a critical limitation in that sibling correlations cannot get at neighborhood processes. Moreover, these correlations, even when large in size, may have little bearing on whether corresponding effect sizes are small or large. It is worth reiterating the same point, made by South (chap. 6, this volume) and by Small and Supple (chap. 11, this volume), concerning the importance of capturing and measuring true neighborhood-effects mechanisms at work. Nevertheless, Duncan and Raudenbush do point out that these sibling-based correlation estimates are potentially helpful in finding out where to look for process-oriented neighborhood effects.

Specific methodological issues such as disentangling contextual-level effects from individual-level effects, accounting for simultaneous effects, biased estimates resulting from unobserved or unmeasured neighborhood characteristics, and biased estimates resulting from models that may not consider the mediating and/or moderating role of families, are all related to the third critical point of *biased estimates of neighborhood effects*. The common link between these problems involves the misattribution of outcomes to particular neighborhood effects. Again, these problems are more likely to occur when studies also do not consider the earlier issues mentioned (i.e., neighborhood sample size and variability). Although Duncan and Raudenbush are not making the case for the "perfect" neighborhood study, they do emphasize that biased estimates of neighborhood effects is a problem researchers have within their means to address and solve when doing neighborhood research. Others in this volume pinpoint additional critical issues worth considering.

In chapter 9, Billy (this volume) points out an important consideration not mentioned by the lead authors with regard to the issue of temporality and neighborhood effects. Neighborhood effects on human development are dynamic processes. Thus, researchers must take into account the possibility that even *past* contexts may have an impact on current social and developmental outcomes. Billy argues that researchers should consider gathering information on individuals' current and previous contexts as well as residential histories that include descriptions of previous neighborhoods. Access to this type of information may provide researchers with the opportunity to explore questions of whether and how changes in past and present contexts coincide with developmental changes and milestones.

Bringing attention to more microlevel issues, Small and Supple (chap. 11, this volume) present a framework using a communities systems approach as a potentially useful tool to help us understand the different levels at which community and neighborhood effects function. They urge neighborhood researchers to take a conceptual step back in the research process, focusing on the different levels and distinct aspects of communities and neighborhoods that have the most immediate and significant effects on individual development. Thus, Small and Supple suggest that organizing neighborhood effects into individual, institutional, and community level factors that can directly impact specific developmental outcomes such as self-efficacy, self-concept, parent-child relations, and peer interactions is a potentially useful way to conceptualize and operationalize neighborhood-effects mechanisms.

Burton (chap. 10, this volume) espouses the value of ethnographic methods to better inform our understanding of the meaning that people attach to neighborhood experiences in their lives, and how these experiences lead to variable outcomes in children and adolescents. Bringing to light innovative and often unobserved issues such as adultification, peerification, and precocious knowledge, Burton focuses attention on how neighborhood conditions and community-based relations in poor neighborhoods can influence out-of-the-ordinary developmental outcomes in children and adolescents. More importantly, Burton's work reveals that some significant child and adolescent outcomes are beyond what traditional structural and demographic indicators of neighborhoods can measure.

This discussion illustrates the innovative and different ways to both conceptualize and capture neighborhood effects, reflecting the dynamic and complex nature of neighborhoods and communities. Taken together, they encompass the essential variety of quantitative, qualitative, methodological, and conceptual issues that researchers must think about in their search for robust and distinct neighborhood effects. Overall, they emphasize that continued and combined innovations in the conceptualization, theory development, and measurement of neighborhood effects are needed, and the examples presented by each author point to promising directions for future research. In the following section, we move on to how others in the fields of policy and intervention have used the knowledge gained from neighborhood research and translated it into effective prevention and intervention strategies.

BUILDING COMMUNITIES FOR HEALTHY DEVELOPMENT: TRANSLATING KNOWLEDGE INTO PRACTICE

Connell and Kubisch (chap. 12, this volume) bring together insights from the youth development field on the necessary ingredients for healthy youth development with a community action framework that delineates the community supports needed to help move youth toward desired ultimate outcomes. Recent experience with comprehensive community initiatives (CCIs), which aim to build both individual *human capital* and community *social capital*, make it clear that initiatives and interventions aimed at improving the well-being of community residents of all ages must take into account the linkages between individual outcomes and the surrounding environment. A framework for implementing and measuring the outcomes of comprehensive initiatives has yet to fully emerge, but the authors suggest three critical areas that such a framework needs to incorporate. The contributions of other authors from this volume reinforce the importance of the three areas Connell and Kubisch identify and provide insights into how these objectives might be attained.

First, because such initiatives are comprehensive and complex, and because the effects on ultimate outcomes may take years to emerge, we need better theories and measures of change—that is, an articulation of the pathways through which ultimate outcomes are achieved, including indicators of short and medium term outcomes, at all levels—individual, institutional, and community. Both direct, linear pathways and indirect precursors and associated measures need to be developed. Duncan and Raudenbush's (chap. 8, this volume) suggestion to consider the mediating and moderating effects of family-level variables is one possible direction. Another is to consider Billy's (chap. 9, this volume) suggestion to incorporate temporal measures of neighborhood effects as a means to assess short term and long term outcomes.

Second, more attention should be paid to developing a better understanding of the *process* through which change comes about—how outcomes are achieved, through what mechanisms, and how such mechanisms work in different contexts. Each of these issues was touched on by others in this volume. For example, Burton's (chap. 10, this volume) ethnographic evidence highlighting the effect of neighborhoods on nonlinear developmental outcomes in children and adolescents, and an emphasis on "whole person" outcomes rather than variable-specific outcomes, can provide insights into *how* and *why* outcomes are achieved. Similarly, Spencer's (chap. 4, this volume) phenomenological framework is specifically designed to address contextual processes and interpret outcomes according to different socio-economic and cultural contexts.

Third, we need a better and more nuanced understanding of the connection between social capital or community building and desired individual outcomes. Sampson's (chap. 1, this volume) three-part framework, linking the structural characteristics of neighborhoods to individual outcomes through the social-organizational mechanisms of social capital, collective efficacy, and routine activities, provides a promising approach. Indicators might include evidence of reciprocated transaction among neighbors, intergenerational closure, residential stability, and links to extra-local institutions.

Connell and Kubisch draw on the youth development field to build a framework for assessing the impact of comprehensive community initiatives on youth and adolescent development specifically. Insights from the youth development field represent the most fundamental elements of a new "theory of change," in that they link the experiences of youth as they grow up with their accomplishments as young people as well as "the probable impacts of these accomplishments in adulthood." Desired long-term (adult) outcomes for youth include economic self-sufficiency, healthy family and social relationships, and community involvement. The developmental corollaries to these long-term outcomes are: learning to be productive, learning to connect with others, and learning to effectively manage and direct their own lives. The youth development field has thus identified what the authors term the *non-negotiables of youth development*—the basic supports and opportunities all youth need to achieve both developmental and long-term outcomes. These are (a) adequate nutrition, health, and shelter; (b) multiple supportive relationships with adults and peers; (c) meaningful opportunities for involvement and membership; (d) challenging and engaging activities and learning experiences; and (e) safety.

Connell and Kubisch's (chap. 12, this volume) main contribution is to link these nonnegotiables to *community strategies* that enhance the chances of all youth to experience these necessary conditions for healthy development. The authors' *community action framework* suggests five community strategies that are linked to healthy youth and adolescent development. First, communities must strengthen the capacities of adults who interact with youth, most importantly parents, but also neighbors and employers. The youth development field has been reluctant to take on issues of parenting directly, as a strong ethos exists discouraging state intervention into "private" matters. The efforts that have involved parents directly tended to focus on the parents of young children; the needs of parents of adolescents— which are considerable—have gone largely unaddressed. As Sampson's (chap.1, this volume) work suggests, efforts to foster *links* among adults, as parents and neighbors, would also serve youth well. Second, integration and reform of institutions that affect youths' lives (e.g., schools, juvenile justice, welfare, housing) is necessary. Currently, institutions and agencies that serve youth operate and are funded in an uncoordinated and unsystematic fashion that undermines youth development. Third, we need to increase the number and quality of activities available to youth when they are not engaged in formal institutions (e.g., home, school). Providing developmental activities during "gap periods," such as after school and on weekends and holidays, as well as the necessary support to strengthen community adults' and institutions' capability of providing such programs, is vital. The work presented in this volume by Spencer (chap. 4), Burton (chap. 10), Korbin (chap. 5), and Taylor (chap. 13) suggests that such efforts should be developed in close consultation with the youth and parents themselves, in order to coordinate with or effectively challenge (depending on the nature) any informal activities already taking place. Fourth, public policies need to be realigned to match all of these strategies.

Connell and Kubisch effectively integrate research, program, and commonsense knowledge about pathways through which communities can affect youth development, and provide a tool for social scientists, planners, investors, evaluators, and community residents involved in implementing and assessing comprehensive community initiatives aimed at youth development outcomes. As Blyth (chap. 15, this volume) points out, an important next step will be to assemble what is known about the specific linkages in the framework in order to help communities put into action the outlined strategies. What does the research literature suggest are the best practices that complement the framework's aims? How do communities go about assessing their ecology and changes to it as initiatives are put into place?

Taylor (chap. 13, this volume) stresses the need for communities to examine the "threats" as well as opportunities and resources in their ecology, and underscores the need for measures to be developed to aid communities in gauging how both resources and threats are changing in the contexts within which children live. He suggests using ecological psychology's concept of *behavior settings* ("standing patterns of behavior—surrounded and supported by a physical environment"). The spatial extent and nature of identified behavior settings, both positive (e.g., supervised sports activity) and negative (e.g., drug markets), could be continually assessed, thereby providing the kind of intermediate outcome measures Connell and Kubisch suggest need to be developed.

Taylor's (chap. 13) discussion of community "threats" and his description of the dominance of the drug corner in the lives of male teens in disadvantaged neighborhoods echo the observations of Blyth (chap. 15), Spencer (chap. 4), Burton (chap. 10), and Korbin (chap. 5), and point to another area in need of development for the framework: the modeling of how the implementation of community strategies might vary across different contexts and cultures (Blyth, chap. 15, this volume). For example, Taylor's discussion makes clear the necessity of examining the *meaning* of objectively identified "threats" to a community for the teens who live there. As he describes, teen males' involvement in the drug trade was motivated as much by a desire for self-respect as for monetary gains. A misinterpretation of this motivation—like a misunderstanding of the hypermasculine response described by Spencer—could lead to critically misguided intervention strategies.

A related point was suggested by Fernandez Kelly's (1994) research, which showed that childbearing for teen mothers in a Baltimore ghetto represented attempts to attain personal autonomy and achieve an adult "milestone" in a context bereft of the means to achieve these goals. "The quest for respect is commonplace among adolescents of all class backgrounds. However, varying outcomes hinge on the attributes of social networks" (Fernandez Kelly, 1994, p. 103). Social capital has been identified as an important ingredient in communities' potential success in achieving desired youth outcomes, and Connell and Kubisch raise important questions about our ability to program its development. As the examples of both Taylor (chap. 13, this volume) and Fernandez-Kelly (1994) suggest, an important component of this assessment should be communities' *connections to other communities and other networks*, particularly those that increase residents' opportunities and resources. As Sampson's work demonstrates, "spatial externalities" matter, perhaps because of the networks embedded within and among neighboring communities.

CONCLUSION

Does it take a village to raise a child? This volume affirms that villages do indeed have an important role in raising a child. Neighborhoods do matter, and they can have profound impacts on developmental outcomes for children and adolescents. In our concluding remarks, we reiterate some key points supporting the role of neighborhoods and communities for child and adolescent development, and we close with critical issues for future research to address.

First, previous neighborhood research focused on identifying relationships among sociostructural conditions of neighborhoods, such as poverty and unemployment, and individual and aggregate level outcomes. However, the mechanisms and processes by which neighborhoods impact and influence human developmental outcomes have been less explored. This volume provides evidence of neighborhood level social-organizational mechanisms, such as collective efficacy and social capital, which mediate the effect of structural characteristics on behavioral outcomes. The search for neighborhood processes extends the research literature beyond questions of whether neighborhood effects exist, to questions of how and why neighborhoods matter.

Second, "objective" variable-centered approaches to studying neighborhood effects are not necessarily the only or best way to examine the relationship between context and individual development. Phenomenologically rooted perspectives that tap into the subjective interpretations and perceptions that individuals attach to their neighborhood experiences can significantly aid our efforts to explain and understand the variability in context-related outcomes among individuals. In the current volume, examples from developmental psychology and ethnography have illustrated the contributions that phenomenological approaches can make above and beyond those of more traditional survey research.

Third, the methods that we use to capture and measure neighborhoods effects must reflect the dynamic complexity and diversity of neighborhoods and communities themselves. Reliance on relatively small, nonexperimental neighborhood samples will, in the end, limit the types of neighborhood mechanisms observed. This volume has highlighted the innovative types of questions and answers that can be addressed using experimental and quasiexperimental research designs. In addition, these new approaches represent promising ways to disentangle confounding neighborhood and individual level effects.

Fourth, research linking neighborhood contexts to individual level outcomes represents a particularly fruitful area for interdisciplinary work. By bringing together developmental psychologists, sociologists, demographers, economists, interventionists, and policy makers, the current volume is a prime example of how interdisciplinary research can advance the overall state of our knowledge by encouraging the pooling of resources and sharing of ideas to address issues that are pertinent to each field individually and collectively. Just as importantly, neighborhood research brings together basic and applied researchers in an effort to address critical social, educational, and economic problems in society.

From these advances, important issues for future research emerge. For example, the work in this volume suggests that more attention needs to be paid to incorporating into our conceptual models the role that families play in mediating or moderating the structural effects of neighborhoods on child and adolescent development. As some of the ethnographic examples demonstrate, family-related factors likely represent a key mechanism through which neighborhood processes and effects operate. Furthermore, the ethnic and cultural diversity found in current neighborhood research literature will have to expand significantly. Particularly in urban areas and inner cities, the growing ethnic and cultural diversity of cities will have to be reflected in neighborhood research. Relatively little information exists on immigrant families and how neighborhood effects impact their transition and incorporation into American society. In addition, neighborhood research needs to move beyond its current focus on concentrated disadvantage to consider the impact of concentrated advantage on neighborhood residents (Massey, chap. 3, this volume).

Finally, future neighborhood research must address the temporal and long-term effects that neighborhoods may impart on lifetime residents. Many interesting and important questions can be pursued through longitudinal studies that can identify and document how neighborhood effects operate throughout the life course. Such an approach would shed further light onto the connection between neighborhood effects and developmental processes.

In its entirety, the current volume represents an important advance in our understanding and conceptualization of how neighborhoods impact child and adolescent outcomes. The question of whether neighborhoods matter is perhaps not as important as the question of *how* neighborhoods matter and *why* their effects are so important for individual and social development. Given the complexity of both people and places, these questions will continue to be topics of great interest for future research.

REFERENCES

Fernandez Kelly, M. P. (1994). Towanda's triumph: Social and cultural capital in the tranasition to adulthood in the urban ghetto. *International Journal of Urban and Regional Research, 18*(1), 88–111.

Manski, C. (1993) Identification of endogenous social effects: The reflection problem. *Review of Economic Studies, 60*, 531–542.

Moffitt, R. (1998). *Policy interventions, low-level equilibria, and social interactions.* Working paper. Baltimore, MD: Johns Hopkins University.

AUTHOR INDEX

SUBJECT INDEX

A

Abbott Adjective Checklist (AAC), 67
Academic achievement
  correlational studies and, 118–120
  predictors for, 63–64
Add Health. *See* National Longitudinal
    Survey of Adolescent Health
Add Health Picture Vocabulary Test,
    123–125
Additivity assumption, 46
Administrative data, 104–105,
    139-140
Adolescent alienation, 52-53
Adolescent Machismo Scale, 69
Adolescents/Adolescent development
  adultification, 151–152
  alienation, 52–53
  community effects perspective
    first order effects, 165–166
    guiding principles in, 163–164
    second order effects, 166–169
    third order effects, 170–172
  correlational studies, 121–127, 132
  criminal activity and, 129–132
  effects of ecological differentiation
      on, 11–14
  female delinquency, 68–69
  fluid family structures and, 153–156
  Gautreaux quasiexperiment, 127–128

modeling of community norms
    and values, 167
Moving to Opportunity experiment,
    128–132
Project on Human Development
    in Chicago Neighborhoods,
    120–121
risk-taking behaviors, 64, 211
sex role development, 62, 64, 65
sexual activity, 91
traditional approaches to, 151–152
See also African American youth;
      Child development; Youth
      development
Adultification, 152–153
Adults
  modeling of community norms
      and values, 167
  perceptions and fears of making
      interventions, 81–82
See also African American
      parents/parenting;
      Parents/Parenting
Affluence/Affluence concentration, 15, 23
  continuum perspective, 48
  PHDCN study and, 26
African American communities
  age of first marriage in, 89
  concentration effects and, 6
  environmental racism and, 67
  metropolitan-wide economic
      restructuring and, 39